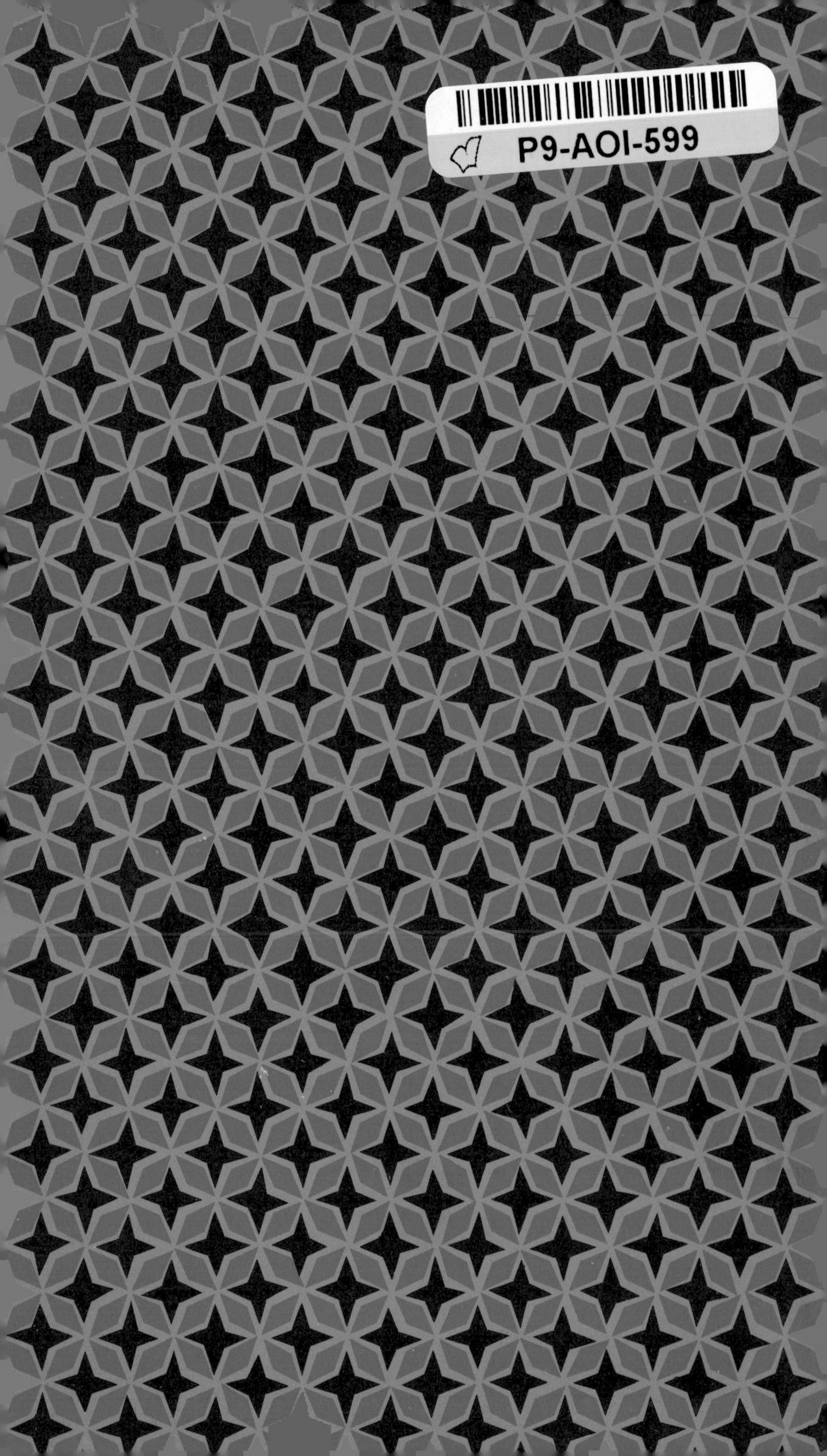
P9-AOI-599

Morning Star

Novels by Elinor Rice

The Best Butter

Action in Havana

Mirror, Mirror

Take the Cash

Elinor Rice Hays

MORNING STAR

A Biography of Lucy Stone

1818—1893

New York

Harcourt, Brace & World, Inc.

First edition

Library of Congress

Catalog Card Number: 61-12349

Printed in the

United States of America

To Frances

because she is a woman

and to Paul

because I am

Acknowledgments

When I consider those who in one degree or another have helped to make this book possible, I feel that a full expression of gratitude would in itself be a book. My thanks go first to Edna Lamprey Stantial. No words can adequately express my gratitude for her permission freely to use the Stone-Blackwell manuscripts which she is preparing for the Library of Congress, for her hospitality, her knowledge, the hours she unsparingly gave. I am grateful to Diana and Lionel Trilling for help and advice, and to Diana for thoughtful and laborious editorial assistance; to my husband for readings and helpful suggestions beyond count; to Miriam Y. Holden for the use of her fine library of books about women and for her generous contributions of time and knowledge. Of Lucy Stone's family I have had the pleasure of visiting Francis Stone Beeman, who lives so near Lucy's own childhood home, and Mrs. Anna Blackwell Belden, of Martha's Vineyard, and have received valuable information by letter from Bowman Stone Beeman.

In every library where I have worked (see bibliography), the librarians have been gracious and helpful far beyond the call of duty, and I am grateful to them. My thanks, too, for permission to quote from manuscripts.

Much of the manuscript material on which this biography is based is still privately owned. Much even of what is public is unknown. The *History of Woman Suffrage*, assembled by Susan B. Anthony and Elizabeth Cady Stanton with Matilda Joslyn Gage, was published while a split in the movement divided their group from Lucy Stone's. This history has become the authoritative document used by all subsequent historians. Lucy Stone's achievements are therefore virtually unknown.

Acknowledgements

No one would wish to detract from the stature of the two great women who made and wrote suffrage history; but surely there is room in the heavens for a third star of equal magnitude. This third is Lucy Stone.

Contents

List of Illustrations

(Between pages 178-179)

Part One

The Lesser Sex

Chapter One

There is no greater tribute to the feminists of the nineteenth century than the fact that today women so frequently complain of too much freedom, or look with nostalgia on the good old Victorian days when the gentle sex was protected and respected as it deserves to be. Most revolutions carry within themselves the germs of reaction; and the fight of nineteenth-century women for freedom was a true revolution. It had its bloody battles and its martyrs. As early as 1792, in England, Mary Wollstonecraft's *Vindication of the Rights of Woman* caused a storm of abuse because it demanded education and political and civil rights for the ignorant, dispossessed and disenfranchised half of the human race. In America, Abigail Smith Adams, the amazing wife of John Adams, wrote to her husband at the Continental Congress, "I desire you would remember the ladies and be more generous and favorable to them than your ancestors." Her desire was unfulfilled. The Declaration of Independence ignored the ladies.

"Bold" women who, in the middle of the nineteenth century, rose to speak in defense of their sex were reviled and physically attacked. They were hosed with water; stones were thrown through windows at them as they spoke. Into the twentieth century women "suffragettes" on both sides of the Atlantic were treated with ridicule and contempt. Yet the more courageous members of the sex fought valiantly on. They won the right to education, to jobs, to the vote.

Then, out in a man's world, they found the struggle a hard one. They had been deprived before. Now they were too much endowed with freedom. The fight to be men's equals had forced them to exist in what might well be called a no man's land in the battle of the sexes. Women had begun to feel that they must not only be men's equals; they must be like men. This impossible effort created new strains and tensions almost unendurable to both sexes. "How much happier we would be without this struggle!" women began to say. And the oversimplified corollary frequently followed: "How much happier our grandmothers and great-grandmothers were."

Though this is fantasy, it would, of course, be equally untrue to say that the lot of every early nineteenth-century woman was miserable. Many women led lives of great happiness, protected and loved by generous, kindly husbands. But this is like claiming that there is no need for prison reform because there are a few model prisons, or like the southern arguments that most masters were kind to their slaves.

That women now retreat from freedom, while the Lucy Stones and Mary Wollstonecrafts might find such knowledge painful, is no rebuke to their efforts. The bitter struggle to free the Negro slaves was no less noble, no less a necessity because today Negroes find themselves in thousands of unhappy predicaments. This means only that the fight is not yet ended, the conclusion not yet reached.

Lucy Stone's fame today rests on a single fact—that she refused to take her husband's name. Yet this act was no more than a symbol, and far less important than the many victories she helped to win for women everywhere. How much she needed a symbol can be seen in a story of her early life. She was only a girl when she joined the orthodox Congregational Church in her home town of West Brookfield, Massachusetts. She had not long been a member when one of the deacons, an outspoken abolitionist, was expelled from the congregation for his antislavery activities. When the first vote on the deacon's fate was taken, Lucy raised her hand in his support. The minister was standing, dark and stern, supervising the vote. Suddenly he turned to the man counting the show of hands, and, in a voice which to

Lucy seemed filled with scorn, told him not to count the woman's vote. The man protested that she was a member of the congregation. "Yes, but not a voting member," the minister announced, settling the matter. Six other votes were taken that day. Each time Lucy held up her hand, and each time it was ignored.

Lucy Stone was born on August 13, 1818, into an age which was different in many ways from ours. It was different for men and women, for rich and poor; but there was a special difference in the lives of women, for from birth to death their status as the inferior sex affected every aspect of their lives.

In affirming women's inferiority, men could clothe themselves in religious virtue. The church's view of women, stemming from Paul, was a low one. Women were daughters of Eve, the temptress, and forever to be condemned. A sixth-century church council had seriously debated whether or not women had souls. By the nineteenth century, the church had decided to admit women to the human race, though on a somewhat restricted basis.

Women were trained from childhood for their subservient role. As late as 1790 in Boston girls were taught in public schools only in summer when the boys did not need the buildings or the teachers. Later they were allowed two hours in the afternoons, after their superior male contemporaries had left for the day; but it was not until four years after Lucy Stone was born that girls were finally desegregated and admitted freely to Boston's "common" schools. Private schools for girls were scarce and very bad indeed. The curriculum, usually taught by some impoverished and uneducated lady, consisted of such subjects as sewing, reading, writing, spelling and the making of samplers.

Conditions in Quaker schools were somewhat better, because Quakers allowed women more privileges than the rest of the population did; but even in Quaker schools girls were separated from boys, and though they paid the same fees, received less education. If they became teachers, they worked for half the pay.

This blackness had not always and everywhere existed. Among the upper classes in medieval times an infinitesimal number of women received a higher education—not only abbesses but a few lay women too. The University of Bologna gave degrees to women; Portia was no figment of Shakespeare's imagination. In later centuries there were a few *salonnières* in France, a few Blue Stockings in England. Here and there in America a rich father with eccentric views might provide exceptional education for his daughter.

The low level of general education for girls was based on a conviction that the less women knew the better for them and for their future husbands. In 1840 *Godey's Lady's Book,* that popular magazine of the time, quoted the advice of an old mother to a young one, "Stimulate the sensibilities of your boys, and blunt those of your girls." And as late as the 1860's the Reverend John Todd wrote a series of articles decrying the growing tendency to educate women. Dr. Todd's popular thesis was that "man's chief end is to glorify God and enjoy him forever," and "woman's chief end is to complete man." To judge by Dr. Todd's views on the education of women, man did not need intellectual completion. The girl student, he said, "must be on the strain all the school hours, study in the evening until her eyes ache, her brain whirls, her spine yields and gives way, and she comes through the process of education, enervated, feeble, without courage or vigor, elasticity or strength. . . . Now that we have taken woman in hand, we are in danger of educating her into the grave, taking her out of her own beautiful honored sphere, and making her an hermaphrodite, instead of what God made her to be."

What God intended her to be was married. The deepest objection to education for girls was that it would undermine the entire institution of marriage. It can only be deduced that men supposed marriage to hold so little attraction for women that, if they were wiser, they would give it up altogether. Yet there was no other future for them. No worse fate could await any girl born in the early years of the last century than to be an old maid; and if she had not caught a husband by her very early twenties, she was already assigned that undesirable role. It was unthinkable that an unmarried woman should live alone, and her fate was more than likely to be a lifetime as unpaid housemaid and nurse in the home of a brother, or of a sister fortunate enough to have acquired a mate. Yet strangely enough, even an unmarried woman had certain advantages over a wife. If she earned a pittance, as she might respectably do by teaching school, or perhaps by housework or sewing, the money she earned, if she was of age, was hers. If she inherited land or money, that was at her disposal too.

The status of women in America had deteriorated since Colonial times, when women were scarce and, like any scarcity commodity, highly valued; for though by common law they had no rights, in practice a man was likely to treat his wife with the care he would give to any irreplaceable possession. Yet common law, then and later, permitted a man to beat his wife, though it did limit him to the use of a "reasonable instrument." What was a reasonable instrument? One judge informed a jury it was a "stick no bigger than my thumb." There is no surviving record of the size of the judge or of his thumb.

As time went on and the supply of women increased, their value became less and they sank back to the level of women in England, a very low level indeed; but the phenomenon of scarcity value was observable again when pioneer women gained economic and social advantages which, though slight, their "protected" sisters on the eastern seaboard did not achieve until decades later.

In the settled areas in the East, the early nineteenth-century wife had no legal rights. Though it was possible under the law of trusts for a father to leave money to his daughter in such a way that her husband could not use it, those who knew of this right or availed themselves of it were few. American law was based on English common law, and the handbook of common law was Blackstone's *Commentaries on the Laws of England.* In 1765 Blackstone wrote: "By marriage, the very being or legal existence of a woman is suspended, or at least it is incorporated or consolidated into that of the husband, under whose wing, protection or cover she performs everything. . . ." A married woman was known in law by the graphic term of "feme covert" or covered woman.

This protection meant that a married woman could not sue or be sued, that her possessions, even her clothes, belonged to her husband. A drunkard whose wife worked could demand and get her wages from her employer and could use them as he liked. Drunk or sober, a husband had the sole decision about any property his wife might inherit, and the use for life of all profit from her inherited real property.

In 1845 Mr. Edward D. Mansfield, who had been a professor of history at Cincinnati College, wrote a book suggested to him by "ladies of distinguished intelligence and worth" defining the *"Legal Rights, Liabilities and Duties of Women."* In this book, which Lucy Stone knew and cited, Mr. Mansfield defended the existing laws of property as they were so often defended in those days: they were the will of God. "The first great principle of Scripture, the unity of husband and wife, is repeated by the law. They are *in law, one person.* This great principle has, therefore, all the authority of human and divine law. . . . And it should be further borne in mind, that many of the laws, which seem severe and harsh towards women, are but necessary and inevitable results of this principle." And a little later he details this happy meeting of divine and human will: "The personal property of the wife . . . vests at marriage, immediately and absolutely, in the husband. He can dispose of them as he pleases, and on his death, they go to his representatives, as being entirely his property. Or if he were in debt, his creditors can take them in execution."

In October 1856 *The Westminster Review* recounted an incident in England which, even at that late date, could have occurred as easily in most of the states of the Union. A woman whose husband had been a failure in business set herself up as a milliner. For years she supported her husband, herself and their children. She finally retired, and the family lived on her accumulated earnings. This happy state was interrupted by the death of the husband who, in his will, left every penny of his wife's earnings to his illegitimate children by another woman.

But a husband's jurisdiction did not end with his wife's finances. He was sole guardian of their children. He could take them away from his wife for any reason or for no reason at all; and even if he did not remove them from her care, he could always threaten to do so if she did not act as he wished. If he died before she did, he could will them to some other guardian. It was fairly common for men to name in their wills a responsible male guardian for their minor children, on the theory that their wives, being women, were incapable of making decisions even about their own children.

If by the standards of *Godey's Lady's Book,* a girl's sensibilities still needed blunting after she was married, the constant routine of childbearing must have helped. Families of ten or twelve children were common, and those of twenty or twenty-five not remarkable. Such families frequently required the efforts of more than one mother, for there were not even the simplest sanitary precautions against infection at childbirth, and the chances were great that either mother or child or both would die.

It was not only childbearing that wore away women's lives. There were slower erosions. Perhaps because inventors were men, improvements in household equipment lagged years behind the rapidly expanding mechanical improvements for factories and farms. Water had to be well-drawn or pumped for cooking, drinking, bathing or washing dishes and clothes. It had then to be carried, heated and dumped out again. Heat and cooking depended on wood stoves, so that houses were cold in winter and kitchens unbearably hot in summer, because stoves could not be allowed to grow cold. For lighting there were candles—frequently made at home—or oil lamps which had to be filled and trimmed and tended. Clothes were homemade, and, particularly in the early years of the century, the cloth usually had to be woven before the sewing could begin. What soap there was might well be made at home, and the surfaces to be cleaned were not the smooth plastic, enamel and metal surfaces of today's kitchens. They were wooden surfaces which caught and held dirt and grease. Pots and pans were iron, and there were no disposable paper towels to wipe them with. Preserved foods did not come from supermarket shelves. They were preserved and packed and labeled in the hot summer months.

One of the more amusing aspects of modern woman's retreat from modernity is that many of today's most fashionable kitchens are not the antiseptic white and metal laboratories of a few years ago. Fashionable kitchens may be wood-paneled rooms with stained oak cupboards and gay wallpaper, stoves that are not white but black. And today's bride, surrounded by her automatic washing machine and dryer, her cold-heat oven set flush into the wall, her electric blender, her mixer, her cake mix (a perfect cake every time or your money back) and her concealed fluorescent lights that cast no shadow, thinks how charmingly domestic it is to have a kitchen so like the one dear great-grandmother had when she was a bride.

Chapter Two

Lucy Stone's life spanned a century and an era. She was born in 1818 in a small, predominantly agricultural country less than a generation removed from colonialism, a country which still contained within its borders the outmoded institution of slavery. She died in 1893 in a free nation stretching across a continent, with nationwide industries and networks of rapid communication.

The year she was born into a nation only twenty-nine years old, the newly adopted flag of the United States was raised for the first time over the nation's Capitol. There were twenty stars in the new flag. The number grew rapidly. In that year Illinois was admitted as a state and Missouri applied for statehood, the first territory wholly west of the Mississippi to ask for admission. The march to the Pacific had begun. That year, too, a life pension was voted for veterans of the Revolutionary War—twenty dollars a month for officers, eight dollars for privates.

In its issue of January 7, 1818, the *Columbian Centinel,* a Boston newspaper, after examining the London papers of December 8, a mere thirty days earlier, brought the encouraging news that on the international scene "things everywhere look permanently pacific." On January 28 *Thomas's Massachusetts Spy or Worcester Gazette,* which numbered among its subscribers a family named Stone who lived on a farm some twenty miles out of Worcester, described the funeral of General Kosciusko, an account translated for the *Baltimore Patriot* from the Paris *Journal du Commerce* of October 31, 1817. "On the 2d April," the *Centinel* of June 6 revealed, "an American ship was spoken by the British Ship Conqueror off St. Helena, and informed that Buonaparte was in good health, but had a slight attack of the gout."

The *Centinel* also carried a repeated advertisement for a Young Ladies Seminary: "Instruction given by Miss Heaney in the following essential and liberal Branches of Education, viz:—Reading, Orthography, Writing, Arithmetic, Geography (Drawing Maps, and use of Globes) History, Chronology, English Grammar, Composition, etc. Tuition in the above Studies, will be given during the morning, and in the afternoon exclusively in Plain and Ornamental Needlework, Drawing, Coloring in Crayons and Water Colours, and the relative employments."

Among the most frequently recurring advertisements in the papers were those of lotteries, of molasses and rum for sale, of hats, shoes and boots newly arrived from London, and announcements of available cargo space on ships about to sail. The United States, only a few decades removed from actual colonialism, was still dependent for many of its necessities and most of its luxuries on the culture of Europe.

Headline news, though headlines were unknown, were the Indian Wars on the border between the southernmost Atlantic state, Georgia, and a Spanish possession, Florida, on its southern border. On January 31 Major General Andrew Jackson issued an order to the Volunteers of West Tennessee calling them to arms after a "repose of three years. . . . The savages on your borders, unwilling to be at peace, have once more raised the tomahawk to shed the blood of our citizens. . . ." Four months later there was an unsavory story of how an Indian town had been destroyed by Georgian troops and all the old people slaughtered. The town was unprotected because its young men had gone off in a body, as volunteers, to fight under General Jackson against the warlike Indians on the border. On July 8 there was an unconfirmed, and apparently uncredited, report of June 2 announcing the capture of Pensacola. Yet, in fact, by the end of May the bumptious general had completed his conquest of Florida and was on his way back to Nashville, where he was feted as a hero.

Far to the north of this unsettled border and largely unaware of it, life went pacifically on. On August 13 the *New York Evening Post* carried an advertisement for new music just published: *William Tell; Fanny Dearest; Thine Am I My Faithful Fair; The Soldier's Bride.* The news columns announced a convention to be assembled at Hartford at the end of the month to frame a Constitution of Civil Government for Connecticut, which up to then had "jogged along . . . under the old charter granted by King Charles."

On August 13, too, a baby girl was born on the Stone farm on Coy's Hill, three and a half miles outside of West Brookfield, Massachusetts, and some twenty miles from Worcester. She was the eighth of nine children born to Francis and Hannah Matthews Stone.

Francis Stone came of a strong, stern family with a tradition of fighting for freedom. His ancestor Gregory Stone had emigrated to America in 1635 to seek religious freedom and, as early as 1644, was a member of a committee to protest a proposal that New England be governed by a royal commission. The committee expressed itself as irrevocably opposed to government without representation. More than two hundred years later Lucy was to make a protest against paying taxes, and for the same reason.

Francis Stone's father had been only seventeen when he fought at *his* father's side in the French and Indian War; and when the father was killed at the Battle of Quebec, the seventeen-year-old boy was sent home as the only remaining support of his family. Later he became a captain in the Revolutionary Army and in 1787 leader of a group of men in Shays' Rebellion.

Hannah Matthews' ancestry, the Forbish (later Forbes) and Bowman families, were also public spirited and well educated, so that on both sides of her family Lucy had a heritage of independence and determination.

Though Lucy's grandfather Stone, after he returned from

the wars, had settled down as a tanner in North Brookfield, Lucy's father in his youth had rejected the family trade to become a teacher. He is said to have been a good teacher; but perhaps because teaching was a miserably paid profession for a man with a family to maintain, Francis Stone returned to his father's trade and set up as a tanner in New Braintree, Massachusetts, his wife's girlhood home. Two years before Lucy was born, however, he left the tannery and bought one hundred and forty-five acres on Coy's Hill for the large sum of $3,200, by a deed which, in feudal terminology, defined the sellers as yeomen and gentlemen. At the time of Lucy's birth he was successfully farming this land.

The night before Lucy was born one of those crises occurred which are constant in a farmer's life. A sudden shower sent the men of the family rushing to the hayfield to save the hay. The pregnant woman was left alone, and that night had to milk the Stones' eight cows. It is not surprising then that when she was told her new baby was a daughter, Lucy's mother said, "Oh, dear! I am sorry it is a girl. A woman's life is so hard." Nor that, with these words, before she was a day old, Lucy's long, arduous path was sketched out for her.

In spite of her belief that a woman's lot was hard, it seems never to have occurred to Hannah Matthews Stone that the pattern could be changed. For the rest of her life, after they moved the less than ten miles to Coy's Hill, her husband never found time to take Hannah Stone back to visit her old home, a drive of two and a half hours, and she never went. "There was only one will in our home, and that was my father's," was the way Lucy later put it. The Stone family was fortunate that theirs was a more benevolent ruler than most. Yet he was a harsh man, with little ability to express tenderness toward his wife and children, though he seems to have loved them.

When Lucy was being weaned—she may have been two or three years old at the time, for children were weaned late in those days—she woke one night to find her mother gone. Hannah Stone was sitting up with a sick neighbor. Lucy began to cry. Her father, wakened perhaps by her sobbing, scolded her so severely that the little girl, frightened, crept out of bed and, wrapping her blanket around her, sat weeping on the hearth. Her father told her to get back to bed or he would "lay on the slaps." She knew even then what his slaps meant, and shaking with fear, climbed back into bed and wept herself silently to sleep.

What made his harshness worse for Lucy was the fact that in rare moments of tenderness her father would take the newest baby, Sarah, on his knee, trotting her and singing to her. How Lucy wished that just once he would trot her like that, but he never did. What this stern treatment meant to her is movingly revealed in a letter she wrote some twenty years later to her brother Bowman about his own child. It is an extraordinary letter for those days. "I want that you . . . should praise Willy if he ever does anything to deserve it. I am afraid that he is injured by too much scolding. Judging from my own experience, and from observation, I know that one word of approval will do more to make a child good, than all the scoldings and whippings in the world put together."

The move from the tannery at New Braintree to the farm on Coy's Hill where Lucy was born seems to have been the sole occasion when Hannah Stone's will dominated a family action. She had decided that the rough characters around the tannery were a bad influence on her growing family, and insisted that they move to a healthier spot. The move surely could not have made life easier for Hannah herself, overworked as she was; but she was right in believing that it would be a blessing to her children. The farm was located on the eastern slope of Coy's Hill, the top of which was famous in Massachusetts for its breathtaking view over gentle green hills spotted by the blue of lakes. Lucy and her three sisters used to climb up to watch the sunset, while their neighbors wondered what on earth those Stone girls found on that hill to "pay them for tramping up there so often."

When she was quite little Lucy and her brother Luther drove the cows to pasture before sunrise. The dew on the grass was so cold, she remembered, that she would stop and curl one bare foot up against her other leg to warm it.

The storybook concept of childhood as a carefree, lazy time seems to have had even less reality in the early nineteenth century than it does today. With large families, low wages and no child-labor laws, children in poor families began to work at an early age. Children on farms were likely to be more fortunate than city children, who often worked twelve to fourteen hours a day in factories and mills. On the Stone farm everyone, adult or child, worked hard. Hannah Stone, besides her household duties of cooking, cleaning, and washing for her family and the farm hands, also wove the cloth for the family's clothes. One of Lucy's earliest chores was to help with the weaving. Her job was to sit on the floor under the loom and hand up the threads to her mother as they were needed.

Hannah Stone had a large family to care for. The family register, engraved in an elaborate flower design, lists nine children, seven of whom lived to grow up. There was Francis, bearer of the name handed down from father to son through the generations; William Bowman, named Bowman for his mother's ancestors and always called Bowman by his family; Eliza; Rhoda; Luther; Lucy; and Sarah, the youngest. There was also Father Stone's half-sister, Aunt Sally, the inevitable unmarried aunt of those days who lived with the family and helped with the work.

Often, too, there were visitors. Father Stone had three cronies of school days, who over the years had become heavy drinkers. Now they liked to do their drinking at the Stones' home. They would appear singly or together for visits of varying duration, and since it was a rule of the house that they were never to be turned away, one or more of the three was usually at the farm. But Francis Stone's hospitality meant that Hannah had to cook for the sometimes rowdy guests and, of course, wash their clothes as well.

Even when the children were very little they shared the almost limitless work, helped their father with the planting and their mother with household tasks. Lucy often shared chores with her brother Luther, the child next older than she, and he was the source of one of her earliest resentments at being a girl; for though she did everything better than he, the fact that he was a boy won him many privileges she was not allowed.

The Stone farm was like most farms. There were more good dairy products and fruit and bread and honey than they could eat. What was lacking was cash. In order to have enough money to pay for goods which must be purchased from the store, extra work had to be done. It fell to Lucy and her sisters to sew rough shoes of the kind worn by laborers and slaves. These were paid for by the local store at the rate of four cents a pair, and the money used to settle the Stones' account. Lucy, because she was the fastest worker, had to sew nine pairs a day.

How much of this was necessary to the family economy is hard to judge. Father Stone was a tight-fisted man, as skimping with money as with love. Lucy later told her daughter, though it was a matter of which she rarely spoke, that her mother finally grew tired of asking for what little cash she needed and, when it became necessary, would help herself to six-and-one-half-cent bills from the pocketbook her husband kept under his pillow night and day. Sometimes she would even take a cheese out of the cheese room and secretly sell it.

Recreations, when there was time for them, were simple. The family were orthodox Congregationalists and had religious scruples against such sinful frivolities as dancing. The children shared the simple country pleasures. They had a loving knowledge of every rock, flower and bird on their hill and in the valley below. They had pets to play with too. Their favorites were a dog known as old Bogue, which helped them to herd the cows, and Top, a pet lamb which joined in Lucy's games. It even lowered its head and kicked up its hoofs when she jumped rope, a game she loved to play and at which she was extremely skillful.

In the winter evenings the whole family sat around the huge living-room fireplace, for which Lucy and Luther carried in the wood, memorizing hymns dictated by their mother as they did so. A mug of cider was brought up from the cellar and passed around, and everyone drank out of it in turn. Sometimes the children were allowed to roast apples or pop corn. On Sundays everyone on the farm went to church. There were two wagons, and when these were filled those left over had to walk. This was carefully arranged so that those who walked one Sunday were always sure of a ride the next. So long as there were still children too little to go to church, their mother read them Bible stories at home.

To keep up with the news of the world around them the Stones subscribed to two publications when Lucy was little. They were the *Advocate of Moral Reform* and *Thomas's Massachusetts Spy,* which was published in nearby Worcester.

Chapter Three

What kind of child did these surroundings breed? A passionate and willful child, whose passion and will were sternly, even dramatically, controlled. A single story gives both sides of this picture. Lucy was racing through the house one day in furious pursuit of her sister Sarah. Her black hair was flying, her gray eyes blazing. Lucy was in one of those rages which came upon her violently, uncontrollably.

On this day Sarah's terrified flight and her wild pursuit brought Lucy, as she turned a corner, suddenly face to face with a mad and murderous creature. It took her a moment to realize that she was facing a mirror, that the face which had so terrified her was her own, distorted by fury. Shaken, she gave up the chase and went instead out to the woodshed, where she could be alone. When she left the woodshed, after what moral struggle can only be imagined, she had resolved never again to turn into that wild, hideous animal which had faced her from the mirror. She knew of only one way to control her temper: never again to speak when she was angry.

With determination surely too great for one so young, she never did. From that day on, when Luther teased her—and he was no less a tease than most young brothers—her face grew tighter and brighter with suppressed fury. Her upturned nose went higher and higher, but she did not speak.

Was it this concentration of passion which, turned to broader fields, motivated her life? In those days a woman given to anger could find abundant cause for indignation in the world around her. Even as a child Lucy was troubled because in the homes with which she was familiar it was taken for granted that men should rule their households and dictate the actions of their wives. Then one day, while she was reading the Bible, she came upon the words, "Thy desire shall be to thy husband and he shall rule over thee."

Since this was in the Bible she knew it must be true, but if it was true, what kind of world had she been born into —and born a girl? It was always to her mother that Lucy went when she was troubled, so she went to her mother now to ask if there was anything she could take which would kill her. The question was entirely serious, and her mother responded gravely. What could have happened to a little girl, she asked, that should make her want to die? Lucy told her.

Hannah Stone tried to console her daughter, but even in such a cause she could not lie. She told Lucy that Eve had placed a curse on every woman, that again and again the Bible confirmed the lowliness of the female sex. "Wives submit yourselves unto your husbands, as it is fit in the Lord." But Lucy's untamed mind refused to believe that half the human race was born to rule and half to be ruled. If she must not kill herself, she would dedicate the life she did not want to finding out exactly what the Bible said about women. Perhaps the translators, who were, after all, men, had falsified the text. She made up her mind to read the holy words in the original. This would require her to go to college, to study Hebrew, Latin and Greek.

It was an amazing decision, for when Lucy reached it—only a hundred and thirty years ago—no woman in the United States held a college degree. Her father's reaction was what any average man's would have been in those days. Although he thoroughly approved the college plans two of his sons had already made, a girl who had any such idea must be, quite literally, insane.

What life he did expect for his daughter it is hard to imagine. To him she was far from pretty. Her face was too round and her cheeks too red and healthy. "Luce's face," he said openly, "is like a blacksmith's apron; it keeps off sparks." Her response to this, whatever young-girl misery it may have covered, was, on the surface, that the last thing on earth she cared about was how she looked. In any case, she was never going to marry and be ruled by a man.

Yet Lucy was in fact far from unattractive. She was small and nicely built. She had dark hair, clear gray eyes and a glowing complexion. Daguerreotypes of her show a face at once warm, soft and strong. But her most remarkable characteristic, the quality which drew people to her throughout her life, does not appear in the pictures. Her power to win people was in her voice, described in lyrical terms by those who heard it. It was a soft voice, "so sweet, so musical that people who entirely disagreed with her would listen for hours."

Lucy was only twelve when her expanding nature expressed itself in a new and striking form. Day by day she had watched her mother wearing her life away with hard work, until it seemed to Lucy that the mother she so loved was growing older and frailer as she watched. Even at twelve Lucy had no doubt that when she recognized a wrong she must right it. The hardest work her mother had to do was the family wash, which included the entire wearing apparel of ten or twelve people. Now, at the age of twelve, Lucy decided to do the family wash herself.

Each weekday the children walked a mile to school, taking their lunch with them. Now, on Mondays, Lucy got out of bed before dawn and scrubbed away until the family laundry was clean. After that, before setting off on the mile walk to school, she hung it on the line to dry. Now, on Mondays, she walked home at noon, took the clothes down and made them ready, then walked the mile back to school. Throughout the evenings she ironed, and late at night did her homework. It was an overwhelming task for a twelve-year-old, and Lucy began to show the strain. For almost the only time in her life she grew pale and drawn, but she continued to do the wash.

Lucy's fight for education was long and strenuous. She was still in her early teens when her father decided that she had had enough schooling for a girl. Even earlier his philosophy and his Yankee thrift joined happily in a refusal to buy textbooks for her. He told her she could make do with her brothers'. So she was still quite little when she began to go barefoot to the woods to gather berries or nuts to sell whenever she needed a book.

Outside of the Bible there was little enough reading matter at home. Besides the periodicals to which Farmer Stone subscribed there were borrowed copies of *The Youth's Companion*. Lucy's favorite book among the few the family owned was Guthrie's *Geographical, Historical and Commercial Grammar of the World*. The Stones also owned one novel, *Charlotte Temple*. Published in 1790, it was the most popular novel of a generation in England and America, the story of a well-bred English girl who was seduced by the man she loved and whose horrid fate included desertion, an illegitimate child, madness and death. In the preface the author expressed the pious hope that her words might save even "one hapless fair one from the errors which ruined poor Charlotte"; and with this hope it was given to young girls to read.

Otherwise, in the Stone home, fiction was considered a product of the devil. Once Lucy's elder sister Rhoda, who by then was teaching school in a nearby town, lent her *The Children of the Abbey* by Regina Maria Roche, a sentimental tale published in England in 1798 and still enormously popular then on both sides of the Atlantic. Why it should have been considered more harmful to a young girl's morals than *Charlotte Temple* is hard to imagine. Never was virtue so set upon by vice, never was vice so humbled by virtue, never was true love so constant or so bitterly tried, never were faithful lovers parted by such strategems or brought together after six hundred pages of suffering by such turns of fate.

Lucy took the book to her room and, hidden there, read

it in secret. But there are no secrets in a house full of children. Her little sister Sarah tattled, and Lucy's deception was discovered, fortunately by her mother rather than her father. Where did they interrupt her? At "Fitzalan burst into tears; the enthusiasm of virtue warmed them both; hallowed are her raptures, and amply do they recompense the pain attendant on her sacrifices?" Or, "Much rather would I have my babes wander from door to door, to beg the dole of charity, than live upon the birthright of the orphan?"

Happily, though, Lucy's pleas met with success, and she was permitted to finish the book down to its last lavish words. "Gratitude has already consecrated their names, and their example has inspired others with emulation to pursue their course." But Lucy was granted permission to finish the book only on the understanding that novel reading was forbidden for the future; and it was many years before she read another novel.

Since the teachers in the local school were inadequate, Lucy and some of the other ambitious pupils of the town joined together to find a college student able to teach them more than the usual reading, writing and figuring. The young man they found boarded with the Stones, and Lucy immediately, and with the full fervor of her nature, fell in love with him. Her worship of Mr. Bartlett was silent and secret. Falling in love did not matter. Lucy had determined, in any case, that she would never marry.

When her father continued to insist that she should leave school, Lucy begged him to lend her enough money to continue a little longer. Then she would be able to teach and earn a living. He was finally persuaded by this practical argument to part with the money, but even then he took her note for the loan. He must have known that a note signed by a minor had no legal weight, but he must equally have known that, to a girl like Lucy, it would have a huge moral significance; and he was right. Though it took her years, Lucy paid off every cent.

At the advanced age of sixteen, Lucy was considered qualified to instruct children little younger than herself and some her own age or even older. She began to teach in the district schools. Teachers in those days boarded free at the homes of families in the school district. Besides her board, at the beginning Lucy received a salary of one dollar a week. Like her father in his early days, she was a good teacher, and was appointed to larger and larger schools until she had attained a salary, unusually high for a woman, of sixteen dollars a month. A man, even a far less qualified man, would have earned much more. "True," she later said of those days, "it cut to the core when the man who taught school no more and no better received $30 for his teaching while his sister received only $4 for hers."

Outside the world of books and of formal learning and teaching, Lucy's education expanded in various ways. Once, while she was still quite young, she joined a church sewing circle which at that time was involved in a project to pay for the education of a needy theological student. Lucy's contribution was to make a shirt.

One day while Lucy was stitching, Mary Lyon, who was trying in the face of indifference and antagonism to raise money for a woman's seminary, came to speak to the sewing circle. Her seminary was to be the first attempt in New England to give women a higher education. It was to offer opportunities for education "so valuable that the rich will be glad to avail themselves of its benefits, and so economical that people in very moderate circumstances may be equally and as fully accommodated." In 1837 Mary Lyon did, in fact, achieve her ambition when she founded Mount Holyoke Seminary at South Hadley, Massachusetts.

Except for her radical conviction that women were not only educable, but entitled to education, Mary Lyon was no radical. Like that other pioneer, Emma Willard, who in 1821 had opened her Academy for Girls in Troy, New York, Mary Lyon was no fighter for woman's rights. Mrs. Willard, in presenting plans for her school, had reassured the New

York legislature that she wished to produce no "college-bred females," and "that public speaking forms no part of female education." Emma Willard's chief problem had been that she could find no women teachers educated enough to instruct her ignorant pupils, so she had studied assiduously in order to teach the teachers in her school the knowledge she had just acquired.

Mary Lyon believed only that women would function better in their appointed roles as housewives and mothers if they were not doomed to eternal ignorance. Her seminary would have a staff and a plant, and not depend, as most women's schools did, on the whim of a single teacher. It would be a permanent institution. Many years later Lucy described Miss Lyon's aims: "The men who were to go as missionaries must have educated wives. It was tacitly understood and openly expressed that Mount Holyoke Seminary was to meet this demand. But whatever the reason, the idea was born that women could and should be educated. It lifted a mountain-load from women. It shattered the idea that they were incapable of education and would be less womanly, less everything desirable, if they had it."

Now, trying to raise money for her daring venture, Mary Lyon stood before Lucy's sewing circle, a woman of medium height, so muscular that she seemed bigger than she was, awkward because of her strange shape, more awkward still because of her badly fitting clothes. She had full, reddish hair, an attractive contrast to her expressive blue eyes, but as always, the hair was almost hidden under a cap. Yet her blue eyes sparkled; her speech was lively and her manner gay. For all her oddity, or because of it, her personality was impressive.

It was particularly impressive to Lucy. Almost fifty years later Lucy remembered her emotions that day, although, with the modesty that always kept her from seeking personal acclaim, she generalized her own experience. "Little sewing circles were formed," she said, "where rich and poor women met to sew, either for a fair to raise money or for garments to be given directly to the young men whom the education societies aided. 'Help educate young men! Help educate young men for ministers and for missionaries!' was the constant appeal made to women. Was it a wonder that as young women drew the needle they also drew the conclusion that if education was so necessary for men who were to go to the heathen, it must be valuable for women who were to stay at home?"

Lucy was never slow in her responses. She was not slow now. As Mary Lyon spoke, Lucy put down the shirt she was sewing. "Those who had sewed and spent time, strength and money to help educate young men, dropped the needle and that toil and said 'Let these men with broader shoulders and stronger arms earn their own education, while we use our scantier opportunities to educate ourselves.' " She never picked up the shirt again.

To Lucy, Mary Lyon's talk was a light burning in the darkness. Up to then she had been alone with her mad idea that women could and should be educated. Today she had found support. Yet she had in fact never been quite so alone as she had supposed. Here and there, unknown to the little farm girl, other brave women were thinking as she was. Revolution was still an active memory. Freedom was in the air they breathed. Women, like men, were beginning to weary of suppression, were beginning to break their chains.

In January 1831, when Lucy was only twelve, William Lloyd Garrison had begun to publish his abolitionist paper *The Liberator* in Boston, and its publication had brought down on his head the condemnation of nearly all the respectable members of the community. A schoolbook version of the Civil War leaves a vague impression of a North, with few exceptions, against slavery, and a South, with even fewer exceptions, in favor of it. But in 1831, and for years afterward, while it was permissible to speak of freeing slaves, or a very small proportion of them, and resettling them in a remote corner of Africa, a man who spoke out in favor of abolishing slavery because it was morally wrong was almost as much in danger of his life in the North as in the South.

The North, like the South, depended for much of its income on slave labor. Many of the elite of northern society had interests in the cotton mills of New England, which relied for raw materials on a crop worked by slaves. The northern newspapers were for noninterference with southern slavery. The northern churches, which with few exceptions were for leaving matters as they were, spoke out against the hotheaded fanatic Garrison who believed that no man had the right to own another.

In the congregation in West Brookfield of which Lucy was a full member the repercussions of this controversy were felt. She had been a member only a short while when a vote was taken on the expulsion of the antislave Deacon Josiah Henshaw, who according to local history had been led into "errors of opinion and indiscretions of conduct." It was then that Lucy raised her hand to vote in favor of the deacon. It was then that her small female hand was not counted. Finally, Deacon Henshaw, "brought . . . into unhappy collision with the majority of the church," was excommunicated.

Lucy's education in being inferior had already been further advanced. In 1837, when she was nineteen, a pastoral letter was published by the Congregational ministers of Massachusetts. The orthodox Congregational Church was the dominant church in Massachusetts, and the words of its ministers had great power. The ministerial conference which issued the letter was held that year in North Brookfield, where Lucy was teaching school. The ministers sat in the body of the church. The balcony was crowded with lay men and women. Lucy sat in that balcony next to one of her cousins, who afterward claimed that her side was black and blue from Lucy's nudges and pokes as she listened with growing anger to the reading.

The document was not calculated to calm the nerves of any independent woman. "We invite your attention to the dangers which at present seem to threaten the female character with wide-spread and permanent injury." The pastoral letter paid lip service to woman's character as it ought to be, to the "mild, dependent, softening influence of woman," to "her labors of piety and love." But "if the vine, whose strength and beauty is to lean upon the trellis work, and half conceal its clusters, thinks to assume the independence and the overshadowing nature of the elm, it will not only cease to bear fruit, but fall in shame and dishonor into the dust. We cannot, therefore, but regret the mistaken conduct of those who encourage females to bear an obtrusive and ostentatious part in measures of reform, and countenance any of that sex who so far forget themselves as to itinerate in the character of public lecturers and teachers."

This was the argument which appeared in every discussion of woman's rights: the idea that freedom for women would somehow cause them to "cease to bear fruit." "I was young enough then so that my indignation blazed," Lucy said years later, "and I told my cousin that, if ever I had anything to say in public, I should say it, and all the more because of that Pastoral Letter!"

But Lucy Stone was not the only person who responded to the pastoral letter with indignation, though the protests of some of the others took more lasting form than the nudges and pokes which were youthful Lucy's only present form of expression. The Quaker John Greenleaf Whittier expressed himself in a long and solemn rebuke to the clergy, reminding them that their predecessors had not contented themselves with words, but had dealt with such matters by "racks, and fire, and ropes." His poem contains the lines:

To silence Freedom's voice of warning,
And from your precincts shut the light
Of Freedom's day around ye dawning.

These are significant words, because the existence of the pastoral letter is one of the surest signs that the fight for women's rights had begun and "Freedom's day" was "dawning." As Whittier recognized in his poem, it had become necessary for the church to declare itself now chiefly because of "Carolina's high-souled daughters," Sarah and Angelina Grimké. These remarkable sisters were rich, pampered ladies, two of the fourteen children of a slave-owning planter of Charleston, South Carolina, who was also a judge. They had been brought up to take their places in an aristocracy based on slavery and the products of slave labor; but slavery horrified them. Sarah and Angelina were total rebels, revolting from everything their life was intended to be.

Sarah's bitter discovery of the disadvantages of being a woman came early. Her father, who said of her that had she been a man she would have been one of the world's great jurists, nevertheless, since she was a woman, refused to allow her to study not only law but even Latin.

Sarah, who was the elder, was also the first to rebel, but as the girls grew older and came North to live and to speak against slavery, it was Angelina who led the way. Contemporary accounts, with rather too much enthusiasm, call her beautiful. Her pictures belie this tradition. Her only beauty seems to have been her great dark blue eyes; but beautiful or not, she was the perfect picture of a southern lady, gentle in breeding and manner, shy in speech, and sought after as any such girl must be. Yet in spite of this and of a timidity which made public speaking painful to contemplate, it was she who first accepted the American Anti-Slavery Society's invitation to talk privately to women's groups.

The two sisters, having agreed to speak to women's groups, now found that their antislavery audiences included men; but they continued to lecture for the cause in which they believed, even though they had been taught that for women to speak in public in the presence of men was indecent, even immoral. Outrage at the brazenness of the two genteel southern ladies was universal. Even the Quakers were horrified. The Congregationalist ministers let forth their bellow of rage in their pastoral letter. As Lucy Stone said, "An earthquake shock could hardly have startled the community more. Some of the Abolitionists forgot the slave in their efforts to silence the women."

But the Grimké sisters were not to be silenced, and they were not content only to speak against slavery. They acted. They could not force their family to free their slaves; but when their father died and the sisters came North to live, they induced their mother to divide the family slaves among her children. As soon as she had done so, Sarah and Angelina freed the slaves allotted to them.

Hounded even in the North, their names were anathema in the South. Angelina's noble "Appeal to the Christian Women of the South," mailed into the South, was publicly burned by southern postmasters. The Grimkés were forbidden to return home even for a private visit to their mother. A return to South Carolina, they were told, would mean official imprisonment and probably unofficial physical attack.

Difficult, then, as it was for a young woman to attain a formal education in Massachusetts in the late 1830's and early 1840's, for a girl who kept her eyes and ears and mind open, education in the ways of the world was inescapable. If Lucy had never heard of the Grimkés in any other way, the church's violent opposition would have brought them to her attention.

Alternately teaching and studying, taking her small accumulation of dollars to go to school for a while, returning to earn a few more, Lucy Stone passed her late teens and early twenties. For one term she went to nearby Quaboag Seminary at Warren, Massachusetts, and in 1840 spent a short time at the coeducational Wesleyan Academy at Wilbraham, a private school which in 1836 announced that charges for regular instruction should in no case exceed $5.00 a term, with board of $1.50 a week. Meanwhile the antislavery issue and the problem of women's rights began to confront her at every turn. Her brother Bowman, who had graduated from Amherst in 1839 and was studying for the ministry, was that exception among clergymen, an ardent abolitionist. He subscribed to William Lloyd Garrison's *Liberator* and sent his copies to Lucy to read. She even met and talked to Abby Kelley when that great abolitionist came to West Brookfield to speak.

In 1839 Lucy had managed to earn enough money to fulfill her dream of entering Mount Holyoke Seminary. Mary Lyon's institution was now well established, and she was carrying out her sensational plan of educating the whole woman, with emphasis on physical as well as intellectual and spiritual training. For it was her revolutionary conviction that, beneath her stifling corsets and her layers of cumbersome garments, the pale, languid woman of the day had a body which needed freeing and educating as much as her mind. Besides her studies, each student had a household task to perform, not in order to learn household duties—these were not part of the curriculum of that extraordinary school—but to pay a portion of her board. The intellectual curriculum, which in the beginning was composed of English, mathematics, science, philosophy and Latin, was later expanded to include modern languages and music.

At Mount Holyoke, which was pervaded by a stern religious atmosphere, it was the custom for teachers and students to keep "mite boxes" for foreign missions. Lucy believed that conversion should begin nearer home. Her pittance went into a mite box for the Anti-Slavery Society, a box which had on its side a picture of a kneeling, manacled slave, and the words, "Am I not a man and a brother?"

After Lucy had read the copies of *The Liberator* which Bowman regularly sent her, she would secretly slip into the reading room of the seminary and leave them there for other students to see. But since her mite box, if nothing else, pointed to her as an ardent abolitionist, Mary Lyon soon guessed who was contributing the antislavery literature to her library. The headmistress, so forward-looking in her views on education, was not up to this degree of free thinking. "You must remember," she said, rebuking Lucy, "that the slavery question is a very grave question, and one upon which the best people are divided."

For the time Lucy stayed at Mount Holyoke, her mite box continued to speak for her; but the time was short. After having attained Mount Holyoke, her dream for so long, she had to leave it after only three months. The close-knit Stone family had suffered the loss of the eldest girl, Eliza, a year before. Now Lucy's sister Rhoda died. Only five of Hannah Stone's nine children still survived. Hannah was heartbroken, and Lucy, who even at the age of twelve had taken the burden of household tasks from her mother, now felt it her duty to give up her hard-won education and go home to comfort her.

What comfort Lucy found for this new interruption of her schooling it is impossible to know. That she refused to allow even this setback to swerve her from her purpose is well known indeed.

Chapter Four

In 1843 Lucy entered Oberlin Collegiate Institute in Ohio. She was twenty-five years old. It had taken her that long to save what she considered enough capital to get to Oberlin and spend one term there—the sum of seventy dollars. When she was a girl, "there was but one college in the world where women were admitted, and that was in Brazil." "I would have found my way there," she said with characteristic unbelief in the limits of possibility, "but by the time I was prepared to go, one was opened in the young state of Ohio." In 1843 Oberlin was the single college in the United States which gave degrees to women. The three women graduated from Oberlin two years earlier were the first in the United States to hold *bona fide* Bachelor's degrees equal to those held by so many men.

In 1840 Lucy had written to her brother Bowman, "Only let females be educated in the same manner and with the same advantages that males have, and, as everything in nature seeks its own level, I would risk that we would find out our 'appropriate sphere.'" She was now entering the only school where she might fairly test her theory. "Men came to Oberlin for various reasons; women because they had nowhere else to go," she said later; but it is not too difficult to suppose that even with a freer choice she might still have found her way there.

Oberlin and Lucy Stone had much in common: intensity of moral fervor, the willingness to battle against great odds, and a determination to remodel society into a system of justice for everyone, though about what was just and what unjust they sometimes disagreed. Oberlin's first circular appeared on March 8, 1834. "The grand objects of the

Oberlin Institute are, to give the most useful education at the least expense of health, time, and money; and to extend the benefits of such education to both sexes; and all classes of [the] community as far as its means will allow. . . . Prominent objects of this Seminary are, the thorough qualification of Christian teachers . . . and the elevation of female character, by bringing within the reach of the misguided and neglected sex, all the instructive privileges which hitherto have unreasonably distinguished the leading sex from theirs."

A little less than a year before this ambitious program was printed, the land on which Oberlin stood had been unbroken forest in Lorain County, Ohio, twelve miles from Lake Erie, in Connecticut's Western Reserve. The moving spirits of the community were the Reverend John J. Shipherd, pastor of the Presbyterian Church of nearby Elyria, and Philo P. Stewart, a former missionary. In 1833 these two men, mystically inspired, they believed, to undertake the enterprise, broke ground for a colony of Christian families willing to pledge themselves to sustain a school from infant grades through college, dedicated to physical, intellectual and moral education, and agreeing to live with "industry, economy and Christian self-denial" so that all funds not required for necessary expenses should be given for "the spread of the gospel." The result was, not surprisingly, an institution aggressively Christian and missionary in spirit. The religious demands were even more intense and restrictive than at Mount Holyoke, but at Oberlin they stood side by side with, and apparently unimpeded by, ideals of racial and sexual equality and by an assortment of health and food fads.

The four early leaders of Oberlin were convinced health reformers, followers of Sylvester Graham, whose philosophy was based on two tenets: gluttony is a worse sin than drunkenness; cleanliness is next to godliness. Graham had conceived the idea that vegetarians were sober people; it was eating meat that caused a desire for stimulants. Even dieticians in those days became universal reformers; and Graham's doctrine did not stop with diet. It prescribed every detail of physical life. Clothing must be adequate and decent, but never too heavy or too tight. People must sleep seven hours a night, but never in feather beds. Vegetables and fruits were to be the chief elements of diet. There were to be no stimulants, no tea, coffee or tobacco, and, of course, no alcohol. There were also to be no fats, pastries or condiments. He has left us a small heritage in graham crackers and graham bread.

It was characteristic of the reform movements of the nineteenth century that a crusade against tea and coffee could, without embarrassment, march hand in hand with an impassioned commitment to antislavery; a commitment which went so far as to make Oberlin an important station of the "Underground Railroad," the system for concealing escaped slaves and, if necessary, forcibly protecting them from seizure. In Oberlin there was even a move to boycott any product of slave labor, though this could hardly be successful since cotton was the basis of almost all clothing. But Oberlin carried its rebellion as far as it practically could, even raising sugar beets in order not to use southern-grown sugar.

This belief in the importance of correcting every evil great or small in every aspect of life appears again and again among nineteenth-century rebels. Later, in *The Woman's Journal,* the suffrage paper which Lucy Stone founded, her colleague, the great William Lloyd Garrison, regularly endorsed a chemical toilet, because, as he proclaimed in its advertisement, "Everything which concerns the health, comfort and welfare of the people is a matter of interest to me, as it should be to every other person. I therefore commend the Earth Closet system as, in my judgment, the most important sanitary discovery of the age. . . . The one I purchased fulfills all my expectations."

The movement for reform in every sphere was typical of early nineteenth-century North America, where freedom to build a new world was so dramatically projected in the westward move to new and better lands and, inevitably, to a new and better life. But to a certain extent the Utopian movement was international, having its counterpart in England and even more in France, where an ancient society had recently given bloody birth to a new social order. In France there was founded in 1821 a *Société de la Morale Chrétienne* whose president was the Duc de La Rochefoucauld-Liancourt, modestly described in the society's literature as *"patron banal de toutes les philanthropies de la terre."* In the wake of revolutions and the discovery of the common man's educability, everything was possible. Man was made to be happy, to be free, to be good. If he were permitted his natural rights to liberty and the pursuit of happiness, no other outcome was imaginable. The dominant philosophic idea of the Western world was that man was infinitely perfectible, a far cry from our day, only a century later, when the heirs of so much hope are obsessed with his infinite destructibility.

Yet ironically, while philosophers were idealizing the common man, common men, women and children were working limitless hours for almost no pay in unsafe, badly lighted, badly ventilated factories. Their intellectual supporters experimented in the creation of small heavens on earth, self-supporting Utopian colonies which for a while dotted the United States. Within months or years they failed, mankind being not yet perfected, but while they lasted they were proving grounds for those communistic, socialistic or religious theories of the uncommon men who established and lived in them.

In the United States, where a revolution had only yesterday been won and where new horizons gave the illusion of free will, Oberlin, though not a self-enclosed Utopian community, became a meeting ground for reformers, a haven in the West for those free fanatic spirits who found life in the Northeast too conservative, or who were rejected by the civilized East as being too radical. Almost from the beginning its survival was linked to its willingness to sponsor radical causes. In 1834, when Oberlin was barely launched and its financial situation was desperate, nearby Lane Institute, a theological school, was broken up when students were forbidden to hold discussions of the immediate emancipation of the slaves. Forty students, about four-fifths of the student body, and several teachers resigned in protest. Among the teachers were Asa Mahan and the Reverend Charles Grandison Finney, both of whom later figured so largely in Oberlin's history.

In the same year the students of Oberlin voted thirty-two to twenty-six against the admission of Negro students. A majority of the men voted for their admission, but of the twenty-one women only six declared in favor of sharing their newly gained right to education with colored men. At about this time, Arthur Tappan, a wealthy New Yorker with radical convictions, offered $10,000 to Oberlin, and his associates agreed to pay for eight professors at an annual salary of $600, on condition that the Reverend Mr. Finney be given the post of professor of theology. But Finney would come to Oberlin only if Negroes were freely admitted and unrestricted discussion of slavery permitted.

The matter was put to a vote of the trustees who, though the survival of their enterprise depended on it, were split four to four on the issue. The deciding vote of President Keep alone admitted Negroes and saved the college. Whether it was financial or moral persuasion which prompted his decisive vote, the result was to establish the radical nature of Oberlin. No moderate institution could have contained Finney and Mahan. Both were men of violent emotions, radical beliefs and fighting spirit, the sort of men whom nineteenth-century America, with its free spaces and vast horizons, seems to have nurtured.

Charles Grandison Finney was in his early forties. His had been a strange and dramatic career. He had been a practicing lawyer, a worldly man with so little interest in religion that he did not even own a Bible. He was almost thirty when, in connection with research on a legal matter, he bought a Bible. He began to read, was enthralled, and before he finished had been converted to militant Christianity. So convinced was he that he gave up the law to preach hell-fire and redemption up and down the East in hysterical revival meetings where the old religion met the new optimism, and, with shrieks and wailing, men dedicated themselves at once to the ancient revelation of God and the new aspirations of free men. He is said to have converted whole communities to the gospel.

At the time he became an evangelist Finney was a man of extraordinary appearance: six feet two, very handsome, very masculine, with almost frighteningly hypnotic eyes and a warm and sympathetic mouth. He had, as well, enormous energy and intelligence. By the time Lucy first saw him at Oberlin this description no longer fitted him. She said that "he was the crossest man I ever saw"; and a daguerreotype of him seven years after she met him shows none of his earlier physical attraction. He was scrawny of body. The hair was entirely gone from the center of his head, but grew in a long straggling fringe around the edges. His expression was worried, unpleasant and intense. He was the very symbol of a fanatical New England clergyman.

At the time he came to Oberlin his influence was so great that not only did thirty-two of the Lane students follow him, but the magic of his name and Oberlin's radical stand caused a rush of entries among young people who believed that the world was to be saved and that they were sent to save it. Nearly three hundred new students applied during 1835.

It was Asa Mahan, however, even more than Finney, who set the tone of Oberlin Collegiate Institute, for though Finney was professor of theology, Mahan was president of the college through its early years of growth from 1835 to 1850. A picture of him in his later years shows a man with sad, benevolent eyes, less stern in appearance than Finney, perhaps only because he looks better fed or because he allowed himself the concealment of long though receding hair and a full white beard. He was, like Finney, violently emotional, even fonder of controversy, and overbearing in manner. His guardianship of Oberlin was a stormy one. Asa Mahan, and Oberlin following in his footsteps, believed that the true reformer was the universal reformer. Mahan was prepared to fight "Whatever is . . . destructive to the true interests of humanity." This included "intemperance, licentiousness, war, violations of physical law in respect to food, drink, dress," as well as "ecclesiastical, civil, and domestic tyranny."

Such was the nature of the institution to which Lucy Stone, with her own ideas of freedom and perfectibility, applied; or rather, to which her brother Bowman applied for her. Women's position in those days can hardly be more dramatically symbolized than by the fact that even Lucy could not summon up the brazenness to address august college officials. So at her request Bowman, with the authority of his masculinity and his new ministerial position, wrote asking that she be admitted. His application was accepted, and at the end of August 1843 Lucy arrived at Oberlin.

The trip had been hard and, in Lucy's terms, expensive too. Even so, on her arrival she invested another twenty-five cents for postage to mail a reassuring letter to her mother, who had been uneasy about the pitfalls which might beset a young woman traveling alone. She said however that she would not be so extravagant soon again. Next time "I will send a paper and dot it." With first-class postage so high, the poorer members of the population habitually took advantage of cheaper newspaper postage by dotting words or letters to make up a message.

Expense was much on Lucy's mind. She had had no help from her father in what he considered a reckless and undesirable enterprise. "The whole expense of getting here," she wrote, "including food, was $16.65." She had, after due consideration, invested an extra dollar and a half to travel by train, since by doing so she would save three days. She rode day and night in "the cars," changing trains only once, whereas "by the packets I should have to change boats 3 or 4 times." It was still something of an adventure to travel in the cars, for the first railway passenger service had been put in operation only thirteen years before and had then covered a total distance of fifteen miles.

There was no trouble about traveling alone. She had heard such stories that she "did not know but there might be something, but there is not a mite." She even spoke to a stranger, "an elderly gentleman," who sat behind her and looking over her shoulder saw that she was studying Greek. He asked her why, and when she told him it was to find out what the Bible really said about the status of women, he suggested she might better learn more practical matters. "How many bones do you have in your hand and arm?" he asked. When she answered correctly, he admitted that she might be ready to study less practical subjects.

The "elderly" gentleman was Francis Elias Spinner, then about forty years of age, a major general in the New York State Militia, who was later appointed Treasurer of the United States by President Lincoln and who served in this capacity under three Presidents. He was so impressed by his single conversation with Lucy that years later, when she was famous, it became his habit to send her official documents from Washington. As Treasurer of the United States he was the first person to employ women in the Treasury Department. Perhaps his indoctrination by Lucy on that train ride long before had some effect on this decisive act.

General Spinner left the train at Herkimer, where he lived, and Lucy continued to Buffalo, the end of the first part of her journey. There was still Lake Erie to be crossed. She had only money enough for "deck" passage, so instead of spending the night in a stateroom she slept on deck along with horses, freight and other passengers, women among them, who like her could afford only the minimum fare. Fortunately the lake was calm.

"We . . . passed, I presume, fifty schooners. They looked

very grand, under full sail. . . . At night I put my trunk beside another, and my carpet-bag at the end, and lay down and slept sound all night, the other ladies did 'ditto,' and one elderly lady, who could not sleep, kept watch. There were several men on the other side of the deck 'camped down,' but we were not disturbed at all." They landed at Cleveland, where Lucy took a stage to Elyria, eight miles from Oberlin. There she changed stages and was joined by "four other ladies [who] got in to go to visit Oberlin."

What did she see when she reached Oberlin at last, after the years of work and saving, after the long journey? A drawing of the college three years later shows a group of seven white buildings: a church, a four-story hall and five smaller buildings, one no larger than a cabin. The campus is a fenced-in green, described as being twelve acres in size. Outside the fence, except for a boardwalk leading to the church, there is nothing but a flat area of bare soil, which must have been dusty in dry weather and soggy when it rained. "I don't think the land here is half as good as it is at home," the farmer's daughter wrote. "It is all clay." The pioneers had been thorough in clearing the forest. Of the vast wilderness only two trees were left standing on the green.

No one could spend even a day at Oberlin without becoming aware of its reformist nature, since food reform governed the diet. The effort to outlaw meat was never entirely successful, but tea and coffee were anathema, and their disastrous effects were pointed out in terms which might better have applied to the evils of alcohol or drugs. Lucy described the fare. "We have things 'sort' of regular here, breakfast at six, dinner at twelve, supper at half-past six. We have had meat once a day, bread and milk for supper, pudding and milk, thin cakes, etc., for breakfast." She seems to have been undemanding, for her comment on this diet was, "We shall live well enough."

Even by the time she wrote this first letter she had received her religious initiation. Abolitionist though Professor Finney was, she had already heard him attack as irreligious and therefore doomed the antislave group which she supported. "Of all the reformers this side of Hell," she quoted him as saying, "the Come-Outers most need reforming." The Come-Outers he referred to were William Lloyd Garrison's group of abolitionists, who refused to support the United States Constitution, which sanctioned slavery, or give allegiance to a church which countenanced human bondage. The term Come-Outers derived from their habit of leaving church in mid-sermon and slamming the door behind them to show disapproval of the preacher's views. But though Lucy was still very religious, fire and brimstone in the hereafter did not frighten her so much as oppression here and now, and on the wall of her room in the Ladies' Hall she defiantly hung a picture of Garrison, and one of her schoolmates said that she came near to worshiping it.

The antagonism of antislavery Oberlin to the Garrison abolitionists is not remarkable, given Oberlin's strong religious principles; and so complete was it that for a long time Lucy was the only person at Oberlin who subscribed to *The Liberator*. Later, in spite of the college's stand against Garrisonianism, she became the Oberlin agent of the *Anti-Slavery Bugle,* the magazine of Garrison's western followers.

Money was a problem not only to Lucy, but to most of her fellow students. Men and women alike did housework at the college and boarded there at the low rate of a dollar a week. But even a dollar a week was too expensive for Lucy, though she supplemented her small capital by working; and for most of the first year she cooked in her own room, reducing her food costs to fifty cents a week.

For housework in the Ladies' Hall she was paid three cents an hour. She made the most of her time by propping her Greek book on a ledge where she could study while she washed the dishes. Teaching brought greater returns; but teaching in the preparatory school was not permitted to college students until their second year. However, on Bowman's recommendation, and because Lucy had been a full-fledged teacher for so many years, this regulation was waived by the college authorities. Lucy was assigned to teach two hours a day, and for this she received twelve-and-a-half cents an hour, more than four times what she could earn by housework.

She never expressed resentment at her father's refusal to help her. On the contrary, years later, without any reference to his general penuriousness, she attempted to exonerate him. "Even their own fathers did not know it was wise and safe to educate women. Good fathers, with pathetic earnestness, still clinging to the old way said to their daughters, 'Your mother can read and write and reckon all the accounts she will ever be called to settle. This was good enough for her, and it is enough for you.' They quoted, 'If a woman would know anything, let her ask her husband at home.' " But what if she had no husband, Lucy asked, or if she had one who could not answer her questions? Later Lucy also told about a girl at Oberlin whose rich father gave her magnificent clothes but refused to contribute a cent for her education, so that she had to sell her beautiful silk dresses to pay for her schooling.

But it was not only rich fathers who took a dim view of education for women. Penniless Negro men shared their prejudice. Oberlin's Negro population was large. There were freed slaves and fugitives, some who settled there, some who stopped on their way farther north. The Negro children went to the regular schools, but the adults were so ignorant that they had to be placed in a special school "designed chiefly for adult persons who have been debarred in earlier life, by slavery or prejudice, from the advantages of education."

In the long winter vacation, arranged so that students might earn money to continue their studies, Lucy was assigned to teach at this school. But when she was introduced to her pupils an indignant murmur went through the room, and a tall Negro rose and said that he for one thought it wrong for grown men to be taught by a girl. They could not read or write. Until very recently they had owned nothing, not even their own bodies; but they knew their rights. They knew that men everywhere and in whatever condition were superior to women.

Lucy stood her ground. She explained gently but firmly that learning to read and write was so important that they should be willing to learn from anyone capable of teaching them. They listened and reluctantly decided to give her a chance. It was not long before they became her ardent admirers and supporters.

Some time later while Lucy was away there was a fire in the Ladies' Hall where she lived. When she returned she was told that during the fire a whole procession of Negro men had appeared asking where Miss Stone's trunk could be found, each interested only in saving her possessions. She had won another battle.

Chapter Five

It is not easy to draw maps for a brave new world. Where is one to set the boundaries? Lucy, embattled—or battling—throughout her life, was too drastic a reformer even for reformist Oberlin. Yet in the hodgepodge of reform they agreed on many issues. Lucy, for instance, was enough the creature of her childhood training to be a leading spirit in Oberlin's Female Reform Society, of which in 1845 she became secretary-treasurer. The nature of this society is illustrated by an essay which one of Oberlin's first women graduates wrote for it in 1836: "What is the proper treatment of licentious men?"

The same year the agent of the New York society had listed the causes of immorality as "Impure imagination, Dress of Females, Slavery. . . . Females receiving visits of gentlemen protracted to a late hour, Low prices of labor in cities, Voluptuousness. . . ." Further causes were parties, the study of Greek and Roman classics, and that old satanic tempter of Lucy's youth, novel reading. The *Advocate of Moral Reform,* to which Lucy's family subscribed, and the *Oberlin Evangelist* carried columns repeating over and over the words "Put down that novel. It is endangering your morals. Put down that novel. It will ruin your soul."

Even the curriculum at Oberlin was influenced by such moral taboos and was far less radical than other phases of life there. The Latin students read not Vergil and Horace but Hugo Grotius's *De Veritate Religionis Christianae.* And in 1845 the trustees passed a resolution that no student should fail to graduate because of "any want of knowledge in the heathen classics." There is no indication that Lucy objected to these restrictions.

Her first recorded brush with authority in her first year at Oberlin was not the result of opposed convictions. She suffered from severe headaches, probably migraine, a striking fact in view of her otherwise extraordinarily good health. "Weigh 119 pounds," she wrote to her family, "more than I ever did before. I have but very little headache." Yet in another letter she told of investing the huge sum of four dollars for "a large rocking chair, with a study leaf on it." She apologized, "It is worth a great deal to me to rest my aching head on sometimes."

Every Sunday morning students were required to attend the lengthy church service; but Lucy soon found that keeping her bonnet on gave her a headache, so, with her usual logic, she took it off. Immediately she was called before the Ladies' Board. To sit in church bareheaded! She replied by asking how, if she had a raging headache all day, she was to account to God for her wasted Sunday afternoons. This so worried the board that they agreed to a compromise. If she would sit in the last row, she might take off her bonnet when the pressure became unbearable. Surely Lucy was the winner of this first small skirmish.

The year 1845 was an eventful one at home and at college. In that year Lucy's baby sister Sarah was married. Father Stone wrote to Lucy, "I do not think she loves him as she ought." And Mother said that the young man, Mr. Lawrence, was teaching in New York "at 21 dolars [sic] a month and wants her to help him. Father and I are not very well pleased but must submit." Father was acting in his usual fashion. "I am astonished that Father did not give you more," Lucy wrote to her sister, "for he must have known that you *needed* more, but he did just so to Eliza . . . and then kept making it up afterwards. . . . In regard to Father's will, giving you and me only two hundred dollars apiece, I don't care a particle about it, for I know that Father has not done it because he loves his sons more than he does his daughters, and though there is no justice in it, still I feel that it is less Father's fault than it is the fault of the time when his impressions of what is right in such a case were formed. When he was young it was the universal custom to give the property principally to the sons, and he probably is only acting in accordance with what he thinks is right."

It is significant that Lucy, who had determined never to marry, felt qualified to advise her sister on how a wife should act. It is perhaps the first indication that Lucy's sense of knowing what was right for herself was expanding into a belief that she also knew what was best for others. "I am anxious that my *only sister* should have all the assistance she can secure to enable her to *begin,* and *continue* right . . ." she wrote.

"In the first place, Sarah, let there be the most perfect openheartedness between you and your husband . . . if he finds that after you are married you conceal, and do things without letting him know, don't you see that he must necessarily become distrustful?" Sarah must discuss expenditures, even for a dress, with her husband, "take a *real interest* in the *interests* of *his relatives,*" keep his *"wardrobe in order."* "Order" is underlined three times. She must set regular days for each household duty. And then the girl breaks through; "I cannot repress the bitter tears that come briming [sic] to my eyes."

The same year two other events took place which made 1845 perhaps Lucy's most important at Oberlin; she won a major battle and gained an ally. In January her father finally admitted defeat in his campaign to make Lucy a model lady. Her courage in attaining an education against his will and without his help had at last won his respect, the tribute of the vanquished to the victor. "When you wrote that you had to get up at two o'clock to study your lesson, it made me think of the old tanyard where I had to get up at one and two o'clock. I little thought then that I should have children, or a child, that would have to do the same; not the same work, but perhaps as hard. I had to work late and early. I was hardly able to live; and you have been under the same inconvenience as far as money is concerned. Let this suffice. There will be no trouble about money; you can have what you need, without studying nights, or working for eight cents an hour."

But his capitulation did not make him reckless. He lent her the money; he did not give it to her. Luther wrote, "Father has taken up your note to Wm Johnson and says you must send *him* your note for the amount you rec'd in all, viz: the 40 dollars to Wm Johnson with three years' interest, the 20 dollars I let you have and the eight dollars you receive in this. Please let us know what amount of money you will want this fall and winter. . . . Father has taken up the note you gave Sarah, and will hold it." Yet there seems in fact to have been a lack of ready cash, for "Brother B. has let Father have fifty dollars, and will let him have more in the fall." Her mother, womanlike, had different financial concerns. What about Lucy's clothes? They were quilting a cloak that had been Rhoda's and would send it to her, but weren't her "bonnets, stockings, flannel petticoats" almost worn out? "I want to know if your apparel compares with the rest of the students."

At long last she could stop worrying about whether she would eat and devote herself to learning. She did not stop working, but she no longer worked every waking minute. Her schedule was still crowded enough. "I rise at five o'clock, and am busy until six taking care of my room and person. At six we go to breakfast, which, with family worship, lasts until seven; then I go and recite Latin until eight, from eight to nine recite Greek, from nine till ten study algebra, from ten till eleven hear a class recite Arithmetic, from eleven to twelve recite algebra, from twelve to one, dinner and an exercise in the sitting room, which all the ladies are required to attend. From one to two, hear a class recite Arithmetic, from two to five, I study, from five to six prayers at the Chapel, and supper, study in the evening. The above are the duties of every day except Monday, which is washing day." That was not all. Monday afternoon there was a composition class. Tuesday a lecture by a member of the Ladies' Board. Thursday the students were required to attend an hour's prayer meeting, and when that was over, an hour's lecture by one of the faculty. Even so she was still earning "a quarter of a dollar more than my board costs." As for her studies, "I get along quite successfully . . . though I am not at the *head* of the class."

The second great event for Lucy was the enrollment of Antoinette Brown at Oberlin. The girl who immediately became Lucy's ally was as remarkable as Lucy herself. She had been born in May 1825, when Lucy was almost seven; but when she came to Oberlin in 1845 she was already sufficiently advanced in her studies to enter the third-year class, of which Lucy was a member.

Antoinette, known as Nette, was a vivacious girl, dark-eyed and dark-haired, whose appearance gave little indication of her extraordinary past and remarkable future. She had been born in a log cabin in Monroe County, New York, and at the age of nine had joined the Congregational Church on profession of faith. Even at this early age she had begun to speak at church meetings. She was considered a kind of miracle, and everyone agreed that so religious a child would grow up to marry a minister or a missionary.

In the stagecoach on her way to Oberlin Antoinette happened to meet a trustee of the college who was an old family friend. The chief subject of his conversation was that she must stay clear of a Miss Lucy Stone, who was a dangerous radical. If anything had been needed to make Antoinette seek Lucy out, this of course was it. She caught a glimpse of her the first evening, "a small round-faced girl in a neat calico frock, her hair cut round at the neck and hanging just above the smoothest, whitest, turned-down collar—which, by the way she always washed and ironed herself. . . . She appeared to be about sixteen." She was astonished to discover that Lucy was, in fact, twenty-six.

This was the beginning of a life-long friendship between the two women, who were later to become sisters-in-law as well. They were soon involved in a project to combat one of the college rules. Each week, in the coeducational rhetoric course they both attended, the young men held a debate which the girl students were required to attend, though they were never allowed to take part. It was enough for them to listen and learn from the men. To Lucy and Antoinette this discrimination was intolerable. They protested to the head of the department, Professor Thome.

They were fortunate. Professor James Thome, who had come to Oberlin from Lane Seminary as a student, was a Kentucky gentleman who had dedicated himself to antislavery. One of the freest of the Oberlin reformers, he agreed that Lucy and Antoinette might debate each other. Their debate, so novel a form of entertainment, drew a large audience. It also drew the fire of the ubiquitous Ladies' Board and of the college authorities. There were to be no more public debates for women.

This was too much for Lucy and Antoinette. Both expected to use public speaking in their future lives and they needed experience. They organized a small group of the most daring girl students to practice debating. At first the little group of five rebels stole into the woods for their secret meetings, taking turns as guards to warn of approaching intruders.

Such a venture was at least exciting, and could be endured as long as the weather was warm; but as winter approached it grew more and more uncomfortable. Lucy, as usual, saved the day. She asked an old Negro woman, mother of one of her pupils, to let them meet at her house on the edge of town. The old woman was reluctant. Why should young women wish to come secretly to her house unless they were up to no good? But when, to her amazement, she discovered there were no men in the debating society, she agreed to let them use her home. Even then the girls made their way separately to their meeting place, afraid their wicked design might attract the attention of the Ladies' Board.

Yet Lucy soon found an opportunity to make a public appearance. The Negroes had organized a celebration, which became one of Oberlin's yearly events, to commemorate the freeing of the West Indian slaves. A program for August 1, 1846, lists as one of its attractions, "Why do we rejoice today? An Essay by Miss Lucy Stone, West Brookfield, Massachusetts." The speech was full of purple passages and ended with a rhetorical burst. Shall we not vow "that we will not abate one jot or tittle from our efforts so long as one fetter remains unbroken?"

Whether this speech stirred up a storm is uncertain. Antoinette Brown recalled long afterward that the next day Lucy had been called before the Ladies' Board and questioned by Mrs. Mahan herself as to whether she had not felt "embarrassed and frightened" to find herself on a platform with so many men. Lucy is supposed to have replied, " 'Those men' were President Mahan and my professors. . . . I was not afraid of them a bit." Yet only two weeks later, when memory was fresh, Lucy wrote home, "I have not been scolded at all." Possibly, to Lucy, used by now to head-on clashes with authority, so mild a rebuke did not constitute a scolding.

Close friends and fellow rebels, Antoinette and Lucy yet disagreed on many subjects. Lucy dressed almost like a Quaker; some of the narrow white collars which were the only trimming for her dresses still exist, witnesses to her sedate neatness. But Nette, religious and serious though she was, was pretty and feminine enough to like gay clothes. Once when she appeared in a flowered hat, Lucy told her scornfully that she ought to be above carrying a flower pot around on her head, and cried when Nette refused to give up her frivolous adornment.

There were far more fundamental disagreements. Antoinette was a Trinitarian Congregationalist. Lucy, reacting against Finney's violent and narrow-minded doctrines, was leaning toward Unitarianism; and later she did, in fact, become a Unitarian and remained one the rest of her life.

This was an important divergence, particularly since Antoinette was a most pious girl.

Both ardent abolitionists, they disagreed even on that subject. Lucy's beloved Garrison was too much an anticleric for the devout Antoinette, who on the issue of antislavery came closer to the accepted Oberlin view. Yet even this did not protect her from Finney's rage. He expressed the suspicion that she and Lucy were atheists or something very like. Degrees of abolitionist thought, like shades of religious or political feeling, could in those days cause violent disagreement and vituperation.

Lucy was so far from being an atheist that it was faith in the Bible which had first moved her to demand an education; and even now, when the passive role of the church in the antislavery battle had made her distrust organized religion, she never fully subscribed to Garrison's Come-Outerism. Yet Garrisonianism was one of the two basic issues on which Lucy and Oberlin did battle. "They hate Garrison and women's rights," she wrote her parents. "I love both, and often find myself at swords' points with them." She was disillusioned to discover too that some of her professors were willing to concede that "war is sometimes right." This was a far less rigorous stand than Garrison's, for though he passionately believed that slaves ought to be freed at once, he was convinced that the only instrument of this change must be moral persuasion.

It is not surprising that the fanatically religious authorities of Oberlin considered Garrison beyond the pale. What is more significant is that, among the multitude of reforms to which Oberlin gave allegiance, feminism found no place. Women were to have the right to equal education, itself no negligible reform; but that was the only right they were to have. Two years after Lucy's graduation, Professor James H. Fairchild, who called the woman's rights movement "the Rozinante of reform," told his Oberlin students that "it is a thing positively disagreeable to both sexes to see a woman a public character." And time after time a phrase which appeared in Oberlin's first circular was repeated; men were the "leading sex." The student body, the faculty and the community were opposed to the fight for women's rights.

Antoinette and Lucy were determined to be content with no less than perfect equality. Early in their friendship Antoinette confided her secret aims to Lucy, for whom she had not only the love of a friend, but the adulation of a girl for a woman seven years her senior. The prophecies of her fellow church members that she would grow up to be a minister's wife fell far short of her intentions. Antoinette Brown was determined that she herself would be an ordained minister. Even Lucy, who was bold enough to aspire to be a speaker for the antislavery movement, told Antoinette that she did not believe any woman could ever become a minister.

At Oberlin Lucy had the opportunity to meet abolitionists of every degree, including men and women so radical that they believed in equality not only for Negroes but for women as well. Outstanding among them were Abby Kelley Foster and her husband Stephen S. Foster, who came to speak at Oberlin. Lucy had met Abby Kelley before. She had lectured in the church in West Brookfield and had even invited Lucy to sit in the pulpit with her. "Oh, I can't," Lucy had replied, with refreshing femininity. "I have ridden three miles, and my hair is all blown about." "Oh, Lucy Stone," Miss Kelley had said then, "you are not half emancipated."

Abby Kelley was herself one of the most emancipated women of her time. She was the first American woman, after the Grimké sisters, to lecture to mixed audiences, though the young Scottish noblewoman, Frances Wright, had scandalized the country in the late twenties by speaking publicly on various unpopular subjects, including education for women; and another foreigner, Ernestine Rose, a bright-eyed Polish girl married to an Englishman, was beginning to make her unwelcome presence felt as an active reformer. Like the Grimkés and Abby Kelley, they were attacked and reviled, but probably because Abby Kelley expounded the most radical form of anticlerical abolitionism she suffered even more abuse than the Grimké sisters, and suffered it without their heartening presence, for their short careers as antislavery speakers had ended. Sarah's voice had failed her; and Angelina had sustained an injury which forced her too to give up regular public speaking. This was in 1838, shortly after her marriage to the abolitionist Theodore Dwight Weld, who had been a pupil at Oberlin for a short time after the breakup of Lane Seminary.

Three days after her marriage, Angelina Grimké Weld made her last speech in Philadelphia, where a beautiful new hall built by Pennsylvania abolitionists was being dedicated. At the same meeting Abby Kelley first spoke in public. It was a meeting made hideous by a mob protesting the appearance of women on a public platform, on a platform moreover where Negroes were also appearing. Three days of dedicatory programs had passed peacefully enough. On the fourth women were to appear. Freedom for slaves might be tolerated. Freedom for women was carrying radicalism too far. A mob gathered outside the hall. They screamed; they threatened; they hurled stones through the windows. Angelina Grimké and Abby Kelley continued to speak, and the meeting was carried to its conclusion. The next night the beautiful new hall was burned down.

This initiation, almost literally by fire, was Abby Kelley's entrance on the public scene. She was a Quaker, born in Worcester, Massachusetts, in 1811. A fair-haired, attractive girl, she had rejected the easier road of early marriage to become a teacher. While she worked, she turned over the money she inherited from her father and everything she earned or was given to the abolitionist movement. But she could not be content until she dedicated her life to the cause. She resigned from her teaching position and became a speaker. For this sacrifice she was almost universally condemned, denounced from the pulpits as a new Jezebel, "a servant of Satan in the garb of an angel of light." She had trampled on God's commandment that women should "keep silence in the churches, for it is not permitted unto them to speak."

In 1887, at the memorial service for Abby Kelley Foster, Lucy Stone told of the outcast life Abby Kelley had lived, so insulted once in a home where she was staying that she ran away, and for a day and a half was not even able to find food. The reputation of this gentle Quaker lady was so frightful that in 1850 the Woman's Rights Convention at Worcester argued for some time as to whether she should be invited to speak, because was she "so odious."

Even at Oberlin in 1846 her appearance caused recriminations and public attack; but by then she was no longer alone. The year before she had married Stephen S. Foster—the reformer, not the composer—and now they lectured together. Lucy was delighted to see them and told her family that she "had a grand time with them." They had lectured three times, "set the people to thinking, and I hope great good will result." What resulted first, however, was that the town and college were so incensed that they refused to allow another meeting. Stephen Foster was even more violent than Garrison in his attacks on a clergy indifferent to slavery; and Abby had entered into an angry debate which Professor Fairchild afterward described as a shocking "specimen of what woman becomes when out of her place."

To Abby, Oberlin's treatment was a bitter blow. She wrote an impassioned letter to Lucy complaining that they had been treated like "low, degraded, licentious vagabonds . . . infidels of the blackest dye." She had never, it seemed, come to accept the ostracism which was her daily life. And if she could not be received in Oberlin, in what community could she hope to find a place?

Yet even with so discouraging an example, Lucy grew more and more determined to lead a life in which public speaking would play a leading part; and it was this which caused her final battle with the college authorities. It was a custom at Oberlin for essays to be read at graduation by leading members of the class, chosen by their classmates. Before the Commencement of 1847, Lucy was selected by a large vote.

There was only one difficulty. Though the men delivered their own essays, the women had to sit silent while the rhetoric teacher read their contributions. When President Mahan and Mr. Whipple, principal of the preparatory department, met with the class to count the votes, and Lucy was found to be one of the winners, she told them she could not submit an essay—not without a "sacrifice of principle that I [have] no right to make."

The class begged her not to resign, and President Mahan, himself a man of principle, admitted that he believed she should be allowed to speak; but he had been unable to persuade the faculty. Mr. Whipple, walking home with Lucy after the meeting, also urged her not to withdraw. He warned that the faculty might even refuse to let her graduate. But "I told him that by so doing I would make public acknowledgment of the rectitude of the principle which . . . denies to [women] the privilege of being co-laborers with men in any sphere to which their ability makes them adequate; and that no word or deed of mine should ever look towards the support of such a principle, or even to its toleration."

Though President Mahan assured the faculty that he had never had a student more worthy to represent her class, they could not be budged. In protest, all the selected women except one refused to write essays, and two of the men joined them. The students appointed to replace these rebels also refused to submit papers. It was a victory, not indeed for Lucy, since she was not allowed to speak, but for her principles, always more important to her than herself.

She was, however, permitted to graduate without submitting an essay, and decided that it would not betray her principles to attend the graduation ceremony, where she received the first Bachelor's degree ever given to a Massachusetts woman. She even had a new dress, her second in the entire four years at college. For this important occasion she sent all the way to New York for black bombazine, a fashionable fabric of mixed silk and wool. The dress, which she must have made herself, cost her four dollars and sixty-six cents. Like her other dresses, its only trimming was a small, white, Quakerish collar.

At Commencement time that year a group of abolitionists happened to be lecturing at Oberlin. Among them were William Lloyd Garrison, Stephen Foster and Frederick Douglass. They arrived in time to hear two of the graduates read papers denouncing Come-Outerist fanatics. They arrived in time too for Garrison to meet Lucy. "She is a very superior young woman," he wrote to his wife, "and has a soul as free as the air, and is preparing to go forth as a lecturer, particularly in vindication of the rights of women. Her course here has been firm and independent, and she has caused no small uneasiness to the spirit of sectarianism in the institution." He could not then have guessed at the life-long association he was to have with her.

In the four years Lucy had been at Oberlin she had never had enough money to return home; and at first it seemed she would not be able to go even now, for she had determined to pay her debt to her father and have enough money for her fare before she started east. Then Sarah wrote, "Father says you had better come home when you get through . . . he will furnish you money." But Father Stone was no more openhanded than usual, for the sentence ends, "and take it out of your legacy." Nevertheless, Lucy accepted the terms and started happily for home. It was the end of her formal education. She was to return to Oberlin as an honored guest in 1883, when women, and she with them, had gained enough rights so that she was invited to be one of the main speakers at the Oberlin Jubilee.

Antoinette Brown's battle with Oberlin was not yet over. While Lucy had been carrying on her fight to speak at Commencement, Nette had won that right without argument. Unlike Lucy, she was not a candidate for the A.B. degree, but was enrolled in the Young Ladies' Course, a limited program originally projected as the course all women students were to follow. At her graduation exercises there would be, except for President Mahan, only women on the platform. By the liberal standards of Oberlin it was proper for women to speak under such circumstances, and Antoinette wrote and read her essay.

Her battle came later, when Lucy was no longer there to help her. Nothing could dissuade Nette from her determination to be a minister. Her family refused to finance her in her folly, hoping to force her to come home. Nevertheless, determined to support herself entirely, she applied for admission to Oberlin's department of theology. She was rejected; but if she insisted, she might, she was told, attend classes as a "resident graduate, pursuing the Theological Course." The faculty had no choice, since Oberlin's charter offered its full advantages to women.

Lucy wrote a stormy letter accusing Antoinette of having accepted "dishonorable terms." If it was possible for Lucy to learn that there might be more than one kind of intransigence, Nette's remarkable reply must have taught her then. "You think I have come back to Oberlin upon dishonorable terms?" her friend wrote. "Then you don't know me. I never did a dishonorable public act that could make me blush to look anybody in the face, never! I came back here just upon no terms at all. . . . I came back to study Theology, and get knowledge. I do get it. . . . I am not responsible for their conduct or decisions. . . . And what if they or anybody else think I act unwisely, or dishonorably, or foolishly, what can that be to me?"

Time, a very long time, proved Antoinette right. Six years later she was ordained in her own small church at South Butler, New York, the first woman to be ordained a Protestant minister. It took far longer for Oberlin to succumb. In 1878 the college granted her a Master of Arts degree; and in 1908 she finally received the Doctor of Divinity degree for which she had completed the requirements fifty-eight years before. By the time Oberlin was ready to concede her equality with the leading sex, she was eighty-three years old. Her final triumph came too late for Lucy Stone to see. Lucy had died fifteen years before.

Part Two

I Must Speak for the Women

Chapter Six

Lucy's years at Oberlin had solidified her conviction that she must dedicate herself not only to antislavery, but to "the elevation of my sex"; and that to do so she must become a public speaker. In an age when radio and television convey ideas across the world in minutes, it is impossible to realize how solitary the lecture platform then stood as a source not only of ideas, but of group entertainment. The lyceum of the nineteenth century, like the Chautauqua of the early twentieth, brought this combination of enlightenment and amusement to otherwise uninformed communities.

Yet in spite of the popularity of male lecturers in 1847, for a woman such an occupation was hazardous. To her family and friends she would seem to have demeaned herself. To her audience she would be the butt of ridicule and even of physical attack, particularly if her subjects were as unpopular as antislavery and the shocking idea that the ordinary woman in her ordinary life suffered grievous wrongs.

So Lucy's decision to make lecturing her career caused understandable consternation in her family. They had been forced to accept the fact that their little round-faced Lucy had grown into an eccentric woman who insisted on being educated like a man; but they had assumed that she would now stop such nonsense and settle down. They had given up any hope that she would marry, for though she looked girlish still, she was now twenty-nine. The only ladylike alternative was for her to become a teacher. The controversy about her future raged by mail while she was still at college. To save paper and postage, three or four of the

Stone family would crowd their messages onto one large double sheet of paper. If a wasted margin remained, someone was sure to cover it, or might even turn the paper and write in a sort of plaid design over someone else's letter.

Of Lucy's family only her brothers Frank and Bowman did not attempt to discourage her from a career of public speaking. The women, trained to be timid and withdrawing, were united in opposition. Frank wrote, "If you think you have got brass enough, and can do more good by giving public lectures than any other way, I say go into it." And Bowman said, "I think you should do that which you think to be your duty. No one can be truly happy who neglects to do what he feels he ought."

Her sister Sarah begged her to teach instead of lecturing. "I don't hardly know what you mean by 'laboring for the restoration and salvation of our sex' but I conclude you mean a salvation from some thralldom imposed by man. Now my sister I don't believe woman is groaning under half so heavy a yoke of bondage, as you imagine. I am sure I do not feel burdened by anything man has laid upon me. . . ." Frank's wife could not resist adding a note to his letter. "Mother . . . feels dreadfully about it . . . and if you think you must lecture, she wants to know if you don't think you could do more good by going from house to house. . . ."

Her father seems not to have entered the discussion, except on her mother's behalf. "Now, Miss Lucy, you will hear what Mother thinks about your Public Speaking. Mother says she had rather you would married Walker and had a pair of twine [sic] babies every year." Then with an unusual burst of humor, "She did not say how many years." But Lucy, in spite of an almost fanatical devotion, could not let even her mother's feelings sway her. She could only try to make her mother understand, and through understanding lighten her unhappiness.

"Because I know that I shall suffer, shall I, for this, like Lot's wife, turn back? No, Mother, if in this hour of the world's need I should refuse to lend my aid, however small it may be, I should have no right to think myself a Christian, and I should forever despise Lucy Stone. If, while I hear the wild shriek of the slave mother robbed of her little ones, or the muffled groan of the daughter spoiled of her virtue, I do not open my mouth for the dumb, am I not guilty? Or should I go, as you said, from house to house to do it, when I could tell so many more in less time, if they should be gathered in one place? You would not object, or think it wrong, for a man to plead the cause of the suffering and the outcast; and surely the moral character of the act is not changed because it is done by a woman. . . .

"But, Mother, there are no trials so great as they suffer who neglect or refuse to do what they believe is their duty. I expect to plead not for the slave only, but for suffering humanity everywhere. Especially do I mean to labor for the elevation of my sex."

She told Sarah she was "pained and surprised by her views in regard to women's position in society. . . . I would almost infinitely prefer your approbation in this matter, but I *can* do without it, since I have an approving conscience."

How unlike Lucy was to the picture of a proper nineteenth-century female is evident from a question she asked her now-married brother Luther. Her question is lost, but his highly moral reply remains. "In answer to your inquiry about sexual intercourse . . . God made the whole of man for his own glory. . . . Our generative organs should never be used except for propagation." Nine-tenths of the men who are underdeveloped in body and mind "have become what they are by their own or their fathers indulgence in the Beastlike use of their generative organs. . . . *I Think It As Great A Sin To Not Suffer These Organs To Be Used At All As To Use Them To* [*sic*] *Much.*"

That she was not a proper nineteenth-century female she continued to prove. In spite of her family's warnings, she delivered her first public address outside of Oberlin in the winter of 1847, the year she was graduated. What was more, she delivered it in her brother Bowman's church at Gardner, Massachusetts. She spoke on women's rights; and the speech became history. It was the first time an American woman had delivered a speech dedicated solely to that subject, though a few forward-looking men had even gone so far as publicly to advocate women's enfranchisement.

Later, when Lucy lectured in West Brookfield, her father, drawn perhaps by some belated sense of loyalty, came to hear her. He came with so great a sense of shame that he sat in the audience literally hiding his head in his hands. But as his daughter spoke, he began to raise his head. She was a splendid speaker; as an honest man he had to admit it, and her audience was silent, interested, respectful. Suddenly, in spite of himself, he was proud of his rebellious daughter. By the end of the lecture he was sitting straight and firm.

Though at Oberlin Lucy had been asked by both the Massachusetts and the Western Anti-Slavery Societies to become a regular lecturer, when she returned East she heard nothing from either group. Then, in the spring of 1848, on the way home from some antislavery meetings in Boston, Lucy stopped at Worcester to visit Abby Foster, who asked her why she had given up her plans to lecture. Lucy answered unhappily that she did not know how to begin.

Abby never wasted time when something needed doing. She wrote at once to ask the Massachusetts Anti-Slavery Society why they were not using Lucy's talents. Samuel L. May, general agent of the society, immediately wrote to Lucy, offering to pay her expenses and whatever in addition she thought was right. Lucy told Bowman that Father and Mother Stone said she "would disgrace the whole family" and would never afterward be able to earn an honest living. "I however thought differently, and concluded to go."

Now began Lucy's long personal association with William Lloyd Garrison, Wendell Phillips, Francis Jackson and Theodore Parker. These men lived in Boston within five minutes' walk of each other, and the new young lecturer visited them, sometimes staying with the Garrisons and living for a while in the wealthy Jackson's charming home when she herself was pitifully poor.

The two great pillars of the movement, Garrison, so long Lucy's idol, and Phillips, the golden youth turned reformer, were so dramatically contrasted that it seemed some celestial casting director had chosen them for their roles. Garrison was a tall, dark man, full-featured, lips almost sensual, brown eyes large and kind; but the kindness of his face was lost in a larger sadness, and the sensuality in a restraining sternness and asceticism. Yet Wendell Phillips, who knew him as well as any man did, said, "I never knew him unhappy"; and though in public controversy he was uncontrolledly violent, in personal relations he was courteous and reasonable.

Such contradictions were characteristic of him. He was a man of excess no less because his excesses were on the side of virtue. He was intemperately moral. Though his public words were violent, he was in principle opposed to violence; and for years maintained that slavery must and could be overthrown by moral persuasion. A religious man, he became an anticleric when he found the church could not be swerved from its proslavery stand. A patriotic man, he turned against the Constitution because the government countenanced slavery. "Friends of liberty and humanity must immediately withdraw from the compact of bloody and deceitful men."

His inability to reject a cause brought him into constant battle with his fellow reformers. His wholehearted espousal of women's rights frightened his antislavery friends, who believed, probably correctly, that their cause was threatened by alliance with an even more unpopular crusade.

His intransigent stand against slavery often placed him in physical danger, not from southerners but from northerners. In Boston, on October 21, 1835, he was barely saved from lynching. On that day, the Boston Female Anti-Slavery Society was holding a meeting in the Anti-Slavery Hall. The mere announcement of this gathering had caused such indignation that before the meeting began a furious mob had gathered around the building. The mayor made no effort to give the ladies police protection, but appeared at the hall and asked them to disperse because *they* were causing a disturbance of the peace. They had no choice but to leave.

The crowd outside permitted the women to go unharmed, but once they were safely away burst into the building, where Garrison was in his office. They grabbed him and were about to throw him out of a window, when someone appeared with a rope and they decided to drag him through the streets instead. They had pulled him for some distance when the mayor at last decided to intervene and, to protect Garrison, sent him off to jail for disturbing the peace.

While Garrison was being dragged through the streets, a young lawyer, drawn by sounds very unlike the usual quiet of a Boston morning, came out to see what was happening. Horrified, he saw the screaming mob and the man they were mauling. The young lawyer was an officer in a Suffolk regiment. With relief he saw his colonel standing near him. "Why not call out the guards?" the young man said. "Let us offer our services to the mayor." The Colonel answered, "You fool! Don't you see that the regiment is in front of you?" It was true. The rowdy men of this mob were the elite of Boston, inheritors of a tradition of revolution and free speech, fighting so valiantly now to keep one man from expressing the opinion that Negroes should be free. The young lawyer was Wendell Phillips, who later said, "It is a singular result of our institutions that we have never had in Boston any but well-dressed mobs."

William Lloyd Garrison had grown up in extreme poverty. Wendell Phillips was equipped at birth with every advantage a man could hope to have: family, money, beauty, intelligence. As became a scion of one of Boston's first families, he was educated at Harvard, where he was leader of Boston's society youths. If he had any thought of reform, he gave no outward sign. He was as warm and gentle as Garrison was stern and forbidding. Across the years descriptions of him create an image rarely found outside the pages of a romantic novel. "He was possessed and moulded of grace." "To my mind then," wrote a classmate, "he was the most beautiful person I had ever seen—handsome, indeed, in form and feature; but what I mean by his beauty was his grace of character, his kindly, generous manners, his brightness of mind, his perfect purity and whiteness of soul." The *chevalier sans peur et sans reproche!*

He was, besides, one of the great orators of his day. His voice had "the penetrating mellowness of the flute and the violin." In a time given to oratorical effects, his style was simple in content and delivery. He was later paid large fees as a lyceum speaker on many subjects: travel, finance, science, foreign affairs; but he always offered to lecture without charge if he might talk on abolition. He and his wife were both well-to-do, and Phillips made a fortune as a lecturer; but they gave everything to the cause of antislavery, and he ended life a poor man.

These were the leaders of the movement for which Lucy began to work in 1848. If Garrison could be almost lynched, if an antislavery hall in Philadelphia could be burned because women lectured there, what, her family wondered, would happen to quiet, demure little Lucy? Could she possibly survive?

They did not overestimate the dangers. They did, however, underestimate Lucy. They knew her courage. What they did not realize was the appeal of her manner, the power of her voice, which had such ability to charm that the rowdiest audiences, after shouting down speaker after speaker, fell silent when they heard it. Yet it was not the strong voice of a public speaker, and its soft, musical tones sometimes failed to carry across large halls. For the quality of her lectures we must depend on current accounts. A letter in her own small, spidery handwriting tells the reason. "I can give the substance of my late lecture next Tuesday evening. I cannot *repeat,* for I never write my lectures." Elizabeth Cady Stanton says more. "In her early days she was an impassioned, extemporaneous speaker. As she did not write [her speeches], no reporter could do her justice; hence we cannot judge of her power and eloquence by any printed word of history. Her sweet voice and simple girlish manner made her first appearance on the platform irresistible."

It was characteristic of Lucy that she never had any sense of herself as history. Later, Mrs. Stanton and Susan B. Anthony were to preserve with loving care the documents of the woman suffrage movement and were to write huge and valuable volumes on its development, in which, naturally enough, they justified their own roles. Lucy Stone seems never to have thought of her role in the future except in its effect on the fate of those for whom she worked. Yet enough of her remarkable speeches remain so that, though the soft, beautiful voice is lost, it is possible to recover some of the technique which so enthralled audiences. It was her habit to praise allegiance instead of attacking opposition, to admit that women often failed in their duties as wives and mothers. "The blame," she would say, "is on both sides." She did not scorn to woo her audience.

In a speech reported in Horace Greeley's *New York Weekly Tribune* in April 1853, she spoke "without manuscript or notes." "Perhaps I should say at first here, what, to my mind, this Woman's Rights Cause is *not*. It is not to array the interests of men and women against each other, or create any antagonism between them. It is not to rob man of the rights which are his and give them to woman. . . . We leave our sphere to be made by our capacity." She went on to describe the enormous differences in women's spheres throughout the world; how in Eastern countries women were not allowed to sit at table with men or to enter places of worship. "What she can do and do well, we say in the face of the universe, she has a right to do it. We propose to give to woman a higher and nobler life." And again, " 'We, the people of the United States.' Which 'We, the people?' The women were not included." Each generalization was followed by a specific incident, fact by feeling, simple statement by a burst of rhetoric.

Her approach was not always so gentle. "You, in New York, rate the Negro so low as not to consider him your brother man. You will not admit him into the same place of worship with yourselves, nor into the same school with your children . . . you will not permit him to be buried in the same churchyard . . . ; yet if he owns enough of dirt, you allow him to have a vote . . . ; and yet those of whom you would make wives . . . you vote as more degraded than the drunkard . . . and more deeply debased than the Negro."

Contemporary accounts also preserve some record of her extraordinary difficulties and the amazing manner in which she overcame them. First, she must brave the rigors of travel, even in the East not the protected matter it is today. She herself told of a meeting to which she traveled alone. "At Northhampton, the 'team' (driven by a stranger to me, with a long cigar in his mouth) was waiting. It was an open wagon with only one seat and a large barrel in front filled with bottles of mead—the back part of the wagon filled with tobacco and sugar, with both [of] which, the driver stopped to supply the grocers on the road.

"I comforted myself on the way, by thinking that we were in a free country, and that it was a capital thing to be very independent." While she was thinking these noble thoughts, a storm broke. For the last seven miles it poured, and she arrived drenched. "My bonnet," she wrote, "which was almost new, hung round my face like paper."

But if the weather was unkind, men were unkinder still. Often when she reached a town she discovered that although local people had promised to post advance notices they had not done so, and she had to walk through the streets with tacks and a stone, nailing her own posters to trees and boards. Even then she was sometimes followed by boys who pulled down her posters as soon as she put them up. The youngsters were happy; they had discovered a prank to which their elders did not object. But Lucy would stop there in the road and tell the jeering boys how terrible an evil slavery was, how children no older than themselves were torn from their parents and sold into slavery. Often she was able to touch their hearts, and they would go away ashamed, leaving her posters where she had hung them.

In Malden, Massachusetts, a Universalist minister attained a reputation as a great wit when he announced one of her lectures: "This evening at the Town Hall, a hen will attempt to crow." On another occasion a Unitarian minister who had promised to announce her meeting told her, when she reached his town, that he had decided not to. It was so late then that she had to go from door to door spreading the news of her own meeting.

When Lucy finally reached a hall where she was to lecture, she often faced the worst of her trials, a hostile and unrestrained audience. Once as she sat on the platform waiting her turn to speak, a man in the audience hurled a prayer book at her, hitting her painfully on the head. The speaker of the moment turned the incident to advantage, saying that only a man with no better argument would have stooped to use such a poor one; but it was Lucy's head that was hit. Sometimes enthusiastic rowdies would throw pepper about the hall to force the people out; and at least once in midwinter a hose was put through a window and icy water turned on her as she spoke. Shivering, she continued her speech as though nothing had happened.

One day when she and Stephen Foster were among the speakers at an outdoor meeting, a mob appeared so menacing that every speaker but Lucy and Foster disappeared. When the mob seemed about to assail them, Lucy told Foster to run. "But who will take care of you?" he asked, just as a large man with a club leaped onto the platform. Lucy looked up at the threatening man. "This gentleman will take care of me," she said. And miraculously, won by her simple charm and courage, he did. The mob attacked Foster, grabbed his hands, "on one of which was an angry boil," knocked off his glasses, ripped his coat in two; but her belligerent protector helped Lucy away. As he led her to safety she talked to him, explaining how vital was the issue of antislavery, until, moved by her appeal, he stood her on a tree stump and, club in hand, kept the mob quiet while she delivered her message. At the end the shamed crowd collected twenty dollars to pay for a new coat for Mr. Foster.

In spite of such difficulties, the antislavery papers reported that she drew large crowds and converted many people. A letter to *The Liberator* gives the substance of one of her speeches. "Her subject was the causes of the existence . . . of slavery in this land, while it is being abolished, and slaveholders are being branded with infamy, amid the hardest despotisms of Europe. These causes were: first, the government; then the religion of the country. She drew a true, a terribly true picture of the Whig, Democratic and Free Soil parties, showing . . . that all their political remonstrances and votes against slavery are utterly futile, while they consent to sit down with slaveholders as legislators, judges, executives, on terms of perfect political equality. . . .

"Then she took up the Church, and showed how her altars stand in a sea of blood and tears—drawn by deep and unmitigated cruelty and injustice from three millions of slaves."

Lucy Stone had suffered a sad disillusionment with the official representatives of her faith, though not with the faith itself. She had become an anticleric; she was accused of being an atheist. Her brother Bowman, no atheist either, but a man who had chosen to dedicate his life to religion, had to give up his pulpit because, in a day when the churches of the North stood almost solidly together in refusing to take any stand against man's ownership of man, he preached that all men were brothers. And in 1851, three years after she became a regular speaker, Lucy was expelled from the West Brookfield congregation because she had "engaged in a course of life evidently inconsistent with her covenant engagements to this church."

Lucy replied, "It is the first intimation that I have received from any source that either the church or any member of it was dissatisfied with my course. I should be glad of an opportunity to explain to the church the reasons of my withdrawal from its communion, and also to show that my course of life is not only not inconsistent with, but is demanded by, my covenant engagements.

"I regard myself still as a member of the church. . . . But as, by the action of the church, I am, in its estimation, no longer a member of its body, it will feel under no obligation to grant me an opportunity for explanation. Indeed, I would not ask it on that ground, but simply as a matter of courtesy, which sinners even extend to sinners." She never received the opportunity.

Long before this, almost as soon as she began her career of public speaking, Lucy had trouble with the Anti-Slavery Society itself. She pleaded movingly for the rights of Negroes, but could never resist including an argument for woman's rights as well. Once in Boston she was completely carried away by Hiram Powers' statue of a Greek slave. "There it stood in the silence," she said, "with fettered hands and half-averted face—so emblematic of woman." The "hot tears" came to her eyes "at the thought of millions of women who must be freed." At that evening's meeting she "poured all [her] heart out about it."

Though Samuel May, agent of the Anti-Slavery Society, was sympathetic to Lucy's views, he felt constrained to point out that she was being paid to speak on abolition, not woman's rights. But Lucy could no more restrict her speeches than she could her feelings, and after an inner struggle she told him that she would have to resign and devote herself entirely to the cause of women. He had not intended to drive away so good a speaker and now tried to persuade her to compromise. If she spoke for women through the week, could she not then give her weekends to the Anti-Slavery Society? They had been paying her six dollars a week. They would pay her four dollars for weekends alone. To this she agreed. "I was a woman before I was an abolitionist," she told him. "I must speak for the women."

Chapter Seven

Lucy reached the woman's rights movement by the road of antislavery. Other women came by way of the temperance movement, for alcohol was a fearsome threat in a time when, as legal nonentities, women might find themselves at the mercy of a drunken husband from whose jurisdiction there was no appeal. From either of these reforms, it was a short step to demanding greater freedom for women.

The antislavery movement indeed led directly to the first concerted effort of women to better their lot. Shortly before the international Anti-Slavery Convention of 1840, pretty Elizabeth Cady, daughter of Judge Daniel Cady of Johnstown, New York, had married Henry B. Stanton, an ardent fighter for Negro freedom. Elizabeth Cady, who was twenty-four years old at the time of her marriage, came of an aristocratic, well-to-do family and was blessed with a father modern enough to believe that, up to a point, a girl was entitled to education. At Johnstown Academy young Elizabeth was permitted the unusual privilege of studying Greek and higher mathematics, but when, in 1830, it came time for her class to go to college, no college, of course, would take her, and she had to be content with the education offered at Emma Willard's new Troy Seminary.

When her father learned that Elizabeth wished to marry Henry Stanton, he was horrified. Henry was personable and intelligent; but no man involved in so fanatical a dream as abolitionism could hope to support a family. Judge Cady must have regretted, and not for the last time, having permitted his daughter so much contact with progressive ideas, because she married Henry without his consent, and their extraordinary wedding trip was a journey to the World's Anti-Slavery Convention in London.

The call for representatives to this convention had not specified that the delegates must be men, since the possibility of any group's selecting a woman had no more occurred to the organizing committee than that someone would send a horse. But radical circles in the United States had progressed so far that several societies did name women delegates. This incredible development threw the London convention into a turmoil.

A month earlier a similar battle had split the American society, when two ministers had resigned because that perennial storm center, Abby Kelley, had been elected to a committee. Their resignations were followed by many others. Now, in London, clerical delegates from the United States busily agitated against seating the women delegates; and the conservatives among the English, dismayed that the cause of freedom was to be contaminated by the appearance of women, joined wholeheartedly with them. Even before the first meeting, attempts were made to persuade the women delegates not to present their credentials. They had traveled three thousand miles under far from comfortable conditions to do just this. They could not be dissuaded.

As soon as the convention opened, the plight of the Negro was forgotten while men battled to remain masters over women. The women delegates were refused recognition and sent to sit in the gallery, behind a curtain, where they could listen unseen. Only two male abolitionists refused to take seats in the hall under such conditions—the indefatigable William Lloyd Garrison and Nathaniel P. Rogers, editor of a New Hampshire newspaper. So, in a country whose ruler was a woman just turned twenty-one, in the very city where that woman reigned, women were judged not only unfit to be heard in public, but even to show their faces. God save the Queen! God protect the ladies!

But like all suppression, this injustice inspired rebellion. In the lodginghouse where many American delegates stayed,

Elizabeth Stanton met the Hicksite Quaker minister Lucretia Coffin Mott, one of the founders of the Female Anti-Slavery Association. The quiet little woman with the sparkling eyes, whose posture was so erect, whose manner was so demure, was nearly fifty then and the mother of five children. It would have been hard to find a woman less like the loud-mouthed, masculine female pictured by the critics of women's rights.

Young Elizabeth Stanton was instantly drawn to the older woman. Together they sat shut off in the gallery. Together they strolled the streets of London, discussing the indignity of their treatment and planning how, when they returned to the United States, they would find other progressive women to join them in a crusade for women's rights. The resolve did not die; but it was eight years before it found expression in the first Woman's Rights Convention. That year was 1848, the same year that Lucy Stone began her career as a public speaker.

It is not surprising that these separate yet related events occurred at the same time. The year 1848 was one of revolution throughout western Europe. Rebellion was in the air. The *Communist Manifesto* was published. Old governments, old customs were overthrown by common men who had begun to learn that they had power if they dared wield it; and women, inspired by their example, dared newer and greater things.

It was an important year in the woman's rights movement. In 1848 the New York legislature finally passed a limited married woman's property act, an innovation for which a few staunch legislators and such women as Ernestine Rose and Paulina Wright Davis had been working for more than a decade. Now in New York a married woman had made the first step toward being considered a legal adult. She remained in sole possession of her premarital and inherited property and did not any longer, by the mere fact of marriage, become entirely dependent on her husband. Yet among the vast rights she still did not possess were the right to make a will, the right to her own earnings, the right to be guardian of her children.

The New York law is generally hailed as establishing for the first time in the United States the right of a married woman to maintain separate ownership of property. However, aside from the then little-known fact that a father could set up a trust fund for his daughter, there were other exceptions. The dependent status of wives had begun to cause concern among enlightened people, and several states had passed fragmentary laws which offered some slight protection to married women.

In that year of 1848 the plans that Lucretia Mott and Elizabeth Stanton had made in London bore fruit in the first Woman's Rights Convention. They had met again when Mrs. Mott visited her sister, Martha Coffin Wright, in Auburn, New York, not far from Seneca Falls, to which the Stantons with their rapidly increasing family had recently moved. This time the two women decided that opportunity, after delaying eight years, might never knock again. Having made this decision, they acted with almost comic precipitousness. Had they realized the multiplicity of problems they might never have arranged a convention; but in their innocence the two women, with Mrs. Wright and another friend, Mary Ann McClintock, sat down together and wrote an announcement which they sent at once to the *Seneca County Courier*. The call, appearing on July 14, invited readers to a convention to be held on July 19 and 20 in the Wesleyan Chapel at Seneca Falls, to discuss "the social, civil, and religious condition and rights of woman." In less than one week plans were formulated and speeches written. On the nineteenth the convention met as scheduled.

Seneca Falls, a drab factory town in northern New York State, was in the center of an area politically dominated by liberals and antislavers. The Stantons lived on the edge of town on a hill overlooking the river. The river has been dammed and the falls for which the town was named are gone. Today the hall where the convention met no longer exists, but on that corner a small plaque marks the historic spot where for the first time "in the World's history" women met together for the express purpose of winning equal rights with men, including the right to vote. The idea that women should demand the right to vote was so radical that, when Elizabeth Stanton suggested it, even her husband and Lucretia Mott felt that she was going too far; but she found support in the great Negro abolitionist, Frederick Douglass, who knew how important the franchise must be to Negroes and to women, and who, at the convention, spoke in favor of her resolution.

Democracy itself was young and the right of men to vote still far from universal. Yet it was inevitable that in an era of widening democracy and popular education one half of the community could not long be kept ignorant or forever disenfranchised. The *Declaration of Sentiments,* borrowing the ringing words of the preamble to the *Declaration of Independence,* evoked its spirit of revolution and liberty. "We hold these truths to be self-evident: that all men and women are created equal; that they are endowed by their Creator with certain inalienable rights; that among these are life, liberty and the pursuit of happiness."

There followed an indictment of man's tyranny over woman. "He has never permitted her to exercise her inalienable right to the elective franchise. . . . He has made her, if married, in the eye of the law, civilly dead. . . . He has made her, morally, an irresponsible being, as she can commit many crimes with impunity, provided they be done in the presence of her husband. . . . He has monopolized nearly all the profitable employments . . . denied her the facilities for obtaining a thorough education . . . endeavored . . . to destroy her confidence in her own powers . . . and to make her willing to lead a dependent and abject life."

One hundred persons, men and women, signed the statement. Accounts of the convention were widely published and resulted in such a storm of abuse and ridicule that some signers withdrew their names. But most of the group, feeling that much business was left unfinished, called a second convention two weeks later at Rochester, New York, of which the *Rochester Democrat* reported that "The great effort seemed to be to bring out some new, impracticable, absurd, and ridiculous proposition, and the greater its absurdity the better." Yet in spite of ridicule, in various parts of the country little groups of women came quietly together to discuss the possibility of equal rights. And in the next years, woman's rights conventions were held in New York, in Ohio, in Massachusetts, in Indiana and in Pennsylvania.

Lucy Stone, without any connection with the Seneca Falls group, or indeed with any of the groups now coming to the fore as fighters for women's rights, had already dedicated her life to the movement. Elizabeth Cady Stanton, who later fell into serious disagreement with Lucy and whose *History of Woman Suffrage* gives Lucy far less credit than she deserves, described her as "young, magnetic, eloquent, her soul filled with the new idea," and said, "She was the first speaker who really stirred the nation's heart on the subject of woman's wrongs." She was called "the morning star of the woman's rights movement."

For a lone woman to speak about freedom for women was even harder than to speak about freedom for Negroes; but Lucy was doing just that. "When I undertook my solitary battle for women's rights," she wrote, "outside the little circle of abolitionists, I knew nobody who sympathized with my ideas."

Yet in and near Boston, in such close relation to the abolitionist leaders, Lucy must have known of the Transcendentalist group—men such as Ralph Waldo Emerson, Orestes Brownson, A. Bronson Alcott, Nathaniel Hawthorne, Henry David Thoreau and William Henry Channing, nephew of the great Unitarian minister, William Ellery Channing. The abolitionist Theodore Parker was one of them, and they were in contact with other of Lucy's abolitionist friends. Close to them too was a radical woman, the gifted writer and talker, Margaret Fuller (Countess Ossoli), whose eccentric father had given her an education beyond the hope of most educated men. A passionate advocate of women's rights, she was to die in a shipwreck in 1850 just as the woman's movement was beginning to come to life.

The Utopian experiment in Transcendentalist living, the Brook Farm colony near Boston, which had survived through six years of the early forties, had just closed down when Lucy returned from Oberlin. The abortive Fruitlands, which Bronson Alcott had founded and of which his daughter Louisa later wrote a romantic account, was hardly even a memory. But both these colonies, in common with other Utopian experiments, ranked women as the equals of men.

The Transcendentalist thinkers had lifted the prevalent reformist idea of man's perfectibility in a free society to a mystic level in their conception of a rational universe transcending human experience. Believing that the evils of society must be eradicated if man was to realize his potential perfectibility, they accepted woman's low status as one of these evils; but they did not emphasize this aspect of their philosophy, and it is likely that Lucy, with her single-minded, untheoretic view of reform, had neither the time nor patience to pursue their metaphysical speculations.

She was occupied with more mundane problems. Her only income was the small sum she earned by her weekend lectures for the Anti-Slavery Society. In the beginning, either because of shyness or a sense of dedication, she did not charge admission to her woman's rights lectures. She had to pay her own expenses, too, though, trained in frugality, she spent only a few cents each night for room and board. Now she alone tacked up the signs she had had printed at her own expense; she could not afford to pay anyone to do it for her. But after she had spoken she would pass a hat through the audience, and so effective were her speeches that she was always able to collect enough to pay for the hall and for a place to sleep that night.

There was usually a fairly good audience, some who came to be informed, others to whom a woman speaking in public had the same appeal as a trained monkey or a circus parade. "After one of my lectures in Indiana," Lucy remembered, "the morning paper reported that I was found 'in the back room smoking a cigar and swearing like a trooper!' Another said, 'You she hyena, don't you come here.' " In one town the report went round that a big, masculine woman, wearing boots, had arrived to lecture, so when the ladies came to call they were amazed to find Lucy small and dainty, dressed in a black satin gown with a white lace frill at the neck, "a prototype of womanly grace . . . fresh and fair as the morning." During Lucy's speech that day an egg was thrown through the open window of the hall. Her expression, as she wiped her soiled dress, did not change. "If you could as easily remove from your minds the seeds of truth which I have sown in them tonight as I can this stain from my garment," she said, "I should feel that my work here had been in vain. You cannot."

Lucy had three lectures on women's disabilities which she usually gave in each town where she stopped. They covered Social and Industrial, Legal and Political, Moral and Religious Disabilities. Once she joined with the Hutchinson family, a group of antislavery singers, for a joint evening session. The Hutchinsons were accustomed to charge admission, and when they handed Lucy her share of the proceeds that night, she saw that it was enough to pay for the new cloak she badly needed. "Thereafter," she remembered, "I always charged a fee, many times but twelve and a half cents. It kept out the stampers and the hoodlums, and in no wise prevented those who were interested from attending." It also enabled her to put aside seven thousand dollars in three years.

By 1850 Lucy was at last in touch with other women whose convictions were like hers. In April she wrote to a Woman's Rights Convention which was meeting in Salem, Ohio, to bring pressure on the Constitutional Convention assembled to write a new constitution for Ohio. "The lowest drunkard," her letter said, "may come up from wallowing in the gutter, and, covered with filth, *reel* up to the ballot-box . . . but woman, in every State, is politically plunged in a degradation lower than *his* lowest depths." She expressed regret that Massachusetts had not led Ohio in the work for women's rights; but if the " 'Pilgrim spirit is not dead,' *we'll pledge Massachusetts to follow her.*" And that same spring Lucy's name was first on a call for a National Woman's Rights Convention to be held in Worcester, Massachusetts, in October.

In May, after a Boston meeting of the Anti-Slavery Society, nine women had met late one afternoon in the dingy, unlit anteroom to discuss the feasibility of holding such a convention. Among them were Lucy and her inflammatory friend Abby Kelley Foster. "It was decided," Lucy said, "that it was time something was done for the women as well as for the Negroes." The leaders of the antislavery movement, busy though they were with their own work, were understanding and helpful. Mr. Garrison spoke to Lucy with "tender sympathy." "He said to me 'There never was a movement that began so small and so poor as the antislavery movement; but it was rich in truth, and, because it was, it has succeeded so far, and it will succeed. . . . Never be discouraged.' "

The eighty-eight signatures which followed Lucy's on the call included some of the Transcendentalists now—A. Bronson Alcott, R. Waldo Emerson and Wm. H. Channing—along with such abolitionist leaders as Wendell Phillips and William L. Garrison. When the convention met on October 23, 1850, in Brinley Hall, Worcester, over a thousand people were present. The list of authorized representatives included men and women from eleven states, one even from California, whose statehood was only weeks old.

The work of organization had been accomplished almost singlehanded by Paulina Wright Davis, who two years later launched the magazine *Una; A Paper,* its masthead stated, *Devoted to the Elevation of Women.* It was, indeed, the first woman's rights paper. This extraordinary lady, laboriously circulating petitions, had already greatly influenced the passage of New York's pioneer Married Woman's Property Bill. More amazing, she had delivered lectures on anatomy and physiology to women, who then knew, and were supposed to know, nothing about the functioning of their own bodies. To illustrate her lectures Mrs. Davis had boldly uncovered a Paris mannequin, at sight of whose plaster nudity modest women in the audience covered their eyes or left the lecture hall. A few tender souls even fainted.

Twenty years later, in an anniversary report of this convention, Mrs. Davis remembered "Lucy Stone, a natural orator, with a silvery voice, a heart warm and glowing with youthful enthusiasm; Antoinette L. Brown, a young minister." The two friends were together again.

Throughout that summer it seemed unlikely that Lucy would attend the convention. Again family life intervened as she was about to reach out for a goal of which she had long dreamed. She had gone west to visit brother Luther, who had moved to Hutsonville, Illinois. A letter she wrote on July 25 to Samuel May of the Anti-Slavery Society tells the first sad events of that summer. "The brother whom I came on to visit died of cholera on the 18th inst. He was sick twenty-eight hours—hours full of dreadful suffering. . . . The weather is excessively hot, and the water miserable —It will require all our knowledge of physiology to keep well, and perhaps we cannot even then do it."

The words were prophetic. Lucy had hardly started east with her brother's pregnant widow, when the poor woman lost her baby; and several days later Lucy herself fell ill of typhoid fever. "Eighteen days I was not able to sit up at all. . . . We were at a hotel, a very lowly one. The windows were broken, the doors full of cracks. . . . The neighbors would come in and . . . ask 'Do you think you shall live?' "

Fortunately she recovered sufficiently to continue the trip shortly before the date of the Worcester convention. She was still "pale and weak" when she stopped at Cincinnati on her way home. She was also, as usual, short of funds; but this time she had a draft drawn by the treasurer of the Ohio Anti-Slavery Society on a Mr. Donaldson, a wholesale hardware dealer in Cincinnati, and an abolitionist. When she reached Mr. Donaldson's hardware store on Main Street, she was dismayed to find that he had sold out to a group of young men, one of whom, Henry Browne Blackwell, was in the store at the time.

Henry Blackwell, himself an abolitionist, was sympathetic to Lucy's plight, the more so because he was "struck by her brightness and charm of manner, and the wonderful melody of her voice." Mr. Blackwell, who was then only twenty-five, instantly decided that here was the perfect wife for his elder brother. Deciding to play cupid, he told Lucy he could have the money for her the next day, and next day sent brother Samuel to deliver it. But Samuel was not so charmed by Lucy as Henry had been. He paid her the money and went away; and Lucy continued on to Massachusetts, with no knowledge of the impression she had made.

From Coy's Hill she wrote again to Samuel May, telling him that, after all, she would go to the Worcester convention the following week, "though only as a looker on, for I have not sufficient command of mind or nerve to be able to do anything." But Lucy's basic health, her abounding zest for life and her faith in the cause of women took over, and when the convention met, she was one of its leading speakers.

Chapter Eight

The clergy might be outraged that women were stepping from their spheres; the newspapers believed they could laugh them back to their safe kitchens. Neither the high seriousness of the call to the Worcester convention of 1850, nor the intelligence and earnestness of the speakers deterred these crusaders for the *status quo.* With few exceptions the papers called the meeting a "hen convention," and found its members uniformly absurd. *The New York Herald,* edited by James Gordon Bennett, spared no effort to draw attention to the ridiculous occasion. Its October 25 report was headed: "Woman's Rights Convention Awful Combination of Socialism, Abolition and Infidelity," and included among the "objects of the Convention as disclosed today" such modest endeavors as to abolish the Bible, the Constitution and the laws of the land, and to cut throats *ad libitum.*

By October 28 the *Herald* had progressed from simple invention to open frenzy. "In another column," an editorial announced, "will be found the sum and substance of the late gathering of crazy old women, at Worcester, Mass." And the promised account began, "That motley gathering of fanatical mongrels, of old grannies, male and female, of fugitive slaves and fugitive lunatics, called the Woman's Rights Convention . . ."

Among these "fugitive lunatics" were the pioneer lecturers, Ernestine Rose, Abby Kelley Foster, Lucretia Mott and her sister-in-law, Lydia Mott. Among them were such men as William Lloyd Garrison, William Henry Channing and Parker Pillsbury. Among them was Harriot K. Hunt, credited with being the first woman physician in the United States, though she held no medical degree and practiced only within the limits of her restricted knowledge. Among them too were Marian and Ellen Blackwell, sisters of young Henry Blackwell whom Lucy had so fortuitously met in Cincinnati that summer. Another sister, Elizabeth Blackwell, was already famous, having graduated the year before from Geneva Medical College—the first woman in the United States to hold a medical degree.

For Lucy Stone and her heroic colleagues there were heart-warming exceptions to the barrage of laughter and vituperation. One was the support of Horace Greeley, editor of the *New York Tribune*. In appearance a ghost of a man with hair so fair it seemed white, pale skin, pale eyes, an effect he exaggerated by wearing a white jacket, Greeley was in character and intelligence far from ghostlike, a great newspaperman, self-made and self-opinionated. One of the few people who influenced him was his wife, whose friend, Transcendentalist Margaret Fuller, had lived with the Greeleys through much of the early 1840's and had written for the *Tribune*. Mrs. Greeley was an ardent exponent of women's rights.

Greeley's *Tribune* published an accurate account of the convention proceedings which had a dramatic result. Susan B. Anthony, that staunch woman and leader of women who was to become Elizabeth Cady Stanton's closest collaborator, said afterward that the *Tribune*'s report of Lucy Stone's speech converted her to the cause to which she gave the remainder of her long life. The *Tribune,* which introduced other speakers without comment, began its account of Lucy's speech, "Lucy Stone spoke with great simplicity and eloquence. . . . She said Woman must take her rights as far as she can get them; but those she cannot take she must ask for—demand in the name of a common humanity. . . . We want, she said, to be something more than the appendages of society. . . . We want that when she dies, it may not be written on her tombstone that she was the 'relict' of somebody."

In England the following July an article appeared in *The*

Westminster Review, unsigned, but in fact written by Mrs. Harriet Taylor, who in that year of 1851 became the wife of John Stuart Mill. "Most of our readers will probably learn, from these pages, for the first time, that there has risen in the United States . . . an organized agitation, on a new question, new not to thinkers . . . but new, and even unheard of, as a subject of public meetings, and practical political action. This question is the enfranchisement of women, their admission in law, and in fact, to equality in all rights, political, civil, social, with the male citizens of the community.

"It will add to the surprise with which many will receive this intelligence that . . . it is a movement not merely *for* women, but *by* them." And if further evidence of the situation of women in England were needed than the note of astonishment in these words, it would be found in the conclusion. "There are indications that the example of America will be followed on this side of the Atlantic. . . . On the 13th of February, 1851, a petition of women, agreed to by a public meeting at Sheffield, and claiming the elective franchise, was presented to the House of Lords by the Earl of Carlisle."

In the United States meanwhile the press had discovered a new cause for hilarity. This was the bloomer costume, named for energetic Amelia Bloomer of Seneca Falls, editor of *The Lily,* a periodical which she had originated for her Woman's Temperance Society. Amelia Bloomer was the Amerigo Vespucci of the bloomer. The woman usually credited with designing it was Elizabeth Cady Stanton's cousin and friend, Elizabeth Smith Miller, daughter of Gerrit Smith, vigorous antislavery leader and, later, member of Congress.

One day in 1850 Elizabeth Miller arrived in Seneca Falls to visit her cousin. To Mrs. Stanton's delight and almost everyone else's horror, Mrs. Miller was wearing a bizarre costume adapted from a garment worn by the women of the Utopian Oneida Colony for work in the fields. By whom it was adapted is not clear, for in December 1849, before Mrs. Miller's appearance, *The Lily* noted that "in almost every paper we have taken up" for the past two months there is comment on the famous actress Fanny Kemble and her new Turkish costume. Later *The Lily* itself made the distinction that "Mrs. Miller was first to wear the dress in public; *we* were second. . . . Fanny Kemble and others wore a similar dress two or three years ago, but we believe it was only worn on rambling excursions."

The skirts of modish dresses, billowing from tiny corset-pinched waists, were reinforced by numerous petticoats so that they flared wide at the bottom. Often lavishly embroidered or trimmed with lace, the skirts sometimes made in a series of tiers to the floor, they were charming to look at but uncomfortable and impeding. Pinched corseting made it impossible to draw a full breath or to bend over. Trailing skirts fashionably swept dirt from the unpaved streets. Machines especially built at great cost to clean the floors of the Crystal Palace in London, where a "Great Exhibition was taking place, were never used because the building was swept clean by the visiting ladies' fine, silk dresses." They were a proper symbol of woman's place; decorative, silly, useless.

How constrictive this fashionable garb must have been is clear from the cumbersome bloomer costume which was to free women from their bondage to discomfort. The upper part followed contemporary style: a fitted jacket, often with a soft blouse underneath. Outdoors it was worn with a conventional hat or bonnet and the cape then in vogue. The revolution began at the waist, which was not pinched in, but left in nature's dimensions. *The Lily* describes the rest. "Our skirts have been robbed of about a foot of their former length, and a pair of loose trousers of the same material as the dress substituted. These latter extend from the waist to the ankle . . . and may be gathered into a band and buttoned tight round the ankle. . . . Or, what we think decidedly prettier, gathered . . . and drawn up to just sufficient width to permit the foot to pass through. . . ."

It was, of course, the few inches of trouser which caused such consternation. That women should publicly admit that their bodies were built on two legs rather than on a single pedestal, even if those legs were thoroughly covered, was indecent beyond belief. Yet there were otherwise respectable women willing to do so. One of the first was auburn-haired Amelia Bloomer, who was pretty and little and looked well in anything she wore. Seeing Elizabeth Miller one day on the street in Seneca Falls, Mrs. Bloomer had her costume copied and wore it everywhere. More than that, she recommended it in *The Lily,* printed pictures of it and began to receive a barrage of correspondence from women who wanted patterns. So she came to be given credit—or rather discredit—for this radical dress reform. A handful of women throughout the country now commenced the daring adventure of appearing in bloomer costume. Among them were Elizabeth Stanton, the Grimké sisters, Lucy Stone and, a short time later, Susan B. Anthony.

Susan Anthony came to the woman's rights movement somewhat later than these other leaders, perhaps because hers was a Quaker home, where women suffered fewer disadvantages and where voting was in any case discredited. Up to 1851 Miss Anthony's relation to reform had been through the temperance movement.

Of all nineteenth-century feminist leaders, tall, rawboned, heavy-featured Susan Anthony came closest to the popular picture of a strong-minded woman. For one thing, though feminists were said to be overthrowing the foundations of marriage, family and home, she was one of the few early leaders who never married. She had suitors, but never took them seriously, for she believed herself ugly and undesirable. She was the victim of two childhood circumstances: a beautiful elder sister, and a crossed eye which her mother seems to have treated as a tragedy. In pictures taken in later life this defect is not perceptible, an indication that the reality was probably far less than its psychological efects. For this young woman, so self-conscious about her looks, so terrified of appearing in public, to choose to pursue a public career was in itself an act of heroism. In the beginning lecturing was torture to her, and though she grew used to it, she was never the appealing speaker Lucy was, and always depended for her effects on a piling up of detail rather than on personal magnetism.

Throughout her life Susan was a person of deep attachments. Deepest among them was her love for pretty, feminine Elizabeth Stanton, an affection which persisted over years when it seemed that Mrs. Stanton did not always provide the needed love and support. Yet in the early days of the movement, Susan's deeper attachments were to Lucy Stone and Antoinette Brown, who, like her, were spinsters, and who, she seems to have assumed, would never marry. How much the later history of the woman suffrage movement was affected by the intangible emotional elements in these relationships it is impossible to judge.

Susan came in contact with the leaders of the woman's rights group in the spring of 1851 when she went to Seneca Falls to visit Amelia Bloomer, a colleague in the temperance movement, and to attend the antislavery meetings which William Lloyd Garrison and the English abolitionist George Thompson were holding there.

Amelia Bloomer lived across the river from Elizabeth Stanton and within sight of her house. Afterward Mrs. Stanton became a prolific contributor to *The Lily,* and Mrs. Bloomer grew more and more dedicated to woman's rights, but at the time Susan Anthony came to Seneca Falls, Amelia Bloomer was still concerned only with temperance. Miss Anthony and Mrs. Stanton first met accidentally on the street, and it was only later that Amelia Bloomer took her guest to visit Mrs. Stanton.

In the summer of 1851 Susan came to Seneca Falls again to attend the meeting of a group trying to found a coeducational college. Among them were Horace Greeley and Lucy Stone. The plans for the college fell through, but the meeting began a long association between Lucy and Susan. The lines of the woman's rights movement were being drawn up for action.

Now that Lucy had joined with other fighters for woman's rights, she was, if possible, busier than before. Besides her lectures there were now yearly national, as well as frequent local, conventions to be organized and attended. One of her many projects was to have convention proceedings printed in pamphlet form at her own expense; and she carried these *Woman's Rights Tracts* about with her to sell to her lecture audiences. Yet in the midst of other activity, she found time to campaign for Elizabeth Miller's father, Gerrit Smith, and helped elect him to Congress.

In October 1851, a year after the first national convention, Lucy was back in Worcester for the second. The infant woman's rights movement had expanded with astonishing speed. Reports of the 1850 convention had been distributed to reform circles in Europe and England, and an interchange of correspondence had developed. At the 1851 convention a letter from the distinguished English writer Harriet Martineau was read. Poor, brilliant Miss Martineau, ugly, deaf, sickly, born without sense of taste or smell, had the single endowment of an extraordinary mind. She had made a great reputation as a writer of stories illustrating principles of political economy and exposing the injustice of the poor laws and of the English system of taxation. She was well known in reformist circles in the United States, where, during a long visit, she had been active in the abolitionist movement.

From the Prison of St. Lazare in Paris came a moving letter from Jeanne Deroine and Pauline Roland, members of workmen's fraternal associations who had fallen victim to Louis Napoleon's reactionary government. Their letter ended, "Sisters of America! your socialist sisters of France are united with you in the vindication of the right of woman to civil and political equality . . . from the depths of the jail which still imprisons our bodies without reaching our hearts, we cry to you, Faith, Love, Hope, and send to you our sisterly salutations."

The national convention of 1852 which met in Syracuse, New York, was greeted by James Gordon Bennett's *New York Herald* with its usual hysteria. The *Herald* devoted enormous attention to what it referred to as "a very entertaining affair" involving "aggregations of eccentric women" who, it assured its readers, numbered only one or two hundred in all New England and New York. Yet their three-day meeting so absorbed the *Herald* that, besides news reports running to twelve and a half columns, it commented editorially for six days to the extent of more than three columns, far more space than the sympathetic *Tribune* gave the convention. The tone of the *Herald*'s editorials was violent. These women "would not be guilty of such vulgarity as to live with their husbands." "The infidelity and socialism . . . have distorted their weak and silly heads." "They want to be lawyers, doctors, captains of vessels, and generals in the field." "How funny it would sound in the newspaper that Lucy Stone pleading a cause took suddenly ill in the pains of parturition, and perhaps gave birth to a fine boy in court!"

Shortly before the paper went to press Lucy Stone, wearing a bloomer costume, was, without disaster, addressing the Syracuse meeting. "It is the duty of woman to resist taxation as long as she is not represented. . . . There are $15,000,000 of taxable property owned by women of Boston who have no voice either in the use or imposition of the tax." The *Tribune* reported her "a favorite with her audience."

Since the *Herald* mentioned that only two women appeared at the convention in bloomers, it is likely that its further comment was intended to describe Lucy, particularly since her hair was cut in what, among "pioneers" of women's hair styles some seventy years later, came to be known as a straight bob. "One of them was a lady who was considerably on the wrong side of her 'teens' and evidently wanted to be taken for a little rosebud of 'sweet fifteen'. . . . She had her hair cut short like a child; but the effect was rather ludicrous than otherwise."

The bloomer costume was not beautiful; but since, even in radical circles, it was required that women's bodies be covered from head to toe, the possibilities of dress reform were limited. For the women who wore bloomers the reform was considerably worse than the original evil. They were subjected to constant unpleasant attention in the street, to constant biting comment in the press and from the pulpit. Lucy said she had never known more physical comfort or mental discomfort than when she put on bloomers.

The costume as well as the furor had traveled quickly. In England the June 1851 issue of *Punch* had commented on the vogue for women's pants in the United States. By autumn the word bloomer, as well as the style, had appeared in England, and *Punch,* like *The New York Herald,* seemed obsessed. In the next few months its issues were studded with cartoons, articles and verse parodies, sometimes two or three to a page.

Even in radical circles in the United States, opposition to the bloomer was so strong that there was talk of refusing to allow Lucy to speak at an antislavery convention unless she wore decent clothes; and this determination only disappeared when Wendell Phillips announced that if Lucy could not speak, neither would he. Jane G. Swisshelm, a pioneer newspaper reporter who had turned against the woman's rights movement as too radical in its demands, wrote of Lucy that "the way she dresses would disfigure Venus herself until she would be scarcely passable."

If the strange new garb was too much for reformers, the consternation of the general population can be imagined. Lucy was stared at, commented on, mocked. The simplest expedition became a public trial. In New York one day she and Susan Anthony started to the post office at midday, when the streets were crowded. Soon such a mob of boys and men collected that the two women could not move. The mob was not hostile, only amused and teasing and a little vulgar. But the women were hemmed in until an acquaintance, happening to pass, ran for a policeman and a carriage, and, as Lucy tells it, "we escaped, with only a little rough treatment at the end."

The unpleasantness was so constant that the women who wore the costume began to confide to each other that perhaps it was too much to endure. Gradually, about three years after the costume first appeared, its wearers began to return to ordinary clothes. Elizabeth Cady Stanton was the first to give up bloomers. For a while she tried short dresses without pants, then gave up the fight for dress reform. On hearing of her decision, Sarah Grimké wrote that she had "done the same, because I found them more trouble to wear and to make."

In the exchange among woman's rights leaders on the subject of bloomers or not, the point was often made that the ridicule they inspired was injuring the movement. Lucy never held this view. To Susan Anthony she wrote, "It is all fudge for anybody to pretend that any cause that deserves to live is impeded by the length of your skirt . . . audiences listen, and assent, just as well to one who speaks truth in a short as in a long dress." But "when I go to a new city, where are many places of interest to see, and from which I could learn much, if I go out a horde of boys pursue me and destroy all comfort. Then, too, the blowing up by the wind, which is so provoking, when people stare and laugh."

She had bought herself a dress, she said, to save herself and her friends embarrassment. When she had visited Lucretia Mott, Lucretia's daughters had begged her not to wear her bloomer costume and had even refused to walk on the street with her. And when Antoinette Brown, recently installed in her own church in South Butler, New York, had invited her to speak there, Lucy had refused for fear of embarrassing her friend by her costume. Nette had pooh-poohed the idea, but later, when Lucy was considering giving up bloomers, Nette, always less readily swayed by passing winds, gave her sound advice: "Don't suffer martyrdom over a short dress, or anything else that can be prevented."

Susan Anthony, ever intense and absorbed, was deeply troubled when her friends gave up the bloomer costume. "But, Lucy, if you waver . . ." she wrote, "why, then, who may not? If Lucy Stone, with all her reputation, her powers of eloquence, her loveliness of character that wins all who once hear the sound of her voice, cannot bear the martyrdom of the dress, who, I ask, can?"

The others, even Susan, finally gave up. Amelia Bloomer, because she was so identified with the garment, and perhaps too because she was tiny and pretty and always looked attractive, wore it longer than the others. The last woman known to give it up was the first to wear it. Elizabeth Smith Miller wore it in Washington when her father was congressman and she his hostess. As Sarah Grimké wrote to Elizabeth Stanton, "dear Gerrit thinks the almost existence of the Woman Cause hangs upon her adhering to Bloomerism."

Chapter Nine

In 1853, however, Lucy was still wearing bloomers. It was to be a new kind of year for her, introducing an element her life had so far lacked—the element of romance. To Nette Brown, she wrote at about this time, "My heart aches to love somebody that shall be all its own . . . [but] I shall not be married ever. I have not yet seen the person whom I have the slightest wish to marry, and if I had, it will take longer than my lifetime for the obstacles to be removed which are in the way of a married woman having any being of her own."

That May was a particularly busy month not only for Lucy but for the entire reform movement. Lucy was in New York where she gave two lectures, acclaimed as huge successes by Horace Greeley's *Tribune*.

On May 12 New York was also the scene of a World's Temperance Convention, to which, since women had for some time been active in the temperance movement, there were, naturally, some women delegates. Their credentials were accepted without too much difficulty; but when the meeting began and it was suggested that such women as Susan Anthony and Lucy Stone be placed on committees, there was immediate objection. When Abby Kelley Foster rose to speak there was such uproar at the idea of a woman addressing the meeting that she had to sit down unheard. The convention was now thoroughly out of hand. Every woman, and every man who tried to speak in favor of women, was shouted down.

Finally the noisy majority voted to exclude the women delegates, whose credentials they had already accepted. At this, Thomas Wentworth Higginson, a fighting minister who three years before had had to leave his church because of his antislavery preaching, suggested that a World's Convention which did not include women might better be called a Half-World's Convention. As Lucy put it in a letter to *Una,* "Think of it, a World's Convention, in which woman is voted not of this world!!"

After a few more speeches, the convention adjourned with a proposal for the conservative men to reconvene on September 6, without the disrupting influence of women. The pro-woman group had more immediate plans. "On Saturday evening following," Lucy wrote to *The Liberator,* "a meeting was called at the Broadway Tabernacle, to protest against the exclusion of one half the world from a World's convention. An hour before the time appointed, the spacious building was crowded to overflowing, notwithstanding 12½ cents were charged at the door. . . . The meeting was a most enthusiastic one." Arrangements had already been made "for a whole World's Temperance convention, to be held sometime during the World's Fair."

That September of 1853 was a month New York was to remember. Never had the city been so crowded. The prime attraction was a World's Fair which drew sightseers from the entire country; and into the already bursting city there poured delegates to two temperance conventions, an antislavery convention and a woman's rights convention. Fortunately many of the delegates to one of these conventions were also delegates to one or more of the others.

Lucy, for instance, had not only been chief organizer of the Woman's Rights Convention, she had also composed the call for the Whole World's Temperance Convention. Susan Anthony wrote to her, arranging to stay in New York with her and Nette Brown. "Who but Lucy could have braved and conquered the objections of such an array of *men?* I feel so thankful to you for your perseverance."

Mr. Higginson opened the Whole World's Convention. "This is not a Woman's Rights Convention. It is simply a convention in which woman is not wronged—and that is enough." The convention was well attended, and passed off peacefully.

The "Half-World" convention was more spectacular. Its members, eager to discourage the "Whole World" group, now kept insisting that this time they would accept accredited women delegates. There was frank disbelief among the women who had attended the spring meeting, and ever-courageous Antoinette Brown decided to test their claim. To her surprise, they did accept her as a delegate, but when she tried to say a few words of appreciation for their generous action the clamor that broke out made it impossible for her to speak. Next day she determinedly returned, asked to be heard and was recognized by the chair. Again she was shouted down, as she put it, by a group near the platform who "were incessantly raising 'points of order'—the extempore bantlings of great minds in great emergencies. For the space of three hours I endeavored to be heard."

On the third day the meeting passed a resolution that "common usages have excluded women from the public platform." The *New York Tribune* succinctly reported the proceedings of the convention:

"*First Day*—Crowding a woman off the platform.

Second Day—Gagging her.

Third Day—Voting that she shall stay gagged. Having thus disposed of the main question, we presume the incidentals will be finished this morning."

But the convention had not only excluded women. It had, more silently, refused to accept the credentials of Dr. James McCune Smith, a graduate of Edinburgh University, who happened also to be a Negro.

Meanwhile the Woman's Rights Convention went on. At the evening session on the first day Lucy told a story of a woman whose husband had kept her locked in their home for three years, never letting her leave the house, and of how no one could rescue her, because he was her master and could imprison her without breaking any law. "We call this a Woman's Rights movement," she said, "but I think it ought to be called a Woman's Wrongs movement; for in every relation she is treated as inferior."

In another speech she illustrated her thesis by a case then causing a great stir in England, the case of Lady Caroline Norton. Eighteen years before, Lady Caroline's ne'er-do-well husband, during a trivial marital argument, had thrown her out of their home and spirited away their three children, refusing his unhappy wife any contact with them. He had then brought entirely unsubstantiated charges, probably politically inspired, against her friend Lord Melbourne for "criminal conversation" with her. The case was absurd and distasteful, and its absurdity was soon emphasized by a young man named Dickens who satirized it in his *Pickwick Papers.*

The aftermath was more serious. Lady Caroline, a black-haired, olive-skinned beauty, was also a successful writer who earned about a thousand pounds a year. Now it was revealed that during the many years of their separation her husband had collected her royalties, allowing her four hundred pounds to live on, and had finally refused her even that amount, leaving her to exist in poverty while he enjoyed her earnings. Inevitably Lady Caroline had fallen into debt and, by an irony of that law which deprived married women of legal existence, her creditors were now suing her husband for what she owed them.

Throughout the conventions the New York press had conducted a campaign of such vilification and derision that crowds, in search of amusement, packed the meetings. On the second day of the Woman's Rights Convention the auditorium was crowded by a mob so noisy and rude that the speakers could hardly be heard. When Sojourner Truth, a giant Negro woman known to her admirers as the Libyan Sybil, rose to speak, the combination of Negro and female inspired the mob to greater efforts than ever. Yet the spectacle did not cause *The New York Times* to lose its urbanity. "Row No. 3," it said of this incident, "was a very jolly affair. . . . Let us be thankful that in such hot weather there is something to amuse us." Lucy was less tolerant. "We shall have a Woman's Rights Convention in New York, less disturbed than this," she ended her speech, "when mothers shall have taught their sons to act better than those who are here to-night."

Between the May and September conventions, Lucy had been far from idle. In Massachusetts that spring she addressed the New England Anti-Slavery Convention in a speech that asked of others her own fine courage. "The base are always cowards. . . . Throw off from your spirit the fetter that makes you stop to ask 'What will people say?' . . . strive faithfully to know the right, and then, if the heavens fall, DO IT! Then will the slave come out of his prison-house—and not till then."

In Boston a convention had been assembled to revise the Massachusetts constitution. Abby May Alcott, mother of Louisa and the other Little Women, had headed a petition, signed by Lucy and others, to have the new constitution include "the extension to women of all civil rights," and the convention had agreed to hold hearings on the petition. *The Liberator* reported that when Lucy spoke about the plight of women, "the whole assembly was deeply moved and men and women alike freely shed tears." Yet tears seemed to suffice them, for the Committee of the Whole reported that "it is inexpedient to act on the petition." And one of the representatives to the convention expressed the opinion that woman exerted great power by the exercise of her feminine graces and virtues, which she would lose if she stepped beyond her proper sphere and mingled in affairs of state.

The only woman who had spoken for the petition seemed not to have lost her "feminine graces and virtues," for sitting in the audience was a gentleman who then and there decided to marry her. Henry Blackwell had not forgotten Lucy since that day three years before when she had walked into his hardware store in Cincinnati, but he had not seen her again until he came East in the spring of 1853, when he met her at the Anti-Slavery office and heard her speak at several conventions.

The following year, while he was courting Lucy, Henry Blackwell wrote to her sister Sarah that, though on first seeing Lucy in Cincinnati, "I felt strangely attracted towards her—I purposely avoided seeing her again, until, several years after, I yielded to my inclination and went East on purpose to see her. . . . I am not naturally very patient, nor very slow in my movements, but I can wait a good while to get Lucy. . . . Jacob, you know, waited patiently 14 years for Rachel."

How much this was a lover's afterthought it is hard to know. There seems to have been no reason why he should "purposely" have avoided seeing her. Besides, he had certainly come East for at least two other reasons; to attend antislavery meetings in New York and Boston, and to try to find a publisher for a volume of poems he had written. Yet for whatever purpose Henry went East, the effect was unquestionable. On June 2 he wrote to his brother Sam, "I shall endeavor to see more of [Lucy] before I come West if practicable, as I decidedly prefer her to any lady I ever met, always excepting the Bloomer dress which I *don't* like practically, tho theoretically I believe in it with my whole soul—It is quite doubtful, however, whether I shall be able to succeed in again meeting her, as she is travelling around—having been born locomotive I believe."

After the legislative hearing he wasted no time before launching his campaign to persuade Lucy to marry him. A day or two later he went to William Lloyd Garrison, who had been his father's friend, to ask for a formal letter of introduction—though it seems strange he should have felt the need for an intermediary. Garrison gave him a letter to that same Josiah Henshaw against whose expulsion from the church Lucy had so valiantly tried to vote years before, but warned Henry that it would do little good to meet Lucy again. He said, Henry remembered, "that Mr. Samuel Brooke of Cleveland, O., and several others had made advances, but that Lucy was resolved never to marry and to devote herself exclusively, body and soul, to the woman's rights reform. He did not think that she was likely to change her mind."

Henry said he would take the letter anyhow. It is odd that he should have fixed so firmly on Lucy as his wife. She was seven years older than he, though she still looked far younger than her years; and he was much interested in a young and beautiful widow, when, as he put it, "Lucy's larger mental and moral and affectional nature put an end to that affair." Henry was an unusually attractive young man, who might have had almost any woman without pleading. Though quite short, he was good to look at, with black, curly hair and beard, blue eyes, very white teeth; and he was an interesting companion, worldly, literary, witty, and with that gaiety and zest for life which are so often the reverse side of a thoughtful and troubled nature. To recommend him further to most ladies, he was an astute businessman. But he had a virtue more likely to attract Lucy; he was an ardent reformer.

He came by his liberal viewpoint, as by his business astuteness, naturally enough. Even in writing poetry he was following his father's pattern. Samuel Blackwell, who had been a successful sugar refiner in Bristol, England, had been also a Liberal and a Dissenter. In 1832, when Henry was seven, his father, after a business crisis, had emigrated to America so that his children, ranging in age from twenty-two to one year, could be brought up among the democratic institutions he idealized. With him came his wife, his eight children (three others died in childhood, one was yet to be born), three sisters, a governess and two house servants. He died six years later, just after moving to Cincinnati, "a stranger," Henry told Lucy, "in a strange city, leaving a widow and nine children accustomed to comparative luxury and *entirely* destitute." The destitute widow and her three eldest daughters, Anna, Marian and Elizabeth, opened a girls' school to support the large family.

Henry's life had not been easy. He had been able to afford only one year at Kemper College in St. Louis before having to return home to become the main support of his large family. His spiritual struggles had been as stern as Lucy's own, though unlike Lucy's they resulted less from conflict with an alien world than from inner turmoil. The young Blackwells, moving in a cultivated society, had come in contact with the Utopian and socialist theories of the new world and the old. The year he became twenty-one Henry found himself bogged down in religious doubt. When he tried to pray, he felt himself "cold as an icicle." The Blackwells' preacher and neighbor, old Dr. Lyman Beecher, father of Harriet and Henry Ward Beecher, reasoned with him, preached at him, prayed for him. His mother was brokenhearted at his defection. He had long conversations with friends about "the blinding power of sin and of my present dark condition." Finally he returned to God and was even able to help his sister Marian, who having been won over to the philosophy of the French Utopian socialist Fourier, could not reconcile her newfound ideas with Christian doctrine.

Henry was accustomed to remarkable women with minds of their own. His mother and five sisters were as extraordinary a group as might be found in any century. His sister Elizabeth was already famous. At a time when no American woman had been accepted at a medical college, Elizabeth had determined to be a physician. She was rejected by one medical school after another until the medical college at Geneva, New York, reluctantly admitted her. In 1849 she had graduated at the top of her class, the first qualified woman doctor. Courageous as she had been in her fight to become a physician, she could not quite summon up the courage to march in the academic procession at her graduation. "Because it wouldn't be ladylike," she said. She was followed in a medical career by her younger sister Emily; yet Emily had nearly as hard a struggle as if Elizabeth had not paved the way.

After graduation Dr. Elizabeth had gone to Europe to continue her studies and had found that La Maternité, the State School of Midwifery, was the only Paris hospital that would take her. At La Maternité clinic Elizabeth, treating an infant, had contracted an infection which resulted in her being totally blind for some weeks and eventually losing her left eye, though the right recovered. Later she had gone to England where she became a friend of Florence Nightingale, the charming, witty, chestnut-haired beauty who had horrified her rich family by deciding to leave a life of leisure and luxury to become a hospital nurse. Hospitals then were filthy, malodorous sources of infection and disease. Women who nursed in them were the dregs of society, slovenly, drunken and immoral; but Florence Nightingale, who was none of these things, persisted, and her determination changed nursing into a respectable profession and hospitals into places where the sick were cured instead of killed. The two women had much in common.

Dr. Elizabeth was now back in New York, where she was establishing a dispensary. She was to Lucy a symbol of woman's achievement. Henry would have needed little more recommendation than that he was Elizabeth's brother.

However, armed with his introduction, he went unannounced to Coy's Hill, where Lucy and her parents and Luther's widow shared one half of the big house, while Bowman and his family lived in the other. It was fortunate that Lucy was so little a coquette, for when Henry appeared at the back door, no one having answered at the front, he found her dressed in the bloomer costume he so disliked, standing on the kitchen table, whitewashing the ceiling. He offered to take a hand, but she refused. She did, however, let him help her peel potatoes for dinner, though she rebuked him for cutting off too much potato with the skin. When Mother Stone came home she was amazed to find a young gentleman in her kitchen. She also noticed with some surprise that her careful, sane Lucy had, in the embarrassment of introducing her new friend, chopped up the carrots instead of scraping them.

Henry obviously wasted no time suggesting the idea of marriage, for soon after leaving for Ohio, he sent her a volume of Plato and a long letter telling of a visit to Angelina Grimké Weld and her husband, Theodore. "If there was ever a true marriage, it is theirs. Both preserve their separate individuality perfectly." And he went on to the real point of the letter. "I believe, some day, you ought to and will marry somebody; perhaps not me,–if not, a better person."

By the end of July, she was writing to him with the many underlinings and emphases which seem to have characterized correspondence in those days, "The privations I have learned to endure, and the isolation, I scarcely regret; while the certainty that I am *living usefully* brings a deep and *abiding* happiness." She welcomed him as a friend, but he could be nothing more. "Let me thank you for having expressed so fully your beautiful idea of marriage. . . ." But "it would be wrong for me to allow you to suppose that I expect a time will ever come when I shall feel released from the obligation to pursue my present course of life. The objects I seek to accomplish will not be attained until long after my body has gone to ashes."

She told him she was not disheartened, for she believed that what she missed in this life she might still achieve, that this life was "only as a pinhole to the whole of space . . . that every individual will, somewhere in the ages, come to the fullest developement . . . and I can wait– 'Earth waits long for her harvest time.'"

Throughout her life she had charted her own course. At home, at college, she had been uncompromising. She must have assumed that the problem of marrying Henry was settled by her decision; but Henry was no antagonist such as she had met before. He was more sophisticated than she, the product of a cultivated background, of an educated family. His older sisters had been under the influence of the brilliant Unitarian minister and leading Transcendentalist, William Henry Channing, then a preacher in Cincinnati. When Ralph Waldo Emerson came West on a lecture tour Henry had helped to arrange, he was entertained in the Blackwell home. So was Bronson Alcott. Their circle included the Beecher family and Dr. Stowe, who headed Lane Theological Seminary in the Walnut Hills section of Cincinnati where the Blackwells lived—that same Lane Seminary which twenty years before had been accidentally instrumental in saving Oberlin College. Henry's was a gentility which four years of college could not superimpose on Lucy's farmyard childhood. Most important of all, he was not afraid of her.

In August 1853, in a quaint script, with those old-fashioned s's which look so like f's, he was gently chiding her for intransigence. "Dear Miss Lucy . . . For myself I have a horror equally of fanaticism and eclecticism. . . . I think a wise man should be a *many-sided* fanatic—Don't you?" He felt that it was as bad for a woman to be superior in marriage as for a man. He would "repudiate the supremacy" of either. "Equality with me is a passion. I dislike equally to assume, or to endure authority." And then the warning, recurrent in his letters, that she made herself a slave to law and prejudice by not taking her right to a good marriage.

That summer he offered two suggestions for seeing her again. If she would come West that fall to speak on woman's rights, he could arrange a tour for her. He felt the West was ready to hear her message. Meanwhile, he knew she was to lecture at Niagara in September. Might he visit her there?

She consented to both proposals. She realized Henry was well qualified to arrange a lecture tour, because he made frequent trips through the West—Indiana, Ohio, Illinois, Wisconsin—for the hardware firm of which he was a partner. He traveled not by train, but on horseback, through sparsely settled country, unbroken forests and unfinished roads. On these business trips he could easily arrange her meetings.

Her consent to their reunion at Niagara Falls was given with reservations. She warned him that she was never the best of company at the Falls, which moved her deeply and made her silent. She warned him too that, though she was glad of the "friendship of the good, whether they be men or women," she had not the "remotest desire of assuming any other relations. I should incur my own heavy censure if, by fault of mine, you did not understand this. But, since you do, I shall be very glad of the opportunity to have one good, long, frank talk with you."

Henry seemingly accepted these restrictions, because he did meet her; but six months later he confessed that his emotions had been far from restrained. "I met you at Niagara and sat at your feet by the whirlpool looking down into its dark waters with a passionate and unshared and unsatisfied yearning in my heart that you will never know, nor understand. I rode with you in that sacred night with a miserable hack for a temple and the stupid driver for a priest and you, dear Lucy, for my divinity." On his way home, Henry, still idolatrous, attended the Fourth National Woman's Rights Convention in Cleveland, to which Lucy was a delegate. Here love and conviction combined to drive him into action. He made his first woman's rights speech, and was elected a secretary of the convention. "The interests of the sexes are inseparably connected," he said, "and in the elevation of one lies the salvation of the other." Surely he must have addressed these words with special emphasis to one among his many listeners. In spite of confidences to brother Sam about his dislike of the bloomer costume, Henry either allowed his convictions to win out over his preferences, or his desire to win Lucy to dominate his aesthetic feelings, because he also commented favorably on the bloomer costume which Lucy and other delegates were still wearing at this time.

The woman's rights movement had already made great

gains. In January of that year, only five and a half years after Lucy was graduated without reading her speech, the wife of Professor Cowles of Oberlin presided at a temperance meeting of a thousand men and women in Columbus, Ohio. The friend who wrote Lucy of the event added a comment: "Six years ago Catherine Beecher delivered an address in Columbus, through her brother, she sitting silent in the pulpit by his side!"

After the Woman's Rights Convention, Lucy began the busy and successful lecture tour which Henry had arranged for her. From Indianapolis she sent surprising news: "My receipts here are $317." She spoke to crowded auditoriums throughout Ohio; went into Pennsylvania, Missouri, Virginia and Kentucky. She was particularly impressed by her reception in the South, as Lucretia Mott had been by hers a few weeks earlier. Lucy wrote from Louisville, "I am holding meetings here which are wonderfully successful. It would not be strange if this slave state should give political and legal equality to its white women sooner even than Massachusetts." She wrote to Henry, "Received at Louisville, a note signed 'many Ladies' asking me to give an *afternoon* lecture . . . or they would be 'compelled to forgo the pleasure of hearing' me. I suppose because they can't go in the evening alone, or *think* they can't."

At St. Louis, after three woman's rights lectures, she gave one on temperance before a large and interested audience. In the midst of it, to their horror and hers, she made an extraordinary verbal slip, attacking "rum and slaveholders." This, in slaveholding territory, could be dangerous. Lucy recovered quickly. "I meant to say 'rum and rum sellers,' " she said, "but . . . I could not forget the deeper ruin that comes to you by your slaveholding; and in spite of myself, the word came to my mouth." The audience, believing she had switched the words on purpose, were so startled by her courage that, in spite of themselves, they burst into applause.

The Liberator reprinted enthusiastic accounts in local

papers of Lucy's speeches. The conservative press and pulpit continued to attack her, but her audiences were charmed. "It is not often that a single speech reverses the public sentiment of a whole town," but Lucy Stone did just that, one listener said. After an antislavery meeting in Pennsylvania, the comment was "modest and self-possessed . . . she could, with the greatest apparent ease to herself, hold that large audience in a breathless attention for more than an hour at a time. . . . She unites in her style . . . the poetical and the practical; so that while she holds the hearer charmed by the golden thread of fancy . . . she at the same time acquires such a mastery over him by the force of facts, and the conclusiveness of her reasoning, that it is impossible for him to resist her." And again, "The secret of Miss Stone's eloquence is, she speaks from the *heart*. . . . Her *soul* is in the subject. Her heart and mind seem all radiant and luminous with love and truth . . . she holds her hearers in perfect captivity."

During this period, whenever she was near Cincinnati, Lucy stayed with Henry's family in the house he had bought for them out of his earnings when he was hardly more than twenty. May 4, 1854, would be his twenty-ninth birthday; Lucy would be thirty-six in August; but this difference in their ages seems not to have troubled the Blackwells. A great attachment grew up between Henry's mother and Lucy, and Samuel reported that "By her quiet decision, steady purpose and lofty principle, she reminds me strongly of Elizabeth; and by a certain precision and distinctness of utterance, and personal neatness and good judgment. We have quite adopted her."

Lucy, however, was not yet ready to adopt them.

Chapter Ten

That autumn of 1853 Henry received a letter from his sister Elizabeth, which he put to use. Henry had asked Elizabeth if she did not feel that Lucy showed "greater nobility in striking for higher aims, and laying aside lower attractions?" Elizabeth answered, "Again and again it has happened to the noble, young enthusiast, to shape his course according to his conscientious conviction of duty, and shocked by the meanness and selfishness of all around, to disdain the life of the mass, and strive through self-sacrifice and heroic devotion to an ideal, to live a nobler life than others realize. But . . . there is a limit to this power, beyond a certain point, this martyr life, with its struggles, its self-sacrifice, and its devotion to truth fails to inspire. . . . We are bound together by a common humanity, and unless the individual can gather into his own soul all the essential elements of humanity, in their full spiritual significance, his life will be a failure, and the lesson of this first stage of existence unlearned. The love of man and woman is one of those universal facts. . . . Your remark[s] on . . . 'the satisfaction of some portions of the being' are utterly inapplicable to this . . . true wisdom-love. Very few know this love, it is given only to the noble, but Lucy Stone is capable of this grand good, therefore her resolution shocks me." This must have seemed profoundly touching to Henry, for Elizabeth, after the loss of her eye, now thought of herself as deformed, unattractive and unmarriageable. He sent the letter to Lucy.

Elizabeth's words impressed Lucy. Writing from Louisville to her sister, she copied Elizabeth's letter and asked Sarah to keep it for her, as she had to return the original to Henry. But it was not only Elizabeth who became Henry's advocate. His entire family had delighted Lucy. Three weeks later she wrote a gentle letter to Henry, telling him of the pleasure it gave her to be able to visualize him in his lovely home, surrounded by his charming family.

It was a home which must greatly have appealed to Lucy, whose own background so lacked the culture she longed for —the gracious mother, whose name, Hannah, was the same as her own dear mother's; the intellectual daughters, one a writer, one a writer-painter, one a doctor, another, Emily, now studying medicine; the liberal, attractive, effective brothers; the house in the beautiful Cincinnati suburb, where the nearness of Lane Theological Seminary provided intellectual surroundings in which the Blackwells were at home. Yet when Henry, encouraged by Lucy's new warmth, asked whether she did not care for him more than for her other friends, perhaps even more than for her family, she answered only, "You *are* dearer to me than they are, but all that you are to me does not come near my ideal of what is necessary to make a marriage relation."

In December she had advanced to the point of admitting wistfully that she loved him; but she continued to insist that she could not submit to marriage under existing laws. He replied reasonably that she constantly submitted to laws of which she did not necessarily approve. He inaugurated the new year by a new suggestion. "Would it not be a *slavish* doctrine to preach that we *ought* to sentence ourselves to celibacy because men have enacted injustice into a statute—But Lucy dear I want to make a *protest* distinct and *emphatic* against the laws—I wish, as a husband, to *renounce* all the privileges which the law confers upon me, which are not strictly *mutual* and I intend to do so—Help me to draw one up—When we marry, I will publicly . . . pledge myself to never avail myself of them *under any circumstances*—Surely *such a marriage* will not degrade you, dearest— . . . I *wish I* could take the position of the wife under the law and give you that of a husband—I would rather submit to the injustice a hundred times than subject you to it."

Yet in spite of Henry's appeals and her admission of love, in spite of the lock of hair she consented to let him have, at the end of July 1854 her will was still holding firm. "Believe me dear Harry we do *not* belong together, as husband and wife. If we did, I should not so often feel my spirit protesting against it."

Meanwhile, love and her resistance to it had in no measure impeded her activity. She had been traveling about as usual, lecturing, arranging and attending conventions. *The Liberator* reports her lecturing in Washington, D.C., in Bangor, Maine. That April she and Henry took part in an Anti-Slavery Convention in Cincinnati. In April too she responded to an appeal for help from her old friend Amelia Bloomer.

At the end of 1853 Amelia and her husband had moved from New York to Ohio, and in January 1854, Amelia began publishing *The Lily* there. Over the years a gradual transformation had taken place in the temperance paper. Perhaps it was the influence of Elizabeth Cady Stanton, who, under a variety of pseudonyms and initials, had progessively filled more and more of its columns. In any case, at the time *The Lily* began publication in Ohio its masthead bore the single motto: "Devoted to the Interests of Women."

On April 23, 1854, Lucy wrote to Henry from Amelia's home and explained her unexpected presence there: Mrs. Bloomer had employed a woman printer. "Her men printers entered into a 'solemn league and covenant' that they would not teach a woman to print, nor work in an office with one. . . . Mrs. Bloomer sent a most imploring letter for me to come and help vindicate the principle involved. And so I am here." It was in this letter that she told him he might have the lock of hair but, instantly tempering her generosity, added that perhaps it would be better if he did not come East to see her that summer.

The crisis in *The Lily* office was solved by a triumph for

the publisher, who resumed publication with women typesetters. Of Lucy's part, *The Lily* said that she spoke on " 'Woman and her employments' in the midst of the excitement about the difficulties in our office and her words were like soothing oil on the troubled waters."

At the beginning of June Lucy was back in Boston for a New England Woman's Rights Convention. Henry wrote to her about a trip he had just taken to see ten thousand acres of land he had bought in Bad Axe County, Wisconsin, "a new county north west of Wisconsin river." He had encountered a great deal of ill feeling on the part of the settlers against land speculators like himself. But the country itself was magnificent. His description of it is one of many descriptions of natural beauty which appear in both Henry's and Lucy's letters throughout the years.

In July Henry continued his suit from Illinois. "Although the ideal of marriage, as of everything else, *can* only exist in *possibility* . . . I still believe that the *majority* of people may and *many do* realize on Earth an union more beautiful and desirable than any other which the present Stage of the World's developement permits—To undertake that relation is equally a privilege and a duty. . . . Why then are women so terribly oppressed you may say? Because they have not as a class the education, the spirit, the energy, the disposition to be free! Give me a *free man*—he can never be made a slave—Give me a free woman—She can never be made one either."

July 1854 was a month of stress not only for Henry but for another of Lucy's friends. Antoinette Brown, who had been ordained in the Congregationalist Church only a year before, gave up her pulpit. She had succeeded in her desperate struggle only to find that, with the stress of battle removed, she began to be troubled by religious doubts, as Lucy had been earlier. To Nette's mind the only solution was to give up the ministry she had attained at such cost; and this she did, though some time later she became a minister of the less doctrinaire Unitarian Church.

Life was not simple for the new woman fighting her way through uncut forests, and finding sometimes that the unexplored world at the other side was not the haven she had expected it to be. Lucy, moral and thoughtful, and, like Nette, full of determination and of doubts, was entering a new phase in her relation with Henry. By fall she had begun to admit the possibility of marriage. Early in September she wrote that she must see him. She would meet him in Pittsburgh in late October, and there they would decide whether or not to marry. "If there can be a true marriage between us, it is as much for my happiness and interest to assume it, as for yours. . . . Do you suppose, dear Harry, that now when I believe I have a *right* to the marriage relation, after having spent half my days on the barren desert of an unshared life, that I would voluntarily shut myself up to its utter loneliness still longer, if I knew any true door of escape? O, no! . . . If it ever comes to me for you, or for any other, I shall accept it as the best blessing of my life . . . [but] the old paining hesitation lingered, and lingers yet. It does seem to me that there must be some inherent want of affinity which is the basis of it."

A week later she cried out, "You can scarcely tell me anything I do not know about the emptiness of a single life. I have tried it longer than you." Then the woman, more feminine than her demands on herself, appeared. "I will wear a long dress" in Pittsburgh.

No sooner had she admitted the possibility of marriage than she must begin to search her soul. Was she good enough for him? "Dear Harry . . . if I have spoken oftener to you of [my defects] it was because I did not want you to be ignorant of them or to forget them—and that if they *could* alienate or weaken your love for me, it should be *now* rather than hereafter." And she returned to one of those defects which most troubled her, her "very limited literary culture." Then, as though answering him rather than herself, poor serious Lucy added, "It is due, I think, not to any want of taste . . . but to the want of opportunity.

I do not think that the *essential elements* of my being are poor and barren, for with no external helps, and everything to contend against, I have yet wrought out for myself a far better life than thousands who have every facility." And of the difference in their ages: "Harry, excessive toil, and excessive grief, gave me a premature womanhood, and so by a natural law, premature physical decay will come all the sooner. Do not forget either that a man is younger than a woman of the same age."

The mere possibility of marrying Henry brought him too within the scope of her soul-searching. It was not only her faults now, but his, that she must weigh. "We at least have this advantage over younger lovers, who always fancy the object of their affection perfect; who, as the illusion vanishes, awake sadly to the reality, and wear a life-long disappointment. *We* know *some* of our defects, and may by mutual help cure them, IF that all-hallowing love *ever* comes to me through which alone we can accept or share a common destiny."

An event had recently taken place which played a large role in helping her to decide to marry him. The return of escaped slaves to their masters, required by the Fugitive Slave Law of 1850, was agitating both Lucy and Henry in those days. Henry had told Lucy that his brother Sam had rebuked him for "advocating forcible rescue," though Sam had been forced to admit that this was a "failing leaning on virtue's side." Now Henry had taken part in that noblest and most romantic of actions, risking not only his reputation but his personal safety to rescue a slave girl from her masters. Lucy had read the news of the exciting event early in September and had written to Henry, "I would rather have been a helper in her rescue . . . than to be President of any slaveholding confederacy."

Then Henry had written his account of the great adventure. He had been attending an Anti-Slavery Convention at Salem, Ohio, when the convention received a message that, on board a train passing through Salem at six o'clock that evening, there would be a man and wife accompanied by a little slave girl whom they were taking back to Tennessee. The Supreme Court of Ohio had held that a slave brought into Ohio by his master was automatically freed if he expressed the wish to be free.

On hearing the news the entire meeting, some twelve hundred persons, adjourned to the railroad station. A group of five, including one Negro, was selected to board the train. Henry was among them. On the train they found a man and wife with their baby and a Negro girl only eight years old. The committee asked the girl if she wished to be free, and she told them that she did. They believed this was all the law required. According to Henry's reminiscences, "The incursion was quite unexpected. The passengers were indignant; the wife cried 'Murder!'; the women screamed; the men swore; and there was a great commotion. It was all over in a minute." That evening an exuberant antislavery meeting greeted the rescued child.

Cincinnati, just across the Ohio River from Kentucky, had a large proslavery population, and when Henry returned home he found that not all his acquaintances, nor all his customers, some of whom came from across the river, were so pleased as his antislavery friends had been. He was indicted for kidnaping, though the case never came to trial; and at a meeting in Memphis a reward of $10,000 was offered for his capture "dead or alive." For months afterward southern men called at the hardware store with the avowed purpose of being able to recognize Henry if he ever dared cross into Kentucky. The press with few exceptions was vituperative and untruthful. One account even claimed that Henry had attacked the girl's mistress, grabbed her baby and flung it to the floor.

Lucy, who knew these tales were untrue, was overjoyed at Henry's courage. "I felt nearer to you then, dear Harry, in all that constitutes nearness, than I ever did before, and if you had been indeed my husband, I would have gathered you to my heart of hearts, with more love-full trust and tenderness than ever." And again, "What an exciting scene it must have been! How much of intense thought, feeling and action were crowded in that little space of time! What a change in one human destiny! . . . God bless you all, as he will, and as every worthy deed does ever!"

But as she was glorying in these emotions, the image was shattered. "I can scarcely tell you how the radiance of the halo I had thrown around you has been dimmed by your last letters." He had written, she reminded him, "regretting the 'needless loss of influence', the 'obloquy'; the 'indiscretion' &c, &c." When she read these words, she added, "I felt no anger or reproach, but a saddened sense of something *lost* and gone has attended me ever since." It was wrong of him to worry because his business was suffering. "You will be richer with your self-respect, even though you may have less in dollars."

This scorn for Henry's financial problems, even for his business acumen, was a striking element in their deepening relation. She constantly attempted to wean him away from the world of commerce of which she was contemptuous. He wrote so well; he ought perhaps to be an editor. He had a noble soul; he should devote himself to good causes, not to gain. And later, he should be a full-time reformer; she earned enough for both their needs.

Even before he became seriously involved with Lucy, Henry had been troubled by this conflict between the desire for financial success and the impulse to create a better world. His was the great American conflict, sharper then than it is today, though it still exists. The United States was a land of wide horizons. Many men who knew riches were theirs for the earning believed also that man and society were infinitely perfectible. The American myth, even when it is materialistic, is idealistic. To make money, to be a success, while desirable and even expected, is also a degradation of man's high purpose. Henry's was a battle each new generation of American youth fights again. Henry fought the battle throughout his life and never entirely resolved it.

In Lucy, the insistence on uprooting Henry from the world of money-making was the more astonishing, since she herself, having so suffered from lack of money in her early years, was never indifferent to it. She kept precise accounts in little black notebooks which she carried about with her; and her voluminous correspondence is studded with references to receipts and costs, to the amount she has earned by a lecture, to the details of numerous other financial transactions. Yet she repeatedly played on Henry's own sense of the inferiority of a commercial life, and in the end, because he was constantly leaving a business or refusing an offer in order to be able to live where and as she liked, he, who might easily have been rich, lived in almost continual financial difficulty and stress.

The first of these rearrangements, small but indicative, occurred that fall of 1854. They had been planning the reunion at which she had promised their future would be decided. On October 18 she wrote that she would meet him in Pittsburgh or Cincinnati, as he preferred. Her eagerness, though strangely joyless, was unquestionable; and three days later, "I want to see you. I want this suspense which haunts me, sleeping or waking, over. The subject has not been absent from my mind an hour since you left me last June. Bewildered and fearful, I see nothing clearly—and dread lest *any* step shall be a wrong one—" Yet within a few days she was telling him they would have to meet in Pittsburgh. There were people in Cincinnati she did not wish to see now. "I am sorry to interfere in any way with your business or your arrangements for lectures. But I *cannot* go to Cincinnati."

Yet he must have felt that any inconvenience involved in their Pittsburgh meeting was well worth his while, for after that time it was taken for granted that they were to be married. Her capitulation was complete. "Dear Harry, we can and will help each other, and we will be *forever better* for our wedded love." "I love you, Harry, and every day my soul is more and more happy on account of that love." "I read your deliverance from that rail-road disaster—Never until then had I known how *dear,* or how *necessary* you are to me. But when I reflected how barren life would be to me, if you had been killed . . . I felt how much I *need* you." "My heart *yearns* towards you *all the time,* so deeply,—so intensely—and only pray this deep earnest love may last forever."

Chapter Eleven

They were to be married, but when, where and even how they were to be married were not yet resolved. Henry naturally wished it to be as soon as possible; but Lucy, partly because of his help, was now a successful lecturer with an ever busier schedule. When he suggested February, she said she could not be ready by then; May would be better. How about March or April? he asked. Well, possibly she could manage to make it April.

Meanwhile, they must decide where to live. In December he told her it would be better for him to settle in the West. He and his brothers had a plan for starting a wholesale grocery business in Chicago, a plan so sound that he hoped to retire permanently after five years, and live on what he had earned, together with the continuing income from lands he had bought. He agreed with her about the cultural advantages of the East, and if there were no other consideration, he too would choose to live there. Even now, he would move East if she considered living in Chicago "undesirable." His rich English cousin had asked him to come to England to take a partnership in the family's prosperous foundry there, but knowing how Lucy felt about her work in the United States he had refused. Yet he was convinced that he had a talent for business and could, if he determined to, become a millionaire.

She was not to be seduced by dreams of wealth. "I know that you have a good business talent . . . but there are plenty of people who can make money—not so many who can bring the world a high thought. . . . I hoped that we should be able to give ourselves to the great *moral* movements of the age—" And at the end of January, after they had seen each other again, "I revolve the subject a great deal, but after all, see clearly only this—that *no* consideration should ever make us sacrifice our spiritual growth for any *material* good—that which is part of us forever must have the *higher* place."

Two of Henry's sisters had expressed doubts about his marriage to Lucy. Elizabeth, while proclaiming admiration for Lucy's "heroic devotion to an ideal," deplored her method of expressing that devotion, for rebel though she was, Elizabeth was enough the product of her time to find women's appearance in public gatherings a trifle vulgar. In June 1854 Lucy had replied. "You speak," she said first, "of the 'united future' which probably lies before 'us.' Possibly, would have been the truer word." Then she went on to defend her way of life from objections which must have startled her, since she might well have expected Elizabeth to be an ally.

"In regard to the expediency of holding conventions," Lucy wrote, "I, of course, believe in it, or I should not certainly aid in getting them up. It seems to me that you could not consider them a 'waste of time' if you had noted their results, with which I am more than satisfied. . . . Perhaps you will say that much of this is due to individual labor and example. . . . But the individual could not have been so well received, had not the convention paved the way. . . . It seems to me that you cannot know well the women by whom, in the main, the conventions are sustained, or you would not believe that they can ever become 'mere displays of vain oratory, or the theatre of noisy and pretty ambitions.' "

Yet when in December Henry told Elizabeth he was to be married, she said she was as surprised "as if I had never heard of the matter. . . . It is true, I do not know Lucy—she has as yet only come before me in the eccentricities and accidents of the American phase of this nineteenth century, in bloomerism, abolitionism, woman's rightsism—The immortal Lucy who will live and bloom in rich humanity, where there is no slave, no caste, and no mud, I have not yet learned to know, but *she* is your wife, and the woman whom I will joyfully meet when I can."

A far more serious note of disapproval was contributed by Henry's eldest sister, Anna, who had for some years lived almost entirely in Europe. She wrote Henry what he called a "tirade about 'Yankee women' " which, with the childlike simplicity characteristic of his relation to Lucy, he promptly forwarded to her. Lucy, accustomed from childhood to the accusation of inferiority, answered apologetically that she could understand Anna's feeling that she was not good enough for him. "You will never be proud of my polished exterior, nor of my brilliant intellect, nor of my high culture—But in the circle in which you will move, you will of necessity often feel that I am inferior to it—you will be pained. . . . I shall ever be on the unpopular side of unpopular reforms." If you do not want to marry me "let no false sense of honor, or what people will say, prevent you from being entirely true to yourself."

Henry did indeed want to marry her. Anna's disapproval had no more effect than Elizabeth's doubts. In February he wrote, "Dear Little Lucy, I hope you won't be offended by the diminutive, which I so often attach to your name—It is an expression of love which, I know not why, seeks to *surround* and *embrace* the object of affection and so, I suppose, conceives of it as small, in order (not being *very* large myself) to encircle it." The letter went on to more practical matters: He and his partners had been trying to sell their hardware business, and he had "been for several weeks in a state of very unpleasant suspense."

Now they began to discuss the *how* of their marriage. Lucy had said that "marriage is to a woman a state of slavery." She had not changed her views, and Henry knew it. It was more than a year since he had told her that if they married, he would wish to make "a protest distinct and emphatic against the laws."

He had admirable precedent for renouncing his marital

rights. As long ago as 1832, Robert Dale Owen, Utopian reformer and son of the founder of the Utopian colony, New Harmony, had in a civil marriage ceremony "morally" divested himself of the "unjust rights" which "an iniquitous law" gave him. In 1851 John Stuart Mill, when he married Harriet Taylor, had signed a statement relinquishing "these odious powers" and putting "on record a formal protest against the existing law of marriage, in so far as conferring such powers; and a solemn promise never in any case or under any circumstances to use them." Now Henry and Lucy had decided to incorporate a protest into their wedding ceremony. Henry had written a draft and urged her to compose a separate one, so that the final version would contain everything they wished to express.

Lucy had hoped her college friend and fellow rebel could perform the ceremony. "We want you to harden your heart," she wrote to Nette, "enough to help in so cruel an operation as putting Lucy Stone to death." But they were to be married in Massachusetts, and Nette, ordained in New York, could not legally perform a marriage there.

That spring was not solely sunshine and orange blossoms. Lucy was working hard and she was ill. The migraine headaches that had darkened her college days were upon her again. She had been freer of them for some time. Now they were worse than they had ever been.

It is not difficult to find a connection between her submission to love, to the idea of marriage, which since childhood she had seen as the essence of woman's subjugation, and blinding head pains. Connected or not, the correlation in time existed. She decided to marry, and that spring she was in such pain that she began to worry that she was going mad. Late in March she told Henry, "I write [to] let you know that I am still better. My head is so that I have now scarcely a fear of insanity—I feel the power of *self control*, and as long as I can do that, there is no danger." She was growing daily stronger. "And as, for months I have loved you alone, deeply and truly, so I still do. And from our mutual love, we will yet, I trust, realize much of happiness—"

He too had been having troubles. "I do not intend to take any active part in the Anti-Slavery Convention this year," he had written, "although I am doing all in my power to aid it. My partners feel desirous of my not doing so, until we can make a change and dissolve the firm. Of course the odium which attaches to me from the Salem affair has been, to a certain extent, injurious to our business, and much more so to its reputation than to its actual condition . . . and we actually did just miss an opportunity of selling out, a few weeks since, by the purchaser's fear that the business had been greatly injured by the Salem Spree." She must not misunderstand. He had no regrets; and was continuing every day to work for the cause.

Feeling a little stronger now, she replied indignantly, advising him not to remain silent at the convention because of his partners' demands. They "have no right to make you *appear* like a coward." And referred slightingly to "Cincinnati where the interests of trade are held more important than those of freedom."

Yet so strong was her love that, in spite of her preference for the East and her scorn for Cincinnati, she had consented to begin her married life in his mother's home. One of the pleasures of this decision was that her only remaining sister, Sarah, had moved West with her family, and was also living in Walnut Hills. She had agreed to be married in April, too, and had suggested coming to Walnut Hills to be married so that Henry need not make the trip East. He would not consent to this arrangement. She had been ill. "I would like that you should not take the long journey alone." Besides, if she came to him, she might be thought "unfeminine" by "silly, or misinformed people."

Perhaps he was the more sensitive because Elizabeth continued to protest the details of their marital arrangements. "The bad taste," she wrote him, "seems to me to result from dragging of one's private, personal affairs into public notice. . . . I think that Lucy, and you, too, have protested enough, in all conscience, both by public and private parlance, to define your position. You will do so henceforth in the far more effectual fashion of your lives."

Henry ended his own letter to Lucy on an odd note for a bridegroom. "Dearest little Lucy, keep up your courage! Don't let evil forebodings and fears find any hold on you. Trust in God, in yourself, and in me."

The date for the wedding was finally set for May 1, 1855, and Lucy's old friend and supporter, the radical minister Thomas Wentworth Higginson, was chosen to perform the ceremony. It is to him that we owe a precise account of the wedding.

Mr. Higginson and his wife and Charles Burleigh, an eccentric, long-haired abolitionist, were the only outsiders. Antoinette Brown and Marian and Elizabeth Blackwell had been expected, but they did not come. The wedding guests arrived together by train on the day before the wedding, were met at the station by Henry, and "rode three miles over a road among rocky hills till we reached a high little farm house, round which the misty sky shut closely down, revealing only rocks and barns and cattle." Lucy presented her mother, "a fine, hale, sturdy, stout old lady, saying, with an air of love and pride, 'Mr. Higginson, this is my mother, my *own* mother.' "

The men of the family came in later from the fields, "the elderly father as sturdy as the mother, with a keen face, but saying little; the brother looked like Lucy, a plain likeness; an ex-semi-Orthodox minister, now farmer; he has her low, sweet voice, and we liked him very much. Mr. Blackwell also we liked more and more." As for Lucy, "she took such care of everybody that I felt as if some one else in the family were to be married, and she was the Cinderella." Her relation to Bowman's children was charming. "Her word seemed to be law and love together."

Everyone was up early next morning, as the wedding was to take place before breakfast. "Queer old" Father Stone, unusually talkative for him, said of Henry, "When he used to come up to our place first, I never thought it would end in anything; there had been a good many after Lucy, first and last, but she had made short work of them."

Surprisingly, there were the conventional orange blossoms, and cloth of gold roses set in vases to decorate the room. Lucy's dress was a "beautiful silk, ashes-of-roses color," and Henry wore "the proper white waistcoat." They stood together and, before the ceremony, Henry read the protest they had written:

While we acknowledge our mutual affection by publicly assuming the relationship of husband and wife, yet in justice to ourselves and a great principle, we deem it a duty to declare that this act on our part implies no sanction of, nor promise of voluntary obedience to, such of the present laws of marriage as refuse to recognize the wife as an independent, rational being, while they confer upon the husband an injurious and unnatural superiority, investing him with legal powers which no honorable man would exercise, and which no man should possess.

We protest especially against the laws which give to the husband—

1. The custody of his wife's person;
2. The exclusive control and guardianship of their children;
3. The sole ownership of her personal and use of her real estate, unless previously settled upon her, or placed in the hands of trustees, as in the case of minors, lunatics, and idiots;
4. The absolute right to the product of her industry;
5. Also against laws which give to the widower so much larger and more permanent an interest in the property of his deceased wife than they give to the widow in that of her deceased husband;
6. Finally, against the whole system by which "the legal existence of the wife is suspended during marriage," so that in most States she neither has a legal part in the choice of her residence, nor can she make a will, nor sue or be sued in her own name, nor inherit property.

We believe that personal independence and equal human rights can never be forfeited, except for crime; that marriage should be an equal and permanent partnership, and so recognized by law; that until it is so recognized, married partners should provide against the radical injustice of present laws, by every means in their power.

We believe that, where domestic difficulties arise, no appeal should be made to legal tribunals under existing laws, but that all difficulties should be submitted to the equitable adjustment of arbitrators mutually chosen.

Thus reverencing Law, we enter our earnest protest against rules and customs which are unworthy of the name, since they violate justice, the essence of all Law.

The reading was followed by the conventional wedding ceremony, with only the word "obey" omitted. "And," says Mr. Higginson, "I have to add with secret satisfaction that, after this, Lucy, the heroic Lucy, *cried,* like any village bride! . . . It was the most beautiful bridal I ever attended."

Afterward he sent a copy of the protest to the *Worcester Spy*. "I never perform the marriage ceremony without a renewed sense of the iniquity of . . . a system by which 'man and wife are one, and that one is the husband,' " he wrote. "It was with my hearty concurrence, therefore, that the . . . Protest was read and signed . . . and I send it to you, that others may be induced to do likewise."

In *The Liberator* the letter and protest appeared next to a column containing the item, "Death of Currer Bell (Charlotte Bronti [sic]) author of 'Jane Eyre', 'Shirley', and 'Vilette'." Charlotte Bronte had died on March 31, 1855, as a result of childbirth, after only a little more than a year of marriage.

On his wedding day Henry also described his marriage, writing in a tone of mock sorrow to a friend, "I have just entangled myself beyond the possibility of release. . . . I lose no time in conveying information of the frightful casualty. . . . Enter Lucy Stone in silk dress and H.B.B. (of unenviable notoriety) in a mulberry coat and white vest. . . . Tears and wedding cake by all the Company—Departure of the Company—the Unenviable and the Bride taking cars for N.Y. . . . P.P.S. Ora pro nobis!"

The bridal couple spent that night in New York at Dr. Elizabeth's house. A soiree had been planned, but Lucy had so bad a headache that she went straight to bed. They continued next day to Cincinnati, arriving there on May 4, Henry's thirtieth birthday. On May 6 Henry wrote his new mother-in-law an account of their journey and, perhaps remembering Father Stone's wedding advice, "Never both of you get angry at once," told her that "We have not yet had the first quarrel . . . and have made up our minds to not have any hereafter."

When she was a student at Oberlin one of Lucy's professors had quoted the line, "Women are more sunk in marriage than men," and had explained it to an insistent Lucy by saying, among other things, that "Women lose their names, and become identified with the husband's family."

Antoinette Brown afterward recalled how Lucy kept brooding about this conversation. And when finally she decided to marry Henry the loss of her name still troubled her. Why shouldn't she continue to be Lucy Stone? Henry was willing, though the inconveniences would be many. Particularly when they traveled together, they would be suspected of not being married. But like any good principle, it was, to them, worth any effort.

It was a principle applauded by Lucy's colleagues. "Here where we have no titles," Mrs. Stanton wrote, ". . . each man must make himself a name. . . . It does seem to me a proper self-respect demands that every woman may have some name by which she may be known from the cradle to the grave. . . . When the slave leaves bondage, his first act is to take to himself a name." Susan Anthony, though disillusioned because her admired Lucy had succumbed to matrimony, also applauded her decision to remain Lucy Stone.

However, in the early days of her marriage, Lucy's decision not to add Blackwell to her name seems not to have been firmly taken. Her wedding card itself read, Henry B. and Lucy Stone Blackwell; and appended to *The Liberator*'s account of her marriage were the words, "We are very sorry (as will be a host of others) to lose LUCY STONE, and certainly no less glad to gain LUCY BLACKWELL. Our most fervent benediction upon the heads of the parties thus united!" *The Liberator* continued for a year to refer to Lucy as Lucy Stone Blackwell without suffering any rebuke from her, although that spring she had troubled to write to them about an obituary they had printed that it was an "insult to *every man's mother* when *any* woman is written as the relict of any man."

In announcements of meetings, which she must have seen and probably authorized, she continued for some time to be Lucy Stone Blackwell, and the report in *Una* of a Woman's Rights Convention at Saratoga, New York, on August 15, 1855, referred to her as Mrs. Blackwell, and said that Antoinette Brown introduced her as Lucy Stone Blackwell. It was in July 1856, when she had been married more than a year, that Lucy asked Susan Anthony, in arranging the annual Woman's Rights Convention to "Sign Paulina as president, and Lucy Stone *only* as secretary. Leave off the Blackwell."

That fall she expressed her belief that, "A wife should no more take her husband's name than he should hers." The depth, indeed the fever of her emotions at that time appear in a letter to Susan Anthony when Lucy discovered that, after all, her name had appeared as Blackwell on a convention call. "At first it made me faint and sick until a flood of tears relieved me. . . . If it had been from an enemy I could have borne it, but from you and Mr. Higginson when I had so dearly loved you both . . . oh! Susan, it seems to me that it has wrought a wrong in me that it will take many years to wear out. I had faith in human beings and in human possibilities. . . . I have lost something which has darkened all my heavens." She had once more determinedly become Lucy Stone; and Lucy Stone she remained throughout her long marriage, which lasted to the end of her life.

Chapter Twelve

The country was moving swiftly toward one of the bloodiest wars in history. Since that day twenty years before when Garrison had so nearly been lynched by a cultivated mob on the streets of sedate Boston, sectional feelings had solidified. The role of the abolitionists in bringing about this change was small, partly because their views continued to be too radical for the average man; partly because the growing differences between North and South were more political and economic than moral. Yet by 1848 the opposition to slavery had engendered sufficient emotion to give rise to the powerful new Free Soil party, whose slogan was "Free Soil, Free Speech, Free Labor, and Free Men!"

The abolitionists, and Lucy with them, professed scorn for political action. "Why do I hate politics?" Lucy wrote to Henry. "Because they are based on falsehood and must necessarily result in injustice and corruption. The idea that a *majority* have a *right* to control the action of a minority is false, and its actualization is an atrocious usurpation. I believe in freedom, the majority of this country do not, so they pass, over me, a fugitive slave law, and *compel* my obedience or make me suffer. . . . The politician is the creature of the public sentiment—never goes ahead of it, because he depends on it. . . . To make the public sentiment, on the side of all that is just and true and noble, is the highest use of life."

Yet it is in the nature of politics that to attempt social or economic reform is to take political action. For years *The Liberator* had carried on its masthead the words "No union with slaveholders," surely a political slogan. And in June 1854, at an antislavery meeting, Lucy told about her conversation in Missouri with a slave girl. "I never felt so deeply the necessity for a dissolution of this Union, as when I stood there and heard that poor girl's imploring words—'Can you not help me out of the state?' . . . Let the support of the Union be withdrawn from the slaveholder, and the three million of slaves will hew their way to freedom and their inalienable rights." Strong political words even in the free North.

Six months later she expressed annoyance at Frederick Douglass, the brilliant Negro who as a slave had nearly been killed by a trainer because he was "bad," the sole manifestation of his "badness" being that he had learned to read. Handsome, articulate Douglass, Lucy's colleague in the anti-slavery and woman's rights movements, had angered Garrison and his faithful adherents by publishing *The North Star,* an independent abolitionist paper, allying himself with more conservative abolitionists, and in 1854 becoming one of the founders of the new Republican party.

Lucy had more personal reasons for annoyance. Douglass's paper had attacked her for lecturing at the Musical Fund Hall in Philadelphia, which refused to admit Negroes and had turned away Negro friends of Lucy's to whom she had given tickets for her lecture. It was hard for Lucy to believe that anyone who knew her could have supposed she would wittingly have consented to speak in a building closed to Negroes, or have given tickets to Negro friends only to have them insulted. A year later, still angry, she told Henry that Douglass was "so unprincipled and mean, that I cannot *pretend* good fellowship, when I feel none." Time, however, wiped out this disagreement, and Lucy no longer had to pretend a fellowship she sincerely felt.

Perhaps the most effective moral argument for the abolition of slavery came from the Blackwells' old friend and Walnut Hills neighbor, Harriet Beecher Stowe. In 1850, as a demonstration against the new Fugitive Slave Law, part of one of the many compromises designed to save the Union, Mrs. Stowe had led eleven hundred women in a protest march, and then had sat down to write the book which led thousands more to an emotional awareness of the evils of slavery.

Meanwhile the politicians Lucy did not like were busily instituting further compromises to keep the Union intact. At the time Lucy moved to Ohio, the nation was agitated by the latest of these, the Kansas-Nebraska Bill, which destroyed the boundaries of slavery set by the Missouri Compromise and left to the settlers the decision as to whether these new territories would enter the Union slave or free. The result was a rush of free soilers to colonize the border territory of Kansas and keep it free. Among the early Kansas pioneers were the five sturdy Brown boys, who some time later were followed by their father, John Brown.

Henry seems not to have shared Lucy's scorn of politics. In spite of her objections, in Cincinnati, shortly after their marriage, he was still taking an effective part in politics. There were two free soil parties in Ohio then, the Liberty party and the American party. The American or Know-Nothing party was committed to one principle: Protestant Americanism free of foreign or Catholic influence; but in the Northwest it had discovered that, in order to survive, it must take an antislavery stand. Henry Blackwell, in spite of having been born in England, of being, therefore, that most abhorred of men, a foreigner, was able to induce these two free soil factions to take joint action at a crucial moment in Ohio politics. Their coalition at the state convention turned the tide in favor of Henry's good friend Salmon P. Chase, every inch an abolitionist and every inch a politician, who was nominated as governor and won the election.

Lucy's own reformist career was no more impeded by matrimony than Henry's. The house in Walnut Hills was half empty when Lucy moved there. Of the girls, only Marian still lived at home, though Ellen was sometimes there, and Marian often away. Sam, George and Henry were there a great deal of the time.

At the time of her mother-in-law's death, Lucy told a revealing story of a day when she came home to find Hannah Blackwell ill and alone. "I went into her room and just put my two hands each side of her face, and kissing her cheeks, told her that I would do my best to be as good as an own daughter. She drew my hand to her lips and kissed it, and the tears were in both our eyes. . . . But to the surprise of us all, Mother appeared [at supper] neatly dressed, looking as tho' nothing had happened. . . . She needed sympathy as we all do. From that time she seemed very near to me." But much as Hannah Blackwell loved her new daughter-in-law, Lucy cannot greatly have made up to her for the absence of her four career daughters, because even in the first months of marriage, she was frequently away from home and her new husband. What she saw of life in Walnut Hills, however, she must have liked, for she came to know such friends of Henry's as Ainsworth R. Spofford, who later became librarian of the Library of Congress, and personable Governor Chase. Henry remembered years later that Chase "took tea with us one evening and presented us with his picture, which still hangs over Lucy's desk."

The house was pleasant too. Henry described it in a letter to Father Stone as a brick house of "seven or eight rooms," few enough surely, though the large family had begun to go their distant ways years before. Two miles from the city, it had a garden with fruit and shade trees. Across from it was open woodland, and on one side was Lane Seminary with "about ten acres of land laid out as a public square." "We are on high ground some two hundred feet above the Ohio river valley."

"Lucy," he added, "looks well and, though she says that *'Lucy Stone is dead,'* she looks so much like her that you would find it difficult to tell the difference."

Lucy was, in fact, so much alive and so much Lucy that she was already traveling about the country lecturing and attending conventions. From home, her husband wrote to his absent bride, "If you have defects, I am not conscious of them—To me, you are all I want, all I need, all I desire—" Her own letters to her family in Massachusetts were warm and loving, equally concerned with the state of the crops and with her reform activities.

Any group generates differences of opinion and clashes of personality; and the woman's rights movement, filled with men and women of violent opinions and rebellious personalities, generated more than its share. In July Lucy wrote to Nette about their colleague Paulina Wright Davis, editor of *Una,* "I hope she won't be here [for the convention] with her vanity and her jealousy." Yet Lucy and Mrs. Davis had worked together for years and, indeed, had together signed the call for this very convention. Of another convention she complained to her mother, "Our convention is over. We had Mrs. Gage Pres't and she did not know anything how to act." Several years later she was to comment about Ernestine Rose, "I do hope Mrs. Rose will not speak at the meeting. . . . Mrs. Rose is 'known,' but 30 people will stay away who see her name, where 10 will be attracted by it." Yet in spite of internal stresses, it was not until almost fifteen years later, when a difference of principle brought such unrevealed emotions to the surface, that the movement was split in two.

The fall of 1855 was a somewhat quieter time for Lucy and Henry and, partly because the National Woman's Rights Convention that year was held in Cincinnati, Lucy was more at home. Accounts of the convention in the local press included the interesting information that some of the more stalwart women were still wearing the bloomer costume. Henry was there and heard Lucy make one of the most moving speeches of her career. "The last speaker alluded to this movement as being that of a few disappointed women. From the first years to which my memory stretches I have been a disappointed woman. When, with my brothers, I reached forth after sources of knowledge, I was reproved with 'It isn't fit for you; it doesn't belong to women.' I was disappointed when I came to seek a profession. . . . In education, in marriage, in religion, in everything, disappointment is the lot of woman. It shall be the business of my life to deepen this disappointment in every woman's heart until she bows down to it no longer." Shortly after the convention she was off again on a lecture tour.

The new year brought an event which further broke up the Walnut Hills home, though it linked Lucy closer than ever to an old friend. On February 1, 1856, *The Liberator* published an announcement: "Married—At Henrietta, N.Y., Jan. 24 by Joseph Brown, Esq., the father of the bride, Samuel C. Blackwell, of Cincinnati, and Rev. Antoinette L. Brown, of New York. Many friends of Miss Brown will be interested to learn, that the gentleman with whom she has connected herself in marriage is a brother of the husband of Lucy Stone Blackwell."

Lucy and Henry were overjoyed. Two weeks earlier Lucy had written about Henry to her mother, "He is *always* kind and good. . . . It is 36 weeks today since that time [her wedding day]; each Tuesday morning as it comes, is a little sacramental season to me, and week by week, I grow more grateful for Harry's love; more and more he comes to be to me all that I need." They had every reason to hope that these two people so dear to them would be equally fortunate.

They could not go East for the wedding, but Nette and Sam were to return for a while to live in Walnut Hills. In her letter of congratulation Lucy explained that she and Henry would be away when Sam and Nette came to Cincinnati, but she knew they would prefer the additional privacy. Sam, she said in one of her rare moments of humor, might "rejoice in the fact that he alone of all the men in the world has a Divine wife."

In January and February 1856 Lucy and Henry were both away, though not together. Letters flowed back and forth between them, touching every subject, from love to finance, likely to concern two newly married people. His letters were longer and more fluent than hers, but hers managed nevertheless to give a thorough account of her activities, the size of her audiences, the number of tracts she sold and advice on his diet. Mr. Higginson had described Henry at the wedding as rather short and stout; and Lucy's letters contained admonitions to "exercise more control" of his appetite. "Dear Henry—*you ought* to be larger than your dinner." She was also constant in her advice not to worry about money. "Life may be rich without *much* money, and may be very poor *with* much money."

On the day after Nette's wedding, Lucy wrote from Fort Wayne, full of regrets because they still had no home of their own and because she had had to leave Walnut Hills before he did when he was about to start on a "long trip." She told him that in Forrest, Illinois, where she had spent several days, there had been such opposition to her speaking that two "calico balls were got up" to serve as competition. Fortunately the opposition had expected her to appear on Tuesday, and when she actually spoke on Thursday, there was a large audience. "Before the first half hour the truth had triumphed." And then a startling note, "It was such an *infinite blessing* to feel again the old inspiration and *faith* in *myself,* and to see the audience swayed as the wind, the grain."

This is the first indication that more than a return of her headaches had been troubling Lucy in those days of her new-found love. In October 1854, when she was beginning to succumb to Henry's insistent wooing, she had written to him from a convention where she was to speak, "I dread it a little, but never mind! It will be over soon." This sense that she had lost her old powers of persuasion was one which grew and waned over the next years. Another indication of her emotional problems appears in a letter from Henry referring to her "little depression of spirit," words heavily crossed out, either then or later, by some guardian of Lucy's reputation for indomitability, conceivably even by Lucy herself.

In spite of love and marriage, she was fighting as hard as ever for her independence. Some months after their marriage Henry chided her gently for insisting that she must support herself, and if need be, help him too. "Lucy Stone Blackwell is more independent in her pecuniary position than was Lucy Stone." And, "Surely, dearest Lucy, it would not pain you, nor annoy you, if you were without money, to share mine with me. You could not feel humbled or subservient in accepting my earnings, any more than in accepting my caresses, since you know they would be valueless to me unless you shared them . . . and the presence of love makes dependence mutual and financial details simply trivial." And this has particular significance, because in the same letter he told her that he was in the process of doing what she had so ardently urged. He would soon be rid of his business and would join her as a lecturer.

Anna Blackwell, still playing the role of big sister, from across the ocean entered the controversy in favor of a man's right to support his wife. She also rebuked Henry because she believed Lucy had given up bloomers for his sake. Henry told Lucy he was torn between "pleasure in the thought of your love which has prompted you to change [your costume], and pain that you should think it necessary to my happiness to do so. . . . I am not so thin skinned as you imagine. . . . So dearest, I am desirous to meet you next Saturday night . . . in the short dress and pants—I shall find nothing disagreeably masculine *within* the dress and so can easily overlook externals—"

Lucy's and Antoinette's marriages had come as a great blow to Susan Anthony, who grieved for them as though they were forever lost to her and to the woman's rights movement. Now she had written to Nette rebuking her for neglecting her work since her marriage less than a month before. Susan was fulfilling Nette's early impression, when she had written to Lucy, "I like Miss Anthony very much, but poor child she'll never get along smoothly in this world. It's as much her manner as the matter of what she says."

Perhaps it was to defend Lucy from Susan's charges of deserting reform for the softer pleasures of marriage that

Nette, on February 14, 1856, related how in Cincinnati the day before, Lucy had made a "glorious little speech in the Court Room—to the Court in fact—in behalf of the heroic slave mother." *The Liberator* recorded the dramatic story of the heroic slave mother at greater length. She was twenty-two-year-old Margaret Garner, according to Lucy "a beautiful woman, chestnut colored, with good features and wonderful eyes." Margaret and her husband, with their four small children and the husband's parents, had escaped from Kentucky. They had reached Cincinnati safely but were discovered there and, because the courts had now interpreted the Fugitive Slave Law as binding, were to be returned to their master.

When the officers arrived at the house where the Garners were concealed and Margaret realized that they were to be carried back to slavery, she struck two of her children on the head with a shovel, hoping to kill them, and succeeded in cutting the throat of a third before she could be stopped. Her mother-in-law, who was sitting quietly in the room while this was going on, made no attempt to intervene. When she was asked why, she said that in similar circumstances she would probably have done the same.

The young mother who, Lucy said, attempted to kill her children not with "wild desperation," but with a "calm determination," later explained that she "would much rather kill them at once . . . than have them taken back to slavery, and be murdered piece-meal."

At the trial, the Deputy Marshal testified that Lucy Stone, visiting Margaret in prison, had appealed to him for permission to give the young mother a knife so that she could kill herself and the remaining children. Lucy was not permitted to testify, but one day, in the courtroom, a strange little scene took place which was described in the *Cincinnati Columbian*. "After the adjournment of the court, the members and audience resolved themselves into a public assembly. . . ." Lucy Stone "mounted the Judge's desk. She was dressed in a black silk gown, had a brown merino mantle over her shoulders, a bonnet of the same material on her head, and a green veil. She spoke in an easy assured manner, without excitement or violence, never so much as raising her voice beyond the low, penetrating tones peculiar to her."

She told of her visit to the prison, of the emotion aroused in her by the slave mother and her pitiful situation. "Impelled by my feelings," she went on, "I turned to Mr. Brown [the Deputy Marshal] and expressed my wish that she could have a knife to deliver herself, dreading as she did slavery to such an extent, that she had taken the life of her dear child rather than return to it. . . . I had a right to put a dagger in the woman's hand—the same right that those had who seized their weapons to fight about a paltry tax on tea. I hoped to see her liberty rendered her—I hope it still. . . . I make no apology to the Court or to anyone for wishing to give this woman a dagger. . . . I exercise the same right as those who distributed weapons to the combatants on Bunker Hill."

Lucy had appealed to Margaret's owner, Mr. Gaines, and she said that he had promised to give Margaret her freedom, but whatever in a moment of shame he had promised Lucy, more astute consideration decided him in favor of taking Margaret and her family back to slavery.

The story now becomes almost incredibly melodramatic. The Garner family were put aboard a boat going South. On the way, a sudden lurch of the vessel gave Margaret the opportunity to let her baby slip into the water, where it drowned. That was not all. Later there was an accident in which many passengers were thrown into the river, among them Margaret and one of her two remaining children. The child was drowned, and Margaret was thought to have drowned with her. Lucy believed Margaret to be dead and free at last of the slavery she dreaded. *The Liberator,* however, records an even sadder ending to the miserable story. Margaret was rescued and for a while disappeared; but she was finally captured for the last time, and returned to the life of slavery she so abhorred.

Chapter Thirteen

With the hardware business sold at last, the Walnut Hills home was to be abandoned. The family was already dispersed; Howard in business in England, Anna, after experimental stays at Brook Farm and the North American Phalanx, permanently established in England and Europe. Even young Ellen, already a writer, had left for London to study art. George was going to Wisconsin; Antoinette and Sam were moving East; and Lucy and Henry were to follow in a few months. Hannah Blackwell and Marian decided to move to New York to be with Doctor Elizabeth and Doctor Emily.

In the summer of 1856 Henry was still pursuing his dream of becoming rich and retiring to a life of good works. He owned about six thousand acres of forest land in Wisconsin, much of it bought from the state on credit. This large tract must be surveyed and "certified" before he could parcel it out to sell, or to trade for land in the East. He had been traveling during the late winter and spring with one of the new owners of the hardware concern, breaking him into the business; and, since he would now have to spend two months in Wisconsin, he begged Lucy to give up her work for a while and come with him. They had been together so little. She had been speaking at conventions, lecturing, and traveling through Indiana addressing lyceums. He told her that, once his financial situation was in order, he hoped he could live in the East and manage the western lands from there. Meanwhile, "Let us not separate any more but live and act *together*." She agreed to go.

They met in Chicago at the end of May and set out by horse and buggy for Viroqua, in Bad Axe County, Wisconsin. It was a wild, adventurous trip, full of real hardships, but full also of a quality which Henry still recalled when he was old. "The whole incident of that summer's laborious, sequestered life is associated with the memory of my wife, and seems to me like a lovely dream. The cares and privations are forgotten; the beautiful scenery and the sweet, pure air of those romantic highlands will forever linger in my memory."

It was, in fact, their wedding trip, the only one they had in the midst of an existence which rated their own happiness below the need to create a better world for other human beings to live in. Yet at the time the difficulties loomed large. "Monday evening," Henry wrote to Sam, "we stopped at a farmer's house . . . where Lucy was horrified by having to sleep in dirty sheets, and two girls and a dog kept passing through our room." Another night, "We got with some difficulty into bed (while our six roommates stepped out to give us the opportunity)."

The population of the United States was so small then that for two much-traveled people like Lucy and Henry the settlers everywhere were identifiable by name and family. "Indeed, Lucy or I were in every case intimate with everybody's relatives and connections. I knew all the Westerners, Lucy all the Easterners."

Toward the northwest, the country was more and more thinly settled. The trip from Madison to Viroqua, a distance of about ninety miles, took them four days. There were thunderstorms, windstorms, sandstorms. There were mountains, rutted dirt roads, clearings, no road at all. They "crossed the Kickapoo and emerged upon the high rolling prairies of Bad Ax County, just as Lucy was sinking into despair. We lost our umbrella and sunshade at this juncture, and, in trying to find them, lost my overcoat; and in our joy at finding the overcoat felt consoled for the loss of our head-protectors. Reached Viroqua in the afternoon, which surpassed Lucy's expectations, there being at least thirty shanties visible to the naked eye."

Lucy described a trip with a Mr. Grace who was hoping to trade some land with them. Lucy and Henry's horse fell down; Mr. Grace's broke its harness. They drove through fields of high grass "full of sloughs, frightfully deep." When night fell the last house they had seen was five miles back, and it had taken three hours to cover that distance by daylight. To return was impossible. They decided to fasten their horses to a tree and go on by foot. They were soaked to the skin; Henry had torn "his pantaloons (one leg) from the bottom to the waistband, so nettles, briars and bugs had free access." Finally they came to the juncture of two wild and seemingly impassable rivers. They stood and shouted, until at last a young man appeared. He found them a log on which to cross the river and took them to his two-room log cabin, where they spent the night. Next day Mr. Grace and Lucy gave up, and Henry went on alone. He came back that night with ankles so scraped he could not put his boots on, but with the cheering news that land bought last spring for $800 would bring $3000 in less than a year.

The two months were not entirely lost to the causes in which they believed. They stayed with an Ira Hazeltine, who, Henry said, was "a shrewd, money-making reformer, with . . . a general love of lucre and liberty," and who then and there arranged a meeting on women's rights.

Lucy had never felt more strongly the need for preaching women's rights. From Illinois, she had written to brother Bowman that the population of that area was mostly foreign. The women worked as hard as the men, and took no more than four days off to have a child. "In the family nearest us, the wife slept in an out-house all winter, because her husband, who lay snug by the fire, said when the baby was born and it was a *girl* 'if she will have gals, cold is good enough for her.'"

Later, at a Fourth of July ceremony in primitive Viroqua, Lucy was asked to lecture. In the midst of her speech the platform on which she was standing broke, but Lucy turned the accident to advantage, "So will this country fall unless slavery is abolished!" Today in Viroqua there is a plaque commemorating this first place in the northwest where a woman spoke against slavery and for woman's rights.

What she saw of women's lives in the wilderness affected her so profoundly that she wrote to her family with a hysteria she never expressed in public. "I care less and less every day which triumphs, freedom or slavery. In either case, all the women of the land are yet subjects. . . . My heart . . . breathes the prayer that slavery may yet crush every white man into the same condition in which the white men have placed women."

In the same letter she told them the Blackwells were gone from Walnut Hills. So, in late summer, when Lucy and Henry returned from their trip, they too went East to live, boarding throughout that winter and spring with Doctor Elizabeth in New York.

Elizabeth had had a hard and lonely time in her first years in New York. Refused admission to any hospital, attacked, misunderstood, she had managed at last to open a small dispensary. By borrowing money she had bought a house on East Fifteenth Street, renting most of it, keeping a few small rooms as living quarters and medical office. Elizabeth herself recorded that in October 1854 "the utter loneliness of life became intolerable," and she went to the immigrants' depot at Randall's Island to adopt a child from the pauper nursery. She selected Katharine Barry, a red-haired seven-year-old, because the pathetic child had blinking eyes and bad physical co-ordination, and needed her "more than any of the others." By 1856 Kitty had been made healthier and happier by love and medical care.

By that winter Elizabeth must have been far from lonely. She had been joined in her dispensary by her protégée and friend Marie Zakrzewska, newly graduated from medical school, and by her sister Emily, back from postgraduate medical studies in Europe. Emily, who later adopted two daughters, was already living with Elizabeth when Marian and Mother Blackwell joined them, to be followed by Nette and Sam, and then by Lucy and Henry.

It was a busy household. The women doctors had been raising funds for a fully accredited hospital where women could be cared for by women, and the dream was about to become reality. The New York Infirmary for Indigent Women and Children was officially opened on May 12, 1857, the birthday of Elizabeth's friend Florence Nightingale, who was thirty-seven that day, a little less than a year older than Elizabeth herself. Miss Nightingale was now famous, a war heroine who had captured the world's imagination as surely as Joan of Arc. In the Crimean War, just ended, she had for the first time brought care and sanitation to sick and wounded troops in wartime. The hospital which the three women doctors founded on her birthday still flourishes as the New York Infirmary, a large institution in its own handsome building a few blocks east of Dr. Elizabeth's house on Fifteenth Street.

Much as Lucy admired her sister-in-law Elizabeth, she did not wish to board with her indefinitely. From the beginning of her marriage Lucy had longed for a home; but now Henry had put Lucy's money as well as his own into land, and they were almost without cash. Their only hope of buying a house was to trade some of their western land for it. In mid-October 1856 Lucy wrote to her mother that they had been looking at property in Orange, New Jersey, and would like to settle there. Unfortunately, it seemed Henry would have to be in business for a few years more, and this might dictate the place where they would live.

Lucy as usual was having a busy winter. On November 25 and 26 she presided over the Seventh National Woman's Rights Convention in New York. Her speech set the mood of the gathering. "This is a day of congratulation. . . . Our first effort was made in a small room in Boston, where a few women were gathered. . . . The laws were yet against us, custom was against us, prejudice was against us, and more than all, women were against us. . . . Never before has any reformatory movement gained so much in so short a time. When we began, the statute books were covered with laws against women. . . ."

Now almost every northern state had somewhat modified its laws. Maine had given women nearly all property rights except the right to their own earnings; and the legislature had been about to include this when a "certain member grew fearful that wives would bring in bills for their daily service" and persuaded his colleagues to drop that portion of the proposed law. In Massachusetts a woman had had no rights except "fee simple in her real estate." Now broad property rights included the right to her own earnings. In Wisconsin she had every right but the franchise. Vermont, New Hampshire, Rhode Island, Ohio, Illinois and Indiana had materially amended their statutes. In New York a woman had rights to any property except her earnings; in these she still had no rights even if her husband was a drunkard, a profligate or had abandoned her; and she was still not guardian of her children.

Lucy had an engagement to speak in Philadelphia early in December; but she canceled her lecture. "Three years ago," she wrote to the man who had made the arrangements, "I took that Hall, and found to my horror that no colored people were admitted in that Hall. I did not know the fact until two hours before the lecture, and at its close gave the public pledge that I would *never* use that Hall again, until colored people could be admitted. Until this moment I did not know that you used the same place." Toward the end of the month she did deliver the lecture at another hall in Philadelphia and was annoyed to discover that the reason for the change of plans had been concealed, and the newspapers reported that family illness had kept her from appearing on the original date.

Now Lucy, who had so resisted the idea of being a woman, was about to perform the most female of functions. She was to have a baby. About this fact she was extremely reticent in her letters, even in her letters to her husband.

Today on television, women, flashed on the screen for a moment in audience participation programs, announce to uninterested millions that they are about to have babies. In Lucy's time the baby was usually a secret until the secret could no longer be kept, and then the about-to-be mother stayed close to home. Even Lucy, the reformer, could not quite defy this convention.

In the early days of her pregnancy Lucy continued to work and travel. Early in March 1857, from "the old home" in West Brookfield to Harry in New York, she wrote a letter full of love and loneliness, expressing sorrow because "we have been so long without a local habitation." But she assured him that she had been resting, and "if we get us a home soon, I will be as quiet as you desire."

She did not appear to be resting. She later wrote to a friend that she had been in Boston, gone on to Providence, received a "telegraphic despatch" to return to Boston to "give an argument to the Legislative Committee to which our petitions for Woman's right to vote had been referred." In Boston she had received another dispatch asking her to go to Maine on a similar mission. She did not reach home until the middle of March.

That spring they found a house, but Lucy had to borrow $500 from a friend to finance it. The house was in Orange, New Jersey, as she had hoped, "with an acre of ground—young fruit and ornamental trees growing about it, guarded by one venerable old apple-tree. . . . I do so enjoy its quiet, and the dear love that blesses it!" But her hopes for a quiet life were short-lived. "We removed April 1st. The very next week Mr. Blackwell's business compelled him to go West, so that I was here, more than a month, with the entire care. We had to have carpenters, masons, housecleaners and gardener etc."

Henry had had some difficulty finding a suitable business venture, for he had severed his western connections and he "had few connections or friends in the east," where he had moved for Lucy's sake. Now he had bought an interest in a firm publishing agricultural books, and was to travel through the West arranging for the establishment of farmers' libraries which would contain a large number of his partner-employer's volumes.

In June Lucy, lonely in the new home which was to have brought happiness and peace, asked her parents to visit her. "I am sure you would like to see this snug little place, which tho' not at all grand, gives us a good pleasant home. You should see how well I have practiced the farm lessons learned at home."

In July Susan Anthony and Lucy were involved in a disagreement. Lucy, because of her pregnancy and her new home, had been inactive for several months, and Susan wrote to Elizabeth Stanton that she felt deserted; she could not carry on the movement alone. Mrs. Stanton tried to keep Susan from upbraiding Lucy, from creating a situation which might endanger the entire movement; but Susan was driven by her frustration and disappointment and could not be stopped. She believed that Lucy and Antoinette had failed the cause of women, and was determined to say so. Elizabeth Cady Stanton had been married when they met. In fact, throughout their long association she was always Mrs. Stanton to Susan. But Susan was impatient of any spread of matrimony among her friends.

At first Lucy had been tolerant of Susan's foibles. "It is very absurd of you, you little naughty thing," she had written in March 1856, "to feel that you are left *alone*—are all the married ones dead and gone? . . . You are a little wretch to intimate that we are nothing *now*. Let me tell you as a secret that if you are ever married you will find that there is just as much of you as before." Now, as it became apparent that Susan could not organize a national convention for 1857, she grew increasingly bitter; and Lucy responded with increased annoyance.

Susan was not the only friend who was troubled. Mr. Higginson, who had so enthusiastically performed Lucy's marriage ceremony, was unhappy too. When Lucy told him that she could not begin work on a *Woman's Rights Almanac* which they had planned, because there was not enough money to see the project through, Mr. Higginson was flabbergasted. "Never before did you give up anything that ought to be done, for no better reason than that."

In the end Mr. Higginson produced the almanac himself. It appeared only once, in 1858. He could not have been too angry at Lucy, for he included in the short volume the speech she had delivered at the Seventh Annual Woman's Rights Convention on the progress of women.

Toward the end of July 1857 Lucy wrote Susan that she could not attend a convention in Providence, because she expected shortly to be a mother. She was forced to this intimate explanation by two events which had upset and hurt her. One was the letter from Mr. Higginson. "He says you saw me in N.J. and thought I 'did not appear quite right' "; but she was disingenuous enough not to mention that Mr. Higginson had agreed with Susan. The second was a letter from Susan herself. "You wrote Nette and me . . . 'I am terribly afraid lest what everybody says will be true, that like other wives you will flat out, and do nothing.'"

Susan's reply was highly emotional; her plea the one so often made by intense people eager to undo the results of their vehemence. "Lucy, *neither* of us have *time*—for much *personal* matters." She "did not intend anything . . . invidious, or *doubtful* of your *truthfulness* and faithfulness to *Woman*." But a rift had been opened which years later was to cut the woman's movement in two; for in spite of her dismay, Susan never learned the restraint which might have healed the breach. She could never conceal her resentment against feminists acting like women. Several years later, when Nette had had two children (she was to have six, one of whom died in childhood), Susan was still writing, "Now Nette, not another baby, is my peremptory command. Two will solve the problem whether a woman can be anything more than a wife and mother. I do feel that it is so foolish for her to put herself in the position of maid-of-all work and baby tender."

In the late summer of 1857 Henry was still away. He was trying to leave the publishing business, which was not so well managed as he had hoped, and to find work nearer home. In early August he was seeking employment as a "confidential clerk and bookkeeper," and asking a salary of $1500 a year.

From New York on September 8 he wrote Lucy a letter full of the soul-searching and fear so likely to obsess a young husband who is about to become a father. In 1857 the danger of death in childbirth was real, and there was the added worry that Lucy was thirty-nine years old; but surely it was extraordinary for Henry to write to his pregnant wife, "I look out from the dark mysterious shadow in which our present life is veiled and see more clearly the defects of my character and purpose which have thrown so many obstacles in your path and so much bitterness into your cup. Lucy dear—*however* this great crisis may eventuate, whether it result, as I hope and believe, in *our* assumption of new duties and cares, or whether in leaving me *alone* in this strange, uncongenial world—I will try to *meet* my responsibilities *worthily* and *well*—Dearest! You have made me *very happy* in spite of surface cares and excitements." And in contemplation of her early death, "I know of nothing better than to promise to live bravely and honestly and to subject mere material aims to loftier purposes."

However, on September 14, while Henry was at home, and Dr. Emily was in attendance, a healthy baby girl was born to a healthy mother. There was a long period of indecision about her name. Was she to be named Stone for her mother, or Blackwell for her father? Henry told Lucy that, since it was she who had suffered to bring the child into the world, he was willing to have her called by Lucy's name. It was Lucy who resolved the difficulty; the child was to bear both names.

The first name caused more trouble. When the baby was

almost nine months old, in one of those letters even a feminist mother apparently could not resist, a document purporting to be written to papa by baby herself, the signature still read:——Stone Blackwell. "We grew desperate and ransacked the dictionary," Henry remembered. "We tried Maud, Barbara, Ysealt. In vain! Then we settled down on Sarah, and Sarah it remained for thirty days. . . . At length came the bright thought Alice. Eureka! The child was named."

In the early months of the baby's life, it might have seemed more appropriate if she had been named for her mother. Lucy, with the high concept of motherhood learned from her own mother, had stopped working. It was not marriage that fulfilled Susan's fears for Lucy, but the care of a child and a home. In the early days it was for the most part a fatherless home. Henry, still driven by his debts and his sense of obligation to his family, was earning a living at the cost of being away from his wife and child most of the time. And Lucy, who had fought so hard to be free of the burdens of womanhood, was left to bear them alone.

Chapter Fourteen

The historic slogan, "No taxation without representation," fitted the woman's movement to perfection, and feminists made good use of it. At the 1852 convention, Lucy had said that disenfranchised women ought to resist taxation, though such a gesture might involve the loss of friends as well as property. "But let them all go; friends, house, garden spot, and all. The principle at issue requires the sacrifice."

Lucy had owned no taxable property in 1852, but by 1857 she did own the home for which she had waited so long; and Henry always referred to the house in Orange not as "our" house, but as "Lucy's" house.

In December, when Lucy's baby was two months old, while her husband was away on business, Lucy wrote a letter to the tax collector. "Enclosed I return my tax bill, without paying it. My reason for doing so is, that women suffer taxation, and yet have no representation, which is not only unjust to one-half the adult population, but is contrary to our theory of government. For years some women have been paying their taxes under protest, but still taxes are imposed and representation is not granted.

"But we believe that when the attention of men is called to the wide difference between their theory of government and its practice, in this particular, they cannot fail to see the mistake they now make, by imposing taxes on women, while they refuse them the right of suffrage, and that the sense of justice which is in all good men, will lead them to correct it. Then we shall cheerfully pay our taxes—not till then."

Lucy later told her daughter that when the tax bill came she felt as the men of the Revolution must have felt. It seemed to her as much robbery as anything could be. To the

State of New Jersey it did not seem like robbery; and notice was posted of a sale for taxes. In telling the story, her daughter says that Lucy "let her household goods be sold for taxes," and that "according to family tradition, little Alice's cradle was also taken." Yet the actual tax, presumably a personal property tax, was, even allowing for the enormous difference in the value of money then and now, a small one. The wide publicity resulting from Lucy's gesture was immensely valuable to the woman's movement, but even for thrifty Lucy, it could not have taken quite the courage for which she afterward received credit, nor entirely deserved the tone of her own "poor little Alice was a baby in my lap, and her father was away at the West."

The *New York Tribune* of January 26, 1858, reprinted the notice posted at the "railroad depot." "One of the constables will, on Friday the 22d day of January instant, at two o'clock in the afternoon of that day, at the house of Lucy Stone, sell at public vendue, to the highest bidder for cash, the following goods, to wit: Two tables, four chairs, one stand and two *pictures* to make the said tax and costs."

The *Tribune*'s account of the sale continued, "The first article offered was a marble table, worth about $12, which was started at $6 and knocked down at $7.50. The next articles were two steel-plate likenesses, one of Gerrit Smith [Lucy's daughter says it was Garrison] and the other of Gov. S. P. Chase, [probably the one he had presented to them in Cincinnati] which were sold together for $3. From these sales a sufficient sum was realized, and a small balance was paid to Lucy. She told the constable that the same operation would have to be performed every year until the law was repealed, as she would never voluntarily pay taxes for the support of institutions that she had no voice in governing. The officer of the law replied that he would let some one else have the job hereafter, as it was not a pleasant duty for him to perform." What the *Tribune* did not know, what Lucy herself had not known at the time of the sale, was that a friendly neighbor had bought the furniture to return to her.

On February 10 Lucy wrote to her mother, "I know that I deserve to be pounded for not writing you more and oftener. If my daughter serves me so, I'll make her sorry for it. But then, with baby, work, company, and the tax-gatherer, I have been very busy. You saw that I did not pay my taxes. Harry and I had an overflowing meeting about it night before last."

In 1915 a bronze plaque was unveiled at the place where Lucy had defied the tax collector. The last act of the drama was played out in 1956. On March 18 of that year *The New York Times* stated, with some inaccuracy of detail, that the historic building at 258 Hurlbut Street, Orange, which Lucy Stone "let go for taxes" was to be razed to make room for a church parking lot. There is no further record of Lucy's having refused to pay her taxes. Her protest had won the publicity for which she had hoped; a repetition would have been ineffective.

Those early years of marriage were difficult for both Lucy and Henry, a period of separation, of illness, of doubts about their marriage and their future. In the spring of 1858 Henry started, with high hopes, on yet another western trip. He was again full of enthusiasm for the publishing business, which had been reorganized to his satisfaction. Like all Henry's favorite business enterprises, this one had overtones of social reform; and it delighted him that, by paying a dollar or so, a family could have the use of books worth sixty dollars.

In his first enthusiasm he decided to supervise the new libraries himself, though this might, he wrote Lucy, mean "a separation from you of a couple of months annually." A few days later he was stilling her doubts. "It is both your fault (or rather *misfortune*) and *my own*, to look too much at the dark side of things. . . . Let us hope for a happy re-union and for many loving and useful years."

Then he learned that Lucy had been ill, and his failure

to be with her when she needed him changed his mood. His letters were given over to self-recrimination. He had made her move around the country, taken her from her family, fettered her work. Her love for him must be based on the principle that "all men love and prize *what has cost them dear.*"

During that spring she was frequently ill. She had two attacks of pleurisy. She had boils, a prevalent disease in those days before the careful sanitation of the water supply; but she wrote to her mother that boils were said to be healthy, and she took comfort from that. The baby, at least, was well. "She gives me a world of weariness . . . but I *love her,*" Lucy told Harry.

Life was filled with a host of less rewarding difficulties. There were money problems, particularly trying to Lucy, who never forgot those girlhood years when she had to slave for every meager cent. Perhaps she should sell the house. Maybe they should take boarders. Apparently they were suffering from the loss of Lucy's income as a lecturer. There were family problems. Though none of the five Blackwell sisters ever married, Marian was the only one who had not settled on a definite career. It was therefore assumed, with a conventionality surprising in this liberal family, that she would care for her mother; but she was no less intellectual or restless than her sisters, and now felt strained beyond endurance. Lucy told Marian that she and Hannah Blackwell could come to live with her, so that Marian would have greater freedom, and in April they did move into Lucy's house.

Meanwhile Susan Anthony was pleading with her to return to work, and Lucy was replying that she could not arrange for any set speech while she was still nursing the baby. But toward the end of April she gave in and went to New York to lecture, leaving the baby with a neighbor. It was no use. She could not sleep, "but kept awake, thinking of the dear child, and vowing I would never leave her again." And her fears were realized. The baby "took a dreadful cold."

The annual Woman's Rights Convention of 1858 was to be held in New York in the second week of May, a time when that city was regularly a center of conventions. For many years church organizations and Bible and missionary societies had held yearly meetings in what was known as Anniversary Week. Gradually the reform movements began to take advantage of the large numbers of sympathizers and potential converts already assembled, and the temperance, antislavery and, finally, woman's rights conventions came to be held at the same time.

Lucy told Harry she might not go to New York even for this most important event of the year. I will not leave *"your baby* with the girl I have." But she presumably made more satisfactory arrangements because, according to the *History of Woman Suffrage,* she spoke at the convention with her "usual effect."

Her co-workers in the movement must have been surprised when they saw her that spring. Lucy had changed. "I am getting as fat as a duck," she told her mother. "It lies in rolls on my ribs, and my thighs are as large as yours. My dresses that used to be so loose won't meet on me at all now." Pictures of her in her later years show a round, comfortable, solid person, very unlike the small, bright-faced girl of the days before her baby was born.

By May Harry had grown frantic at his continued separation from his family. But what could he do? He had been enormously successful and owed it to his partner in the publishing business to continue until the libraries were installed. Yet all he desired was to settle in Massachusetts and work for woman's equality there. Where "human rights are household words and where the revolutionary spirit burns most brightly—there we will *win for woman absolute equality before God and the Law."*

In May Lucy left with the baby to visit her childhood home. She was there for two months. In June Harry, still in

Chicago, wrote to her, "Hereafter *nothing* must induce me thus to leave you." Yet on July 8, "It seems to me a hundred years since I left you—I *wonder* how I have *borne* it! Alas—on the same principle that a man endures amputation or submits to be hanged—" The following winter, in spite of determination, he had to go West again, but this time, after he had been gone for a while, Lucy and the baby went to join him.

Lucy had never before occupied herself so little with public affairs. Yet the cause was making progress; and in that period of her retirement two financial events of great importance occurred in the suffrage movement, one of which involved Lucy directly. In early November she and Susan Anthony were informed by Wendell Phillips that he had received an anonymous gift of five thousand dollars, to be used by the three of them to support the woman's rights movement. The fund was later known to have been given by the Boston abolitionist, Francis Jackson, in whose home Lucy had lived for a time when she returned from Oberlin. It was, in a sense, conscience money, for the Jackson fortune was founded on textile mills made profitable by the labor of countless disenfranchised and anonymous women. A few months later another Boston abolitionist, Charles Hovey, died, leaving a fund of not less than eight thousand dollars a year to Wendell Phillips and his associates to be used for reform movements, chief among them antislavery and woman suffrage.

The world was making progress too. "We had a great firing of guns and ringing of bells in honor of the telegraph," Lucy wrote her father. "I wonder if Brookfield shouted too." The first Atlantic cable had been laid and Queen Victoria had transmitted to President Buchanan the hope that it would "prove an additional link between the nations whose friendship is founded upon their common interest and reciprocal esteem." The cheering was premature. It was not until eight years and a civil war later that a permanently successful cable was laid.

The first week of December 1858 Lucy and the baby, now definitely named Alice, were in Chicago with Henry. After Lucy's death Henry still kept a tender memory of those days. "Evanston in 1859 was a very pleasant village with a beautiful grove and public park extending to the Lake shore, where we had a bath-house. . . . Every afternoon, as . . . I came from the railroad cars, Lucy was accustomed to meet [me], and as [I] approached the child ran forward. . . . It was a pretty picture."

By the summer of 1859 Henry had taken orders for fifteen hundred libraries and, his work completed, was ready to return East. That summer Lucy lost a baby boy, prematurely born. Again a veil of modest secrecy hung over the event. The clearest reference to it is in a letter Nette wrote to Lucy on August 29, "You must know that I heard of the poor premature little baby and that I sympathize with you deeply. . . . Lucretia Mott's daughter asked me if you had another child. I said no, with a world of pain, and she looked so surprised . . . that I did not know what to say, and so said nothing at all." She could not reveal this intimate secret without Lucy's consent, but she did ask permission to tell Susan, who, as usual, was indignant that Lucy had not been lecturing. Much of Susan's concern seems to have been justified, for in the next years, Lucy gave few speeches. The events of her life were largely domestic, rather than historical.

For several years Henry had been much occupied in the purchase, sale and exchange of land. Now, on his return East, he gave up publishing to occupy himself entirely with real estate, opening offices in both Orange and New York, where he rented and sold houses and land on commission and, when there was an opportunity to do so, traded his own western properties for eastern land. Lucy helped too. Mornings, while Henry was at the New York office, Lucy would take the baby and tend the office in Orange, often going out to show properties to prospective customers.

There are poignant reminders that in those years when

her daughter was a baby, life for Lucy was an almost ceaseless struggle of conflicting impulses and needs. Long after her death, Henry was to say, "When we consider the wrench which marriage and maternity made in a public career, previously so brilliant and successful, the sacrifice of personal independence . . . the pressure of domestic cares,—all coming at an age from 37 to 47 years when most women have outlived their first youth—there is something absolutely sublime in the cheerful serenity . . . and uncomplaining loyalty to husband and child which marked those crucial years."

Yet in the next sentence Henry himself casts a shadow on this "cheerful serenity" which he liked to believe enveloped his wife. "At all times of her life, Lucy was subject to occasional severe nervous headaches accompanied by days of extreme depression, during which she sought refuge in absolute silence. I remember on one such occasion, during our residence in Orange in 1858 or 9—going to New York with the fear that some very serious consequences might ensue. On my return I found my wife bright and cheery and absolutely well. It seems that soon after I left home Angelina Grimké (Mrs. Theodore Weld) came up from Belleville to call on her. The sudden diversion of thought and feeling proved the very antidote needed and in the revival of old associations, the cloud passed away."

On another such occasion, Lucy wrote Henry a troubled letter in which the familiar, recurrent doubts appear. She was trying to be better. She was reading more, trying to be more cultured, more worthy of him. Apparently she had outgrown the taboo against novels, for she told Mrs. Stanton that she had been reading George Eliot, whom she found highly instructive.

To Henry she wrote of the baby, "She has the most radiant little face I ever saw and *is* a very promising child—" But then, "I never feel her little cheek beside of mine, never hear . . . her sweet baby voice without the earnest purpose to gather to myself more symmetry of being—to sustain all my relations better. . . . I *am* trying to be a good wife and mother . . . but I *have* tried before, and my miserable failures hitherto make me silent now. But if I have conquered myself, or gained anything in all these weary weeks, you will find it in my actions—I hope to be more to you and better—when you come to me."

Henry too was having his domestic problems; for she is glad, she says, that you "feel the lack of dignity in the *running* to the station etc. and that you will *try* to mend it. I will have the breakfast earlier, and we may, after all, be a model family yet—We will be patient with each other."

Part Three

Dissension in Utopia

Chapter Fifteen

While Lucy remained enmeshed in the problems of the small world encompassed by Henry and Alice, the turmoil in the greater world around them steadily increased. The passage of the Kansas-Nebraska Bill in 1854 had created a state of civil war in the new territory of Kansas, a rehearsal for the national conflict which was to follow. The free soilers who had rushed to Kansas to insure its entry into the Union as a free state were met by gangs crossing over from slaveholding Missouri, determined not to permit a free state to grow up on their very borders, a temptation to Missouri Negroes to escape or even to rebel.

Two rival authorities with two capitals claimed the right to govern Kansas. There were skirmishes, rigged elections, arson and murder. John Brown and his sons killed five men, became outlaws and continued their raids. In May 1856 while Lucy was on her way to Wisconsin with Henry, a proslavery mob had burned and sacked the town of Lawrence, killing many of its inhabitants. Senator Charles Sumner of Massachusetts, in a violent and provocative speech, called it "a crime without example in the history of the past." The provocation had results. Next day, as Sumner sat at his desk in the Senate, Representative Preston Brooks of South Carolina approached him from behind and beat him over the head with a cane. The cowardly attack continued until Sumner lay unconscious and bloody on the Senate floor. The frenzy of those days could be no more clearly illustrated. The North was scandalized, and Lucy and Henry were deeply affected by this violence against a man whom Lucy had known in the antislavery movement in Massachusetts, and whom they so much admired.

Lucy's connections with Kansas were many. By conviction a passionate free soiler, she happened also to be related by marriage to Charles Robinson, one of the two rival governors of the territory, who later became the first governor of the state. He was a physician who had emigrated from Massachusetts to California and then to Kansas. Lucy's brother Bowman had successively married two of his sisters; and a third, whom many years later Bowman also married, lived with Bowman and his family on the farm at Coy's Hill.

As early as 1855 Sam Wood, a Republican politician whom Henry described as "a rough fellow but with generous instincts," asked Lucy to draft a married woman's property bill for Kansas, a bill which was passed almost as she wrote it. Later, in 1859, Wood wrote to Lucy and to other suffragists asking what the laws pertaining to women should be in the new state when it was formed. According to her daughter, none of the others answered. Lucy did. "Hence Kansas was the first state to give mothers equal guardianship."

Two years earlier, when emotions in Kansas were running high, the Supreme Court had handed down the Dred Scott decision, which had further inflamed exacerbated feelings. The court held that a free Negro was not a citizen; that a Negro taken temporarily by his master into free soil was not thereby freed; and, most important to Kansas, that Congress did not have the power to exclude slavery from any territory. The great majority of northerners were incensed. That year Higginson, Phillips and other abolitionists in a convention in Massachusetts advocated that the free states secede from the Union. In the national capital President Buchanan, weak and indecisive, was willing to make any compromise to prevent further discord. Fearful of northern intransigence, he surrounded himself with southern sympathizers. Washington was, politically and socially, a proslavery city.

In October 1859 John Brown, his sons and a few supporters, seized the government arsenal at Harpers Ferry, Virginia, in the hope of obtaining arms to set up a free Negro area in the Alleghenies. It was a mad and hopeless venture. The raiders were captured, tried and condemned. Six were hanged. People who had befriended Brown and probably encouraged him fell under suspicion of being accomplices. In the house four miles from Harpers Ferry where the Browns had recently been living, there was found, according to *The Liberator,* a letter "from Fred. Douglass, containing ten dollars from a lady for the cause." There was also a letter from Gerrit Smith about "money matters." Douglass, accused of having promised to join the raid, denied giving his approval or agreeing to be there, but did not deny knowledge of the plan.

Governor Wise of Virginia declared in a rabble-rousing speech that "if anyone should bring [Gerrit Smith] to me by fair or foul means, I will guarantee that he will be given a fair trial." This and widespread attacks in the press so terrified Smith that he went completely to pieces and was for a while committed to what was then known as a lunatic asylum. Douglass and other of Brown's supporters hurriedly departed for Canada until the hue and cry should have died; but Lucy's courageous friend Higginson took part in two wildly romantic but unsuccessful plots to release John Brown and his men.

The Liberator, and Lucy too, blamed not Brown's supporters, but the institution of slavery, for inciting honest men to insurrection. When the death sentence was carried out, Lucy wrote to her mother, "Isn't it dreadful to think that Old Brown *could* be hung—such a man! It seems as though the times of the martyrs had come again—I imagine we shall have blood shed in Congress, and may be the dissolution of the Union. . . . We are near a revolution I think."

Because the bodies of the executed were to be relinquished for burial if claimed by their friends, a petition was sent to Governor Wise. "We hereby apply for the remains of Messrs. Copeland and Green. . . . We conclude from the fact that no such application has been made . . . that they are fugitive slaves. . . ." The signers declared themselves "willing and happy to identify [themselves] in life and in death with the proscribed race to which these brave and unfortunate men belong." Lucy and Henry were two of the eight signers.

In October 1859 wide publicity had been given to a letter purported to have been written by Senator Stephen Douglas in answer to an invitation from Lucy to attend a convention for the "promotion of happiness and protection of the interests and rights of the female sex." *The Liberator* printed Lucy's denial of the incident. "The hoax seemed to me so barefaced that I never gave it a second thought . . . it is not to *such men* that the Woman's Rights cause appeals for helpers." Even to aid women, Lucy could not imagine appealing to the author of the Kansas-Nebraska Bill.

The woman's movement had been making great strides. Early in 1860 the New York state legislature, having listened in joint session to an impassioned plea by Elizabeth Cady Stanton, amended its married woman's property law and gave women, among other rights, the right to their own earnings and equal guardianship of their own children.

In 1860, too, a stormy Woman's Rights Convention took place in New York in Anniversary Week. Among the many anniversaries to be celebrated that May, the *Tribune* listed those of the American Bible Society, the American and Foreign Bible Society, the American Tract Society of Boston and the National Woman's Rights Convention. It was the last national convention on woman's rights to be held until after the Civil War.

On the second day of the convention Elizabeth Stanton brought up the tabooed subject of divorce. Like so many nineteenth-century reformers, Mrs. Stanton was for reform in everything, and as she grew increasingly anticlerical and prodivorce, she came into conflict with other leaders who, even when they agreed with her, felt a realistic reluctance to saddle the woman's movement with more disabilities than it already had. In 1854 Antoinette Brown, who certainly did not agree with Mrs. Stanton's theological views, wrote to her, "When you write for yourself, say exactly what you please, but . . . do not compel us to endorse anything foreign to the movement." Nette was in equal disagreement on divorce. In 1853 she had written to Lucy, "It is said you are in favor of divorce on the ground of drunkenness"; she herself was not yet ready to accept such an idea, even if both parties wanted it.

Lucy believed that loveless marriages were immoral. Some years before her own marriage she had told a friend that she believed in divorce, "that a true love may grow up in the soul of the injured one. . . . Whatever is pure and holy, not only has a right to be, but it has a right also to be recognized, and further, I think it has no right *not* to be recognized." In 1856 she had said of Paulina Davis, "She wants the marriage question to come up at the national convention. It seems to me we are not ready for . . . the real question, viz. has woman, as wife, a right to herself? It is very little to me to have the right to vote, to own property, &c. if I may not keep my body, and its uses, in my absolute right—Not one wife in a thousand can do that now . . . but it seems to me untimely now."

Lucy had corresponded with Elizabeth Stanton on the same subject. "If I were only sure what was the right, I can stand by it through fire and flood. I very much wish that a wife's right to her own body should be pushed at our next convention. It does seem to me that you are the one to do it. Can't you come? I will help all I can." On further consideration, she decided that the question should not be brought up, and in July 1857 was writing to Susan Anthony, "Of course, you must use your own judgment about the time and place to discuss the marriage question—But when it *is done,* it seems to me, we must not call it 'woman's rights' for the simple reason that it concerns men just as much." She also continued to plead with Elizabeth Stanton, and a short while before the 1860 convention she again begged her to call a separate meeting to discuss marriage and divorce. Elizabeth Cady Stanton was not to be dissuaded, and Lucy finally gave in enough to say, "It is a great grave topic that one shudders to grapple, but its hour is coming. . . . God touch your lips if you speak on it." She wrote too that she intended to be at the convention, and though she would not be able to prepare a speech, would possibly join in the discussion. There is no record, however, of her having attended.

Mrs. Stanton's speech and the resolutions she offered threw the meeting into turmoil. They brought sharp dissent from Nette and more moderate objections from Wendell Phillips. Both Phillips and Garrison shared Lucy's view that the issue was equally the problem of both sexes. "I would move to lay the resolutions on the table," Phillips said, "but my conviction that they are out of order is so emphatic that I wish to go further than that, and move that they do not appear on the journals of this Convention."

One of the chief targets of Mrs. Stanton's attack was Horace Greeley, whose early editorial support had meant so much to the woman's movement. He was violently opposed to divorce and was much antagonized by its inclusion in woman's rights propaganda.

That autumn a great loss befell Lucy. Her beloved mother died. Henry learned of it in Lucy's letter from West Brookfield on September 14. Through letters of the period the news of death runs in almost casual fashion; a letter was the normal means of communicating, even to closest relatives, the news of birth, death and the events between. Now, recalling her other recent loss, the loss of her baby boy, Lucy wrote that her mother had died today, on "our one wee darling's birthday." She said little more; but her mother's death was a great sorrow. Lucy had loved and admired her mother, and in early childhood had built around her mother's situation her whole conception of what a woman's life was and what it ought to be.

Aware as ever of the need to keep the woman's movement alive, Lucy knew she should be back at work. Two years before she had written to Susan, "Garrison's mother (to say nothing of yours and mine) did the best for the world by taking care of him," a strange comparison, since poverty had forced Garrison's mother to leave him at an early age. Now Lucy's daughter was three years old, and Lucy felt that the time had come to go out into the world again.

Ten years after Lucy's death her daughter still remembered with gratitude the devotion of her mother in those early years and later. "In addition to all that she did and all that she was to humanity at large, she was to her child the best, the wisest, and the tenderest of mothers. Motherhood was to her the crowning joy of life, and its duties among the highest and most sacred, never to be slighted for any cause, however important. . . .

"Two things I have always been proud of—that my mother nursed me from her own breast, and that she made me obey her. Most of the frivolous women who sneer at 'strong minded' mothers seem unable to perform either office for their children."

Now, ready to go into public life again, Lucy was able to conquer her fears and to begin to lecture, and lecture successfully. On January 30, 1861, from Dayton, Ohio, she wrote to Henry, telling him of the warm reception her speeches had received. "I am *so* glad to find again the old inspiration, and it comes to me more and more." But it was too late. Only a little more than two months afterward the Civil War forced abandonment of the woman's rights movement for some years to come.

It was a necessary abandonment, but an unfortunate one. The gains had been spectacular, but they had been neither broad nor solid enough. Whether it was because the pressure of the woman's movement was gone, or because of the atmosphere of reaction that accompanies war, in 1862 the New York legislature amended the 1860 Act, withdrawing most of the property rights granted to married women only two years before, including the right to equal guardianship of their own children. It did, however, recognize a mother's interest in her offspring to the point of conceding that "no man shall bind his child to apprenticeship or service, or part with the control of such child or create any testamentary guardian therefor, unless the mother, if living, shall in writing signify her assent thereto."

Chapter Sixteen

Though Lucy had gone so far as to advocate the secession of the North and an uprising of slaves, the actuality of war came as a great blow. Added to her belief in the wickedness of war were the old dissatisfactions. The government could, she said, without his mother's consent, take any son away to be shot, and without her consent could then "put its bloody hand in her pocket to help pay the bills." Yet even these objections do not explain the fact that such public-spirited citizens as Lucy and Henry continued their lives in the early war years much as if there were no war. From New York in July 1861, after the bitter Union defeat at Bull Run, Henry wrote to Lucy that after the bad news "grossly exaggerated kept coming in . . . hundreds surrounded the bulletin boards at all the offices." But their own lives were largely unaffected.

Other women throughout the country were playing important roles, for it is among the ironies of history that in spite of man-made restrictions, of delicate nurturing and limited education, the United States reared strong women who came to their country's aid in time of need, whether to settle the wild frontier, or to fight a war.

Henry's doctor sisters were leaders among northern women. In the first month of the war, Elizabeth, inspired perhaps by the example of Florence Nightingale, called a private meeting of the managers of the New York Infirmary to discuss the training of nurses for field service. A notice of the meeting accidentally found its way into *The New York Times,* and to everyone's amazement, at the time set, the parlors of the Infirmary were crowded with women eager to help. Encouraged by this unexpected enthusiasm, the Infirmary managers called a public meeting, and the Woman's Central Association of Relief was set up with offices in Cooper Institute. There women collected comforts and necessities for the soldiers, and Elizabeth interviewed applicants and selected those she considered worthy of being given a month's training before being sent out as army nurses.

The movement spread. Women's relief associations sprang up throughout the country. In June 1861, as a direct result of these organizations, the United States Sanitary Commission was appointed by President Lincoln. It had no appropriation and no real power, operating entirely on funds collected by the women of the nation, largely through Sanitary Fairs—a total during the war of at least ten million dollars. The Sanitary, as it came to be known affectionately among the troops, distributed supplies, supported sagging morale and helped to care for the sick and wounded. The army required any aid it could get. In the early days of the war, except for the tiny regular army, the fighting forces were made up of volunteer units organized and equipped by the states. Enlistments were for three-month periods. The confusion was unimaginable, conditions frightful. There were desperate shortages of men, clothing, medicine, food.

The nurses Elizabeth was training or arranging to have trained were sent to Washington to Dorothea Dix, who in that first June of the war had been appointed Superintendent of Nurses. Miss Dix was a Boston intellectual, a teacher who, having discovered the horrible conditions prevalent in lunatic asylums, had set out to publicize and correct them. At the outbreak of war, Miss Dix, then fifty-nine years old, entrained for Washington with the first Massachusetts troops, determined to care for them single-handed if necessary. She found Clara Barton already there, a thin little woman with clear brown eyes and a warm expressive mouth. Miss Barton had given up her job in the Patent Office and now proposed to accompany the troops to the battlefields to nurse the wounded, friend or enemy with equal care. From Ohio came Mary Walker, a physician graduated in 1855. Dr. Walker arrived in a man's uniform at the battlefront, and set up as a surgeon.

In Chicago Mary A. Livermore, a New England schoolteacher married to a Universalist minister, had up to that time taken no interest in the woman's rights movement. Now Mrs. Livermore organized a Ladies Aid Society, and did such effective work that she was made an associate member of the Sanitary Commission.

There was the writer Anna Ella Carroll, whose biography Henry's sister Ellen wrote many years later. Miss Carroll, daughter of an ex-governor of Maryland, freed her slaves and used her considerable influence and her literary ability to keep Maryland in the Union, a crucial matter because, if Maryland seceded, the national capital would be lost to the North. In 1861, invited by the War Department to go to the West to estimate the military situation, she advised against a premature plan to send a gunboat fleet down the Mississippi. "The civil and military authorities," she stated, "seem to me to be laboring under a great mistake in regard to the true key of the war in the South-west. It is not the Mississippi, but the Tennessee River." The capture of Forts Henry and Donelson, a turning point of the war, was the result of Miss Carroll's plan.

While these pioneer professional women gave over their lives to war work, Lucy's only relation to the conflict in those first years was as one of the anonymous women who picked lint for bandages. This cannot be explained by family problems, by emotional complications or by her aversion to war. There were other important psychological factors.

The woman's rights movement had been entirely abandoned at the outbreak of hostilities, and Lincoln's policy of caution was making it far from clear that he considered this a war to free the slaves. Even to the two causes in which she most firmly believed, Lucy's relation was always the same. She was a propagandist. Speaking and writing were her talents and her profession. She never functioned in any other way. Now in the war years she believed the old paths of action closed to her.

That Henry did not go to war is less significant. He was thirty-six when the war began. Later, during the draft, Lucy wrote to him, "Harry dear, if you *should* be drafted, you must buy a substitute at any price—Draw on my credit if necessary!!!!" Harry was drafted and paid three hundred dollars for a substitute; but it was customary for men who had sufficient money to buy a substitute, and no ignominy attached to them for doing so.

The problem which could most readily win Lucy's and Henry's allegiance was freedom for the slaves. Even before the war the abolitionists had found Lincoln too slow in taking a stand on emancipation. But most of the country hated the very idea of abolishing slavery, fearing that such an act would split the Union they still hoped could be saved; and from the time of Lincoln's election it was almost as dangerous to advocate emancipation as it had been in the thirties, when Garrison was so nearly lynched. In the northern seaboard states, when the movement for secession was developing in the South, antislavery speakers were howled down, stopped by riots; and on at least one occasion in Massachusetts, Negroes leaving an emancipation meeting were attacked by mobs.

But saving the country from emancipation had not saved it from war. At last, toward the end of 1862, Lincoln issued the Emancipation Proclamation but, still cautious, freed only the slaves in the rebel states and left slavery intact in the loyal border region. When the proclamation was about to become effective on January 1, 1863, Lucy wrote to her father, "We are here all feeling interested to hear the result of the President's proclamation of freedom to the slaves—I only hope he may be able to carry it out. But so many officers of the army are pro-slavery, and so many of the soldiers hate the negros, that I am afraid the poor fellows stand a poor chance."

It was not until the third year of the war that a cause presented itself to which Lucy could give her full allegiance, and inevitably this was a cause that included woman's rights. In 1863 she joined Susan Anthony and Elizabeth Stanton in forming a Woman's Loyal National League. Though it had been agreed that a time of war was not the moment to press for women's rights, suffrage leaders now saw an opportunity to make themselves felt in shaping national policy, and in linking woman's emancipation to the Negro's.

The New York legislature's withdrawal in 1862 of most of the benefits of its married woman's property bill of 1860 was believed in reform circles to have been brought about by the wartime abandonment of the woman's movement. It was imperative, then, that women should again make their voices heard; and when the Emancipation Proclamation freed Negroes only in the rebel states, it seemed that the time had come to attempt to guarantee that the war should not have been fought in vain, and that slavery should be forever abolished from the land. Elizabeth Stanton and Susan Anthony sent out a call "For a meeting of the Loyal Women of the Nation," to be held in New York on May 14, 1863. "The policy of war, our whole future life, depends on a universal, clearly defined idea of the end proposed." Mrs. Stanton made the opening address. Lucy Stone was elected president of the convention. As in the old days, Angelina Grimké Weld, Ernestine Rose and Antoinette Brown Blackwell were all there and all spoke. Susan Anthony offered a resolution that "There never can be a true peace in this Republic until the civil and political rights of all citizens of African descent and all women are practically established."

This caused an uproar. The very idea that had brought Lucy out of retirement antagonized many of the women who had come from across the country to support the Loyal League. They had not expected either antislavery or woman's rights to be included in the concept of loyalty. Lucy's speech in the spirited debate shows that whatever her doubts she had lost none of the eloquence of her early years. "If the right of one single human being is to be disregarded by us, we fail in our loyalty to the country. . . . We come to-day to say to those who are administering our Government and fighting our battles, 'While you are going through this valley of humiliation, do not forget that you must be true alike to the women and the negroes.' We can never be truly 'loyal' if we leave them out." In the end the resolution was carried by a large majority.

The chief task of the Loyal League was the nationwide circulation of a petition asking Congress to pass a Constitutional Amendment abolishing slavery. An office was opened at Cooper Institute with Susan Anthony as its only paid—and underpaid—worker. The rest of the staff was composed of many part-time volunteers, Lucy among them. By February 1864 the league had collected one hundred thousand signatures. These petitions, divided by states, each roll wrapped in yellow paper and tied with red tape, were dramatically introduced into the Senate by two large Negroes who carried them onto the Senate floor where they were presented by Charles Sumner in a moving appeal.

By its first anniversary the league had five thousand members, of whom two thousand were active in circulating petitions. It had collected over two hundred and sixty-five thousand additional signatures. By then the Senate had already passed the Thirteenth Amendment, and it seemed that the House would soon follow. Its work done, the Loyal League shut its offices that summer, but it was not until early the following year that the House acted, and in December 1865, ratified by the States, the Amendment became law and slavery was abolished.

With Lincoln's first election, the antislavery forces had reached a point of serious disagreement. The intransigent, nonpolitical Garrison now supported Lincoln and counseled moderation. Wendell Phillips and many others demanded far more radical action than the President was prepared to take. Before the 1864 election the Republican party very nearly split on these issues. Phillips wrote, "I would cut off both hands before doing anything to aid Abraham Lincoln's election." The radicals wished to jettison Lincoln as the party's Presidential nominee, and supported John C. Frémont, explorer of the West, a romantic figure who had been the Republicans' first candidate in 1856.

Inevitably a compromise movement grew up in an effort to save the Republican party from a split which would have wrecked it. The hope was that the party could be united under a third, less controversial, figure.

Mrs. Stanton supported Frémont, but Lucy feared that a split in the Republican ranks would mean victory for the Democrats. "And bad as Mr. Lincoln is," she wrote to Susan that summer, "a union with him and his supporters seems to me *less bad* than a union with peace Democrats." Both Lucy and Henry supported Lincoln for re-election, though Lucy wished they could "make Mr. Garrison see that his fulsome laudation of Mr. Lincoln is right against the slave. O, if he would only cry out as in the earlier days!" And after Lincoln's re-election she expressed disappointment that Garrison did not agree with "*nearly* all [Wendell Phillips's] criticisms of the administration."

War or no war, the Stone-Blackwell family were as always involved in the elaborate problems of living and making a living; and in the Civil War years they went through many domestic shifts and changes. Henry's trading in real estate sometimes included the property on which they were living. On their return from Chicago they moved to a new home in Orange, and two years later moved again to a house Henry had bought in West Bloomfield. Meanwhile they remodeled a dilapidated cottage on the land Lucy had acquired before going to Chicago, about which she had then written to her father, "We have exchanged our house and one acre [in Orange] for 20 acres in W. Bloomfield, three miles from here." It is "a place rather run down—with poor buildings—but with good fruit—three good building sites, plenty of good pears, cherries, grapes, apples—a small wood lot and most magnificent view."

Henry, after Lucy's death, remembered their life in the remodeled house in what is now bustling Montclair. "Lucy, a farmer's daughter, tried to make farming our land a source of income. But our abundant crop of cherries and apples scarcely paid for the gathering and the hired help. We kept two men, a horse and carriage, and one hired girl. We found the situation, tho' lovely, too inaccessible for my convenience in business. . . . The roads were deep and miry during the winter and spring." The railroad service was "slow and irregular."

It took Henry, in fact, more than three hours daily to cover the few miles to and from New York, so, as the winter of 1862–63 set in, they rented the house and moved to the city. They did not live in that house again, though Lucy never sold it and it remained a profitable source of income throughout her life and after her death. They boarded that winter of 1863 with a Mrs. Palmer on Gramercy Park, later moving to another boardinghouse.

During these years Henry also moved from one economic venture to another. The real estate business prospered in the early days of the war. Property owners were frightened for the country's future, and were, by Henry's own account, willing to "realize anything unencumbered. But I found the load of interest and taxes so hard to carry that I transferred my real-estate business to my brother George." Brother George proceeded to expand the business and eventually became a multimillionaire, the only one of the three brothers in America not involved in the reform movement, the only one to become rich.

Meanwhile Henry, abandoning the real estate business at the moment of its greatest possibility, had taken a position in New York at $1500 a year as salesman for a furnace company, but had soon left to become salesman and bookkeeper at double that salary for Dennis Harris in the sugar-refining

Lucy Stone as a young woman

Henry Browne Blackwell
in middle life
and in his later years

Lucy Stone in the 1880's

Reunion, in 1886, of leaders of the antislavery movement at the Dor
chester home of Lucy Stone and Henry Blackwell. Front row: Samuel May
William Lloyd Garrison, Jr., Harriet W. Sewall, Samuel Sewall, Wendel

Garrison, Henry Blackwell, Theodore Weld. Back row: (seated) Eliz-
eth Chace, Sarah Southwick, Abby Kelley Foster, Lucy Stone, Zilpha
ooner; (standing) Francis J. Garrison, Alla Foster, George T. Garrison

Alice Stone Blackwell
as a girl and later

Home of Lucy Stone and Henry Blackwell
at Pope's Hill, Dorchester, Massachusetts

Letter from Lucy Stone to Henry Blackwell, January 18, 1855, before their marriage

Boston. Jan. 18 – 1855 –

Dearest Harry – After riding from 3 o'clock yesterday morning, until 8 last evening, I found myself once more here. Went first to the Anti Slavery office, where I got your letter of Jan. 10 – and many others from dear friends congratulating me on our marriage prospects. and sending kind greetings to you. James & Lucretia Mott, Charles Burleigh & wife &c – I was glad of them all but more especially of yours. which spoke so truly to me. as though I was a part of you. Now once more that feeling grows with me that we are a part of each other. and I miss you every where. and feel that something of mine is gone – I am as anxious as you are to assume our marriage – and perhaps be can, earlier than the time I suggested – then in that case, I should not think of coming East to attend the May meetings – I could neither do nor get, as much good as it would cost – I did not want to be in Cincinnati during your convention – I do not think I can ever speak well there again – I know it is very weak and foolish. but I cannot help it – I am glad Douglass is not to be there – He is so unprincipled and mean. that I cannot bear to pretend good fellowship, where I feel none – But we can fix the time of our marriage when we meet – We shall probably start West, next Monday or Tuesday – I would go at once to Cincinnati with Sarah. If I were sure that you would be at home – My appointments in Mich. are not made. and I can

Sebago Lake Apl 30 – 1878

Dearest Wife of mine

If I could only spend the 23d anniversary of our wedding day with you tomorrow, I would gladly assign ten per cent of my (prospective) profits in the beet Sugar business for the privilege. But it seems impossible to do so without injury to others as well as myself – & sentiment must yield to duty. Believe me, dear Lucy, I am glad & only glad of our having united our lives on the first of May 1855. If I were only as sure that you had been the gainer as I, I should be still more happy. I know I have tried you in a thousand ways – but, most of all, by not being able to show you the sincere good will I have had – If it had been necessary I would have died for you at any time, but it is far harder to live so as not to wound & grieve the heart that loves one. Neither you nor my mother can fail to have found

Letter from Henry Blackwell to Lucy Stone, April 30, 1878, on the eve of the twenty-third anniversary of their marriage

"The New Female Costume."
A drawing from *Gleason's Pictorial*, circa 1851

"Woman's Emancipation."
A cartoon from *Punch*, 1851

business. Mr. Harris had worked for Henry's father, whom he had met on the boat coming to America. Mr. Harris had been a Methodist preacher then, but some time later, when Henry's father encountered him on the street, he had still not found a post. Mr. Blackwell made him a foreman in his sugar business, and when the Blackwells moved to Cincinnati in the wake of the depression of 1837, Mr. Harris bought the plant. Henry's position with his father's former employee was his entrance into a business which, throughout most of the rest of his life, was to fascinate him and to prove a will-o'-the-wisp leading to a fortune he never made.

By the summer of 1864 Henry had become uneasy about Mr. Harris's way of doing business and was again deciding to retire from business altogether. Like all Henry's financial decisions, this evoked a complicated series of reactions from Lucy.

That late spring and summer Lucy and Alice spent with Lucy's father, who was an old man now and ill. In June Lucy wrote to Henry that he ought to give up the job he so obviously did not like, and live on the income from the houses he owned. If he stopped working, he could go West to inspect his lands there. Then, when he came back—"I hope you will consider seriously my proposition to lecture this Fall." Yet in August Lucy was again expressing concern about money and suggesting that she could greatly reduce their expenses by living for a year or so with her sister in Gardner, Massachusetts, where Sarah and her family had settled after their Cincinnati venture. Lucy was, of course, eager to have Henry do as he wished and take a rest from business.

Her state of mind had been bad, and she seemed now to be aware of some connection between her marriage and a decline in her powers. A few weeks earlier she had written, "Here with fewer cares and almost nothing to vex me, I hope to get back somewhere near to the state of soul and spirit in which I was when you first found me, and then, when we meet, to begin new." She must stay in some quiet corner where she might "be able *perhaps* to find that better self of me, which, during all the years of my poverty-stricken girlhood, steadily aspired to a life of worthy use—and which, with a patience that no delay wearied, and courage that no difficulty ever daunted, carried me, serene and self-respecting to the port I had toiled to reach, and then kept me there, to work with the same courage and patience. O no, Harry! for the sake of us three, I must keep in some quiet 'cleft of the Rock' till the angels of healing make me whole again."

To Susan she had given a more female explanation. In the quiet of the farm, she had had only one day of headache and "none of the mental confusion that has so tormented me before. . . . If I can only survive the inevitable change of constitution, and be right side up at the end of it, I shall pray again for that great impulse that drove me into the world with words that *must* be spoken." Lucy was forty-six that summer.

On the last day of September 1864 her father died. "He survived mother 4 years and fourteen days. He would have been 85, on the 9th of Nov." She hated to leave Brookfield, she told Harry. "But the old home and Father's house will never be the same again to any of us. We came back from the grave to the empty room with a sense of loneliness that only they know who have felt it." She had been thinking that, if Harry retired, they might buy a place nearby. But, she added, I am beginning to believe "you will not be satisfied to discontinue, for any length of time, the business to which you have all your life been accustomed . . . and we must shape our lives accordingly." In any case, she would remain for a year in the country. She could not bear again to be shut up with Alice in a suite of rooms. "I wish we could live together. I want you all the time, for speech, and for silence, for rest, and sympathy, and all good things, Harry dear." Certainly, whatever demon Lucy was battling in this period, it did not seem to her to involve a failure of her love for Harry. Her letters were full of affection. "Dear

Little Husband of mine." "Dearest Harrykin." "Dear little child." Yet the letters were many and the separation long.

Meanwhile Harry had retired from business. He was now thirty-nine, and he had worked since he was fourteen, when his father died. Now at last he was "out of debt with several thousands in his pocket." After he had stopped working and had "stumped New Jersey for Mr. Lincoln," he came to stay in Gardner for a while with his wife and daughter.

"Alice," Lucy wrote to a friend that December 12, "is seven years old—large of her age, and the image of her father. She reads very well. . . . She is a brunette. Has a strong body." Harry was out West on "personal business," but was hoping to be back in Gardner for Christmas. However, on December 23, when he was on his way home, Lucy wrote to him at Washington suggesting that he might like to stay there until Congress reassembled. He seems to have accepted her suggestion, for on December 29 she again wrote to Washington that she was planning to come to New York to meet him when he reached there.

That summer Lucy had written to Harry, "I wish this infernal war were over. But the nation does not deserve peace, until it respects human rights—" Now on December 10 she said, "Of course, you have read the prest's message—It is good that he suggested the constitutional amendment, and that he announces the end of the war 'when they who began it cease to fight.' " And to her friend, two days later, "I am not going to say a word, how glad I am, that Mr. Lincoln spite of his short comings, is re-elected and Mr. Chase made Chief Justice, and that the Louisville Journal has come out for freedom."

The war was nearly over, and with it, Lucy's partly enforced, partly voluntary retirement. The woman's movement was about to be reconstituted, and Lucy was about to return to the public role which throughout her early years she had fought so hard to attain.

Chapter Seventeen

Abraham Lincoln said, "If all that has been said by orators and poets since the creation of the world were applied to the women of America, it would not do them justice for their conduct during this war." Now the war was over; Lincoln was dead. There was a new world to be made, and articulate women were determined to take part in making it. During the war, to help their country, they had withdrawn their claims. Now they believed the time had come to reassert their demands; but now the great cry in reform circles was enfranchisement for the Negro.

The abolitionist forces had split. With victory and the abolition of slavery, William Lloyd Garrison felt that the battle to which he had dedicated his life was won, and *The Liberator* ceased publication at the close of 1865. Wendell Phillips, far more intransigent now than the formerly intransigent Garrison, believed that freedom would not become a reality until Negroes had the same privileges as all other citizens—except women. They must have the franchise, and illiterate though they were, must have it at once. With this as his purpose, he continued the Anti-Slavery Society, and began to publish the *National Anti-Slavery Standard*. Its editor was Parker Pillsbury, of whom Lucy had said, "I never made a decent speech when his great beetling brow was within sound of my voice."

Most old-line abolitionists, formerly sympathetic to women's fight for equality, were resentful that women should persist in their demands at such a moment. "This is the Negro's hour" was the catch phrase repeated whenever women made their voices heard. Leading Republicans, fearful that the fight for Negro suffrage would be irrevocably damaged by being linked to woman suffrage, urged women to remain silent. Important Democrats, seeing an opportunity to embarrass their Republican rivals, and perhaps agreeing that a link between Negro and woman suffrage would defeat both, suddenly became ardent advocates of woman's rights. This drove such radical Republicans as Charles Sumner, Wendell Phillips and Horace Greeley further into antifeminist positions which, they insisted, were temporary. Many formerly militant women too were convinced that they must wait. Lucy was not among them. She believed that the time had come for women to press their rightful claims again. She also knew that now she must, if ever, overcome her personal reluctance and return to public life.

The first national activity of the reconstituted movement took place on May 10, 1866, when the Eleventh National Woman's Rights Convention opened in New York. Caroline H. Dall, associated with the movement since 1855, spoke on recent changes in woman's status. She was well qualified. Author of several books on woman's position in contemporary society, in 1866 she published another, *The College, The Market and The Court,* for which Alfred University later awarded her the first LL.D degree given to a woman. Mrs. Dall cited many advances. In the past year the American Social Science Association had been formed with two women on its board of directors, and the Boston association with seven. Lowell Institute, connected with Massachusetts Technological Institute, advertised classes for both sexes. Vassar College had opened. Some medical schools now admitted women, and in New York a Medical College for Women had been established three years before.

A significant element of this meeting was a far greater awareness of the growing movement in other countries, particularly in England. Mrs. Dall noted that in 1864 a Workingwomen's College had been opened in London, offering, in addition to ordinary branches, botany, physiology and drawing. In Liverpool Miss Nightingale's Training School for Nurses had been in operation for three years. After being refused by every English medical college, Elizabeth Garrett had obtained a degree at Apothecaries Hall, where she had been charged fifty guineas for single courses which would have cost a man five.

The English movement had started later than the American, the first "committee" being organized in 1855 by Barbara Leigh Smith to collect petitions for the revision of woman's property laws. Miss Smith, who later married the French physician Bodichon, was a tall, handsome, openhearted girl whose enlightened father had given his sons and daughters alike three thousand pounds on their coming of age. But more than any of the courageous women who took part in the struggle, a man was responsible for the early advances in the English movement. He was John Stuart Mill who, when asked to stand for parliament in 1865, made it a condition that he would work for woman suffrage. To his amazement, this condition was accepted and, enthusiastically supported by the small group of radical women, he won. In May 1866, backed by a few thousand petitions, he delivered a speech in favor of suffrage for women householders. However, his constituency, apparently having discovered that he meant what he said, did not return him a second time.

The National Association for the Promotion of Social Science, center of the English humanitarian movement, with such members as Charles Kingsley, Lord Brougham and Lord Shaftsbury, had from its formation in 1857 admitted women to full membership. With its support, a group of women started a woman's journal and opened an employment bureau which became a central meeting place. The movement grew rapidly. It was, if anything, more necessary in England than in the United States, for though marriage was still the only proper career for upper-class women, in the small country of England there were in 1857 almost nine hundred thousand more women than men. The life of hopelessness and boredom which was their lot was added stimulus to action.

When the woman's rights movement in the United States was reconstituted after a lapse of so many years, old names were missing, new names and faces had appeared. By far the most dramatic newcomer was twenty-three-year-old Anna E. Dickinson of Philadelphia. This Quaker girl, hardly five feet tall, so striking in appearance that she seemed beautiful, with her rich voice, magnetic personality and sparkling intelligence, had already become famous on the lecture platform as an outspoken political critic. During the war she had, with more audacity than truth, publicly accused General McClellan not of incompetence, but of treason. The attitude toward women in public roles had so changed since Lucy and others had blazed their courageous trail that in 1863, when the Republican parties of New Hampshire and Connecticut seemed about to lose the congressional elections, they had called on Anna Dickinson to save them. After her speaking tours they won both states, and she became a national heroine. She was a sensationally popular speaker, reputed to have earned as much as a thousand dollars by a single lecture. But Miss Dickinson was always more interested in Miss Dickinson than in any cause, and was not long a dependable supporter of the suffrage movement.

Less spectacular but more important to the woman's movement and to Lucy in particular was Mary A. Livermore, an ardent temperance advocate, who, when the war broke out, was in Chicago helping her minister husband edit a church paper. Her work in the war, which included carrying sanitary supplies to field hospitals throughout the country, had convinced her that for reforms to become realities, women must be given the vote. Only two years younger than Lucy, she came to the movement twenty years later.

Prominent at the New York convention were the dynamic preacher Henry Ward Beecher and his friend Theodore Tilton, young, handsome, poetic, eloquent. Tilton was editor of *The Independent,* which announced that it had "the widest circulation of any weekly religious newspaper in the world." On the floor of the convention Mr. Tilton and Mr. Beecher spoke with great seriousness, but they also entered into a kind of worldly banter unknown until then in the woman's movement.

Before the convention it had been hoped that a suggestion made by Theodore Tilton that the Anti-Slavery and Woman's Rights Associations should merge in a single Equal Rights Association might be realized. Susan Anthony and Lucy had been members of a group which went to Boston to discuss the possibility with Wendell Phillips. Phillips had made a technical objection, which the delegation understood he intended to overcome; but to their dismay, at the time of the Woman's Rights Convention he still refused to join with them.

The women were nevertheless determined to link the two suffrage issues, and at the 1866 convention the name of the National Woman's Rights Association was officially changed to the American Equal Rights Association. Lucretia Mott, now over seventy years of age, was elected president, Henry Blackwell recording secretary and Lucy Stone a member of the executive committee. An address was sent to Congress appealing for universal suffrage and equal rights. It was one of many such petitions presented to that session, the first petitions on woman suffrage ever to be addressed to the United States Congress.

Though Lucy was a member of the executive committee, there is no evidence that she attended either the Woman's Rights Convention or the Equal Rights Association meetings in Boston a few weeks later. A letter from Henry seems to indicate that neither he nor Lucy had been at the Woman's Rights Convention. Lucy's wanderings were over, and they were again living together in New Jersey. Early in 1865 they had settled in Roseville, today part of the city of Newark, first in a rented house, then in a home they bought not far from the West Bloomfield area where they had lived before. The Blackwell clan had begun to reassemble; Sam and Nette had a house nearby; so did Mother Blackwell, Marian and brother George.

In November 1865 Susan Anthony, returning from a long stay with her brother in Kansas, had visited Lucy to discuss collecting petitions against the inclusion of the word *male* in the Fourteenth Amendment. After a stay of several days Susan had gone into New York with Lucy, feeling more friendly and surer of Lucy's dedication to the cause than she had for some time.

Her confidence seems to have been premature. Lucy's difficulties were still keeping her from full activity. In May 1866 Henry urged her to go with him by horse and carriage lecturing through Massachusetts. "Dear Lucikin . . . You shall speak first in all cases, but if you prefer, only for a short time or as long as you feel like—I will follow, filling up all gaps. . . . In short, I will act as your supporter and aid, and we will see whether we cannot do your great work a real service. Lucy dear, I am sure that if you feel able and willing to make the trial, good will come of it! If your head aches and you don't find the spirit move, you will see that I will come up well to the rescue, and if you are in good mood, I will gladly make myself brief and witty in a ten minute speech, you taking the whole time. Let us try to sing the New Song of Humanity together." Although she had done some lecturing in the first year after the war, she was still not free of her fears.

One enterprise she did undertake that spring was to go with Henry to Washington to see Charles Sumner, author of the Fourteenth Amendment, then before Congress. The Amendment would for the first time introduce the word "male" into the Constitution, with the words "when the right to vote . . . is denied to any of the male inhabitants of such State" who is a citizen over twenty-one years of age, the basis of representation of that state should be proportionately reduced. Lucy and Henry hoped to persuade Sumner to omit the offending word. They visited him at his home. "He received us courteously," Henry remembered. " 'I sat up all one night' he said, 'and re-wrote that clause of the Amendment fourteen times, so unwilling was I to introduce the word "male" into the U.S. Constitution . . . but I could in no other way embody my meaning.' " Naturally, since his meaning was that Negro men should vote, and women should not.

Sumner told them he thought women were logically entitled to equal suffrage, but that it would not come yet. " 'How soon do you believe woman suffrage will come?' he asked. 'Mr. Sumner,' said Lucy, 'it is at our very doors.' "

In the following year, with Henry's support, Lucy was as active as ever in her life. In March 1867 she was given a hearing by the New Jersey legislature on a petition for woman suffrage in New Jersey. Henry wrote in his reminiscences that in 1776 all inhabitants worth £50 had been "made voters in that state. Women and Negroes voted there for thirty-one years." But in 1807 the legislature had used election frauds as an excuse to restrict the franchise to white male citizens of twenty-one years or over, and worth £50. After Lucy spoke, the legislative vote to re-enfranchise women was twenty-three for, thirty-two against.

Henry, now devoting his time to Lucy and the woman's movement, in January addressed a long letter, later widely circulated in printed form, to the legislators of the southern states, suggesting that since Negroes were to be enfranchised, the southern whites would improve their political position by giving the franchise to women, because the number of white women enfranchised would equal the total number of new Negro voters.

Later that year Henry arranged a series of meetings in New Jersey under the auspices of the Equal Rights Association, at which he and Lucy spoke in favor of woman and Negro suffrage. Mrs. Stanton joined them in several of these meetings. The idea of votes for Negroes was still very unpopular even in the North, and in Princeton their meeting was "mobbed and broken up by the students, who were mostly 'copperheads.'" In November the New Jersey Woman Suffrage Association was formed with Lucy as president.

In New York a State Constitutional Convention was to be held in June 1867. In January, as soon as the convention was called, Mrs. Stanton appeared before the legislature asking that the revised constitution give women the vote. Henry and Lucy were among the speakers at a series of meetings throughout the state, collecting petitions for universal suffrage. On June 27 Mrs. Stanton and Susan Anthony were granted a hearing before the convention; and on July 10 Lucy Stone spoke.

Horace Greeley, chairman of the Committee on Suffrage, was adamant in his belief that women should not demand the vote at this time and threatened permanently to withdraw his support from the movement if the women persisted in pressing their claims. His wife, Mary Cheney Greeley, disagreed so strongly that she had signed a petition to strike out the word male from the state constitution. Susan and Mrs. Stanton arranged that the petition, with Mrs. Horace Greeley's name first on the list of signers, be presented publicly just before Horace Greeley made his negative report. The resultant derision served further to alienate Greeley. But the retreat of liberal men was in any case the mood of the moment, and even Theodore Tilton, who had originally suggested the merger of the antislavery and woman's rights movements, had now concluded that it was the Negro's hour. The legislature voted 125 to 19 against woman suffrage.

Lucy and Henry had been announced as speakers at the May meeting of the Equal Rights Association, but when May came they were in far-off Kansas, where the legislature had decided to put before the people the questions of whether the words "white" and "male" should be removed from the state constitution. Lucy and Henry arrived in Kansas at the end of March. They had left their nine-year-old daughter with her doctor aunts in New York, and had gone to join their friend, Sam Wood—colonel, state senator and newly appointed judge—in stumping Kansas for equal suffrage. They had with them "250 pounds of tracts," and they "sowed them thick." Their traveling expenses came mainly out of their own pockets, except when transportation was provided by their Kansas friends. With Susan's support, Lucy had outvoted Wendell Phillips and received $1500 from the Jackson Fund for tracts and publicity.

Never did conditions seem more propitious for any crusade. Kansas was a land settled by pioneers who had come there to fight for freedom. The dominant Republican party was officially in favor of votes for women and Negroes, though every effort had been made to cause it to back down. The liberal world had its eyes on Kansas. From England John Stuart Mill, as an officer of the Impartial Suffrage Association, wrote to Sam Wood, "We are accustomed to see Kansas foremost in the struggle for the equal claims of all human beings to freedom and citizenship." But the liberal papers of the East, whose support would have meant so much, remained strangely silent on the issue of woman suffrage in Kansas.

On April 5, from Governor Robinson's home outside of Lawrence, Henry wrote a long letter telling Elizabeth Stanton about a convention in Topeka at which a State Impartial Suffrage Association had been formed after a move to separate the issue of "white" from "male" had been defeated. "Lucy," he wrote, "spoke with all her old force and fire." Both Henry and Lucy wrote frequent, friendly letters to Susan Anthony and Elizabeth Stanton during their trip. "[We go] over the length and breadth of this State speaking every day, and sometimes twice, journeying from twenty-five to forty miles daily, sometimes in a carriage and sometimes in an open wagon, with or without springs," Henry wrote in April. "We climb hills and dash down ravines, ford creeks, and ferry over rivers . . . fight the high winds on the high rolling upland prairies, and address the most astonishing (and astonished) audiences in the most extraordinary places."

Lucy was herself again. "I speak as well as ever, thank God! The audiences move to tears or laughter, just as in the old time. Harry makes capital speeches, and gets a louder cheer always than I do, though I believe I move a deeper feeling." Henry had written that they were "announced to speak every night but Sundays from April 7 to May 5 inclusive. . . . If our voices and health hold out, Col. Wood says the State is safe." Their voices held out, and they were induced to stay and continue their campaign. Lucy sent a telegram to the Equal Rights Convention. "Impartial suffrage, without regard to color or sex, will succeed by overwhelming majorities. Kansas leads the world!" Sam Wood sent one too. "With the help of God and Lucy Stone, we shall carry Kansas! The world moves!"

In his letters Henry described Sam Wood with enthusiasm, as "a thoroughly noble, good fellow, and a hero. . . . It is worth a journey to Kansas to know him for he is an original and a genius." He also said, "We find a very strong feeling against Col. S. N. Wood among politicians, but they all respect and dread him. He has warmer friends and bitterer enemies than almost any man in the State."

The fact was that the eastern suffragists had stepped into a dangerous political situation which they did not understand and about which their friends did not enlighten them. The two rival factions of free soilers in the days when Kansas was a territory had continued in the state Republican party. Bowman's brother-in-law Robinson, an ardent supporter of Negro and woman suffrage, was governor, but the faction opposing him was powerful. Although Lucy and Henry did not realize it, the very presence of Wood and Robinson as their sponsors, by antagonizing a large sector of the Republican party, greatly lessened the chances of success in the fall elections. Years later Henry understood this clearly as one of the causes of failure in Kansas. There were others.

In their letters to Susan and Mrs. Stanton, Lucy and Henry pleaded with them to come to Kansas and continue an intensive campaign. The two women agreed, but feeling that they were needed in New York during the Constitutional Convention, they decided not to go to Kansas until the fall.

On her return East, Lucy was jubilant. "They are surely giving women the suffrage," she wrote to a friend. She was busily engaged in collecting funds so that attractive, dynamic Olympia Brown, who, though the name was coincidental, had followed in Antoinette Brown's footsteps to become a minister, could leave a substitute in her Universalist church and go to Kansas. From July to November Olympia Brown made two hundred and five speeches there.

Lucy continued to work in the East. According to a letter from Susan to "Darling Anna Dick.," Lucy "in her plain, worn, gray Kansas travelling dress," stopped in Boston to ask that woman suffrage be represented on the Anti-Slavery platform. "The Grand Mogul," Wendell Phillips, refused, but did say he intended to make woman suffrage the subject of a speech next winter.

Lucy also went to Horace Greeley, whose *Tribune* was widely read in Kansas, and begged him to come out for the Woman Suffrage Amendment. All he would promise, she wrote to a friend, was that she "might have a finger's length in the Tribune every day for Woman Suffrage." But he said he believed that before the reconstruction was settled, women as well as Negroes would have the vote.

Alice recalled a more intimate story her mother told of this same conversation. Seeing tears in Lucy's eyes as she pleaded with him, Greeley had said, "When you have been whipped as many times as I have, you won't cry about it." "All the same," Lucy told Alice, "when he was whipped afterwards, he not only cried about it, but he broke his heart, and died."

Chapter Eighteen

In September Susan Anthony and Elizabeth Stanton went to Kansas, accompanied by the popular Hutchinson family of singers, whose Kansas suffrage song contained the lines:

We . . . aim by noble, just endeavor
To elevate our sex forever.

Fear not, we'll darn each worthy stocking,
Duly keep the cradle rocking . . .

CHORUS:
Clear the way, the songs are floating;
Clear the way, the world is noting;
Prepare the way, the right promoting,
And ballots, too, for woman's voting.

By the time they reached Kansas, the dissension in the Republican ranks had become clearer. Governor Robinson traveled with Mrs. Stanton; but the majority of the Republican party had become outspoken in their effort to defeat woman suffrage while passing the Negro franchise amendment.

By midsummer there had been no funds for Susan and Mrs. Stanton's trip. The Hovey Fund, intended to promote both abolition and woman's rights, was in the control of Wendell Phillips and his friends, who were refusing support to the woman's rights movement. Susan, with her usual indefatigability, made the rounds of New York business concerns, selling advertisements to be printed in the tracts she would distribute in Kansas.

For most of the time they were in Kansas, Mrs. Stanton, better known and more popular with audiences, toured the state. Susan remained at headquarters in Lawrence where, according to her hostess, she spent her time "planning and advertising meetings, distributing tracts . . . and attending to the minutiae and drudgery of an extensive campaign." A month before the election, when the campaign, in spite of their dedicated efforts, was going badly, an offer of help came from an unexpected quarter. The eccentric crusader George Francis Train sent Susan a telegram offering to come to Kansas at his own expense to join the campaign. With the encouragement of Kansas suffragists, Susan, who was always willing to accept aid for her beloved cause wherever she could find it, told Train to come.

George Francis Train was a self-made man who, still in his thirties, had already made a fortune as a financier. Politically he was a Democrat and a Copperhead, who had been thrown out of Missouri for a traitorous speech in wartime, and who now saw no harm in supporting woman suffrage by reviling the Negro race. Tall, handsome, with curly brown hair, he dressed in an exaggeratedly foppish, almost clownish fashion rarely seen anywhere, and surely never before in the rugged pioneer state of Kansas. His own pamphlet, which tells in glowing terms of his triumphal tour, quotes from a Topeka paper's description of his platform costume. "Mr. Train . . . always appears in Lavander kids, black pants, closely buttoned blue coat with brass buttons, and patent leather boots."

People thronged to his meetings, for his speeches were as dramatic as his appearance. They were a mixture of humor and grotesquerie, combined with some sound sense and a recurrent, only partly facetious suggestion that George Francis Train should and would be the next President of the United States. Their tone was contained in the rhymes he delivered, known as epigrams.

Let your corrupt politicians dance their double clogged jig,
As a bid for the suffrage of the poor Kansas Nig,
For our women will vote while the base plot thickens;
Before barbers, bootblacks, melons and chickens.

His public success made Susan and Mrs. Stanton feel that Train was piling up votes. Others, Henry among them, believed that he was "repelling earnest anti-slavery Republicans by his blatant copperheadism, and intensifying prejudice and misconception by his wild inconsequent harangues." And perhaps by such unsavory remarks as, "Keep your nose twenty years on a negro and you will have hard work to be able to smell a white man again."

Henry, who had returned to Kansas in September, felt that the fight was lost. Wood had been desperately ill and had had to drop out of the campaign. Train was a poor substitute. He "drew immense crowds," but he "made our noble campaign utterly offensive and ridiculous." Lucy's view was even more emphatic. "Mr. Train was a lunatic, wild and ranting, and his presence as an advocate of woman suffrage was enough to condemn it in the minds of all persons not already convinced. . . . He made the cause a laughing-stock everywhere, and excited the greatest grief of the larger part of the suffragists."

Meanwhile in the East other seeds of discord were being sown. Henry and Lucy had gone that summer to Martha's Vineyard, the lovely island off the Massachusetts coast, but had returned at Susan's request to work in the Equal Rights Association office. On October 13, from New York, Lucy wrote to Henry, "I have two characteristic letters from Susan. In one, she gives us a cuff after this fashion—'I fear your release of Parker [Pillsbury, from the Equal Rights office] is "pennywise, and pound poor." He surely brought us a good deal of money, and the work he does, pays richly' —Isn't that rich, after *her urgent* solicitation that we should hurry from the Vineyard, because Parker could not stay in the office, and after Parker himself told us . . . he *must* be relieved! ! !"

In a letter the day before she had indicated still another problem. "If S.B.A. pushes to know about funds, tell her we paid a good deal from our private money—and that Phillips is *willing* we should draw from the Jackson fund, so much as we will give our personal guarantee for." Later, when Henry, Lucy and others questioned Susan's use of Equal Rights funds for Train's unauthorized activities, Susan felt betrayed, but apparently the suspicion was not entirely on one side.

Train was a man who entertained himself with liberal causes and gave generously of time and money while an enterprise held his interest. Now he made two suggestions which seemed to Susan like gifts from heaven. After the Kansas campaign he would travel East with her and Mrs. Stanton, the three of them stopping at seven large cities to lecture on woman suffrage. Train would pay the expenses. Back in New York he would finance a suffrage newspaper. It was almost too much to believe.

The movement had long needed a press of its own. The year before, Lucy and Henry had tried to collect money for a paper to be called *Universal Suffrage;* but when they left for Kansas there were still not enough funds, and Lucy was writing to her friend Elizabeth Buffum Chace of Rhode Island, "In case I am not able to raise funds enough to start a paper, are you willing to give your $50 for the general purpose of Woman Suffrage?" Now the choice for Susan was between no paper or an effective journal plus Train. Susan accepted both of Train's offers.

Meanwhile in Kansas election day came and went. There were 10,483 votes for Negro suffrage, 19,421 against; 9070 for woman suffrage, 19,857 against. It was small consolation that with so many powerful Republican forces openly in favor of Negro suffrage and opposed to female, women had received only 1400 less votes than the far more popular freedmen. Governor Robinson wrote to Mrs. Stanton, "I am satisfied it was fortunate that Train's caravan did not canvass the state thoroughly" for there was so much that was offensive to Republicans in what he said "that large numbers voted against us who would otherwise have voted for us"; but perhaps the governor was consoling himself for the failure of his own campaign.

On their subsequent lecture tour, Susan, Mrs. Stanton and Mr. Train shared the platform, and Mr. Train continued to nominate himself for the Presidency. Lucy and other suffrage leaders were disturbed because the "bill posters of their meetings were printed so that they appeared to have emanated from the Equal Rights Society." There had even appeared in the *Tribune* a notice with the names of leading suffragists, Lucy's among them, "approving Mr. Train and his Kansas escapade."

As soon as the lecturers reached New York they began publication of *The Revolution*. Elizabeth Cady Stanton and Parker Pillsbury (who had resigned from Phillips' *Anti-Slavery Standard* in protest against the withholding of the Hovey Fund from the woman suffrage movement), were editors, and Susan B. Anthony proprietor and manager. The first issue of the weekly appeared on January 8, 1868.

The Revolution, which stated that it was the organ of the National Party of New America, was for educated suffrage (enfranchisement of educated women rather than illiterate Negroes), equal pay for equal work, and the eight-hour day. It was also for cold water and against alcoholic drinks or medicines. Furthermore, it proposed a new commercial and financial policy: "Gold like our cotton and corn for sale. Greenbacks for money." Train, with David M. Melliss, financial editor of the *New York World,* wrote an unsigned financial column, which during the first year covered from two to five of the newspaper's sixteen magazine-sized pages. Letters and articles by and about Train took another page or two, and there were always advertisements of his favorite business enterprises, the Union Pacific Railroad and the Credit Foncier of America. Though the two women did not realize it, the advocacy of a controversial "new financial program for America" added yet another disadvantage to the already overburdened woman's movement.

In its woman's rights fight, *The Revolution* was a forceful and effective paper. It championed not only suffrage, but improved wages and working conditions for women, and their organization in labor unions, a cause in which Lucy throughout her life was surprisingly uninterested, even though workingmen's organizations were among the first supporters of equality for women. The balance of good and evil in *The Revolution* was a matter of judgment. Susan Anthony and Mrs. Stanton believed that to be more widely heard was worth the risk of saddling themselves with Train and his views. Many of their co-workers disagreed.

In its fourth issue *The Revolution* printed a personal letter from Garrison to Susan calling Train a "crack brained harlequin and semi-lunatic . . . as destitute of principle as he is of sense. . . . He may be of use in drawing an audience, but so would a kangaroo, a gorilla, or a hippopotamus." This half-column letter was followed by a vicious four-and-a-half-column attack on Mr. Garrison.

Lucy's old friend Samuel May, one of the few abolitionists who had continued to support the fight for women's rights in the postwar period, wrote to her in March, "Train is a fool or a monomaniac. I never in my life have seen a man make himself appear as ridiculous as he did in our Meeting Hall in the presence of a large audience. And yet Miss Anthony spoke of him as a great patron and main dependence of the American Equal Rights Association."

Train had already created problems. No sooner had the first issue of *The Revolution* appeared than his always volatile interest was turned to an earlier love, the Irish nationalist movement, and, leaving a few hundred dollars and instructions to Melliss to supply more, he crossed the Atlantic to support the Fenians. He was arrested in England and again in Ireland, and in jail or out continued to send articles but no money. Long before he returned, almost a year later, *The Revolution* had accumulated a serious deficit.

Meanwhile the ill-feeling generated within the movement began to take its toll. Lucy asserted that at an executive committee meeting of the Equal Rights Association, "Miss Anthony was asked why she had used the name of the Association . . . and our individual names without our knowledge or consent. Miss Anthony replied, '*I* am the Equal Rights Association. Not a soul of you amounts to shucks except myself.'

"But when she was told that she could not claim to be the persons whose names she had used without their knowledge, she said, turning to me: 'I know what is the matter with you. It is envy and spleen, and hate, because I have a paper—and you have not.' "

Whatever personal unpleasantness was exchanged, an important difference of principle existed. When Susan said that she would "take money from the devil" if it were for the suffrage cause, Lucy properly objected that Susan had taken not only the devil's money "but the devil too." And writing to Garrison she commented, "I felt the hurt of this action of theirs, as tho' it had been a blow to my own child." Susan and Lucy were, in fact, engaged in the age-old argument as to whether the end justifies the means.

At the annual May meeting of the American Equal Rights Association in 1868 matters came to a head. Susan, finding her group in the minority, and considering herself, as she had said, to *be* the association, privately formed a so-called national society which for a while functioned as the Woman's Suffrage Association of America. It is surprising that this action did not at once split the movement beyond redemption, but it did not. The organization hobbled along and called its annual meeting the next year.

Chapter Nineteen

"Our victory is sure to come, and I can endure anything but recreancy to principle," Lucy wrote in March 1869. In the past year she had had ample reason to formulate this opinion.

Aside from such tactical disagreements as the alliance with Mr. Train, the chief divergences in the suffrage forces after the war concerned the relative importance of Negro and woman suffrage; and Congress's decision to supplement the Fourteenth Amendment with a Fifteenth magnified these dissensions. The old-line abolitionists, formerly almost unanimous in their support of the woman's rights movement, were increasingly convinced that to link Negro and female suffrage would defeat both. In 1867 Lucy had chided Abby Kelley, so long her idol and her friend. "You, and Phillips, and Garrison, and the brave workers who for thirty years have said, 'Let justice be done, if the heavens fall,' now smitten by a strange blindness, believe that the nation's peril can be averted if it can be induced to accept the poor half-loaf of justice for the negro, poisoned by its lack of justice for every woman in the land. As if the application of a *universal* principle to a single class *could* suffice for the necessity of this hour! . . . Oh, Abby, it is a terrible mistake you are all making!"

Susan and Mrs. Stanton, taking the opposite view from the abolitionists, were determined to keep Negroes from voting as long as women could not vote, and began to turn from the conception of universal suffrage to that of educated suffrage.

Lucy and Henry stood between the two. Lucy supported the abolitionists in their demand for a stern reconstruction.

When President Johnson was impeached for trying, with extraordinary lack of political tact, it is true, to carry out Lincoln's plan for reconstruction without vengeance, Lucy wrote to Garrison, "What a blessed thing it is that Andy Johnson is being impeached! One may now hope for a speedier and better reconstruction—" Unlike the abolitionists though, she did not abate her demands for woman suffrage. She merely persisted in her lifelong conviction that both women and Negroes were entitled to equality. When Susan said, "let the question of woman be brought up first and that of the negro last," Lucy answered, "We are lost if we turn from the middle principle and argue for one class. . . . I will be thankful in my soul if *any* body can get out of the terrible pit."

The Fifteenth Amendment declared that "The right . . . to vote shall not be . . . abridged . . . on account of race, color, or previous condition of servitude." The women had lost their battle to include "sex"; but they had not surrendered easily. *The Revolution* and women's societies throughout the country had circulated petitions to Congress. Lucy, Henry said, had gone again to Washington "during the 'heated term' to secure from as many influential congressmen as possible an 'appeal' for the inclusion of women with men in the suffrage reconstruction. It was signed by quite a number."

Lucy, contemplating defeat, was yet able to understand the abolitionists' position. "I think God rarely gives to one man, or one set of men, more than *one* great moral victory to win. Hence we see the old abolitionists generally shrink from the van of our movement, tho' they are in hearty sympathy with it. If Mr. Sumner 'don't want to be in this fight,' as he told me, in my heart I yet say, 'God bless him'. Our victory is sure to come, and I can endure anything but recreancy to principle."

Mrs. Stanton and Susan came out against the ratification of the Amendment. Disgusted with the Republican party for its Negroes-first stand, they continued to work with

Democrats, although any help from the Democrats probably came, as in Kansas, from their hope that a link with woman suffrage would defeat Negro enfranchisement.

In January 1869 the Anthony-Stanton group held a woman suffrage convention in Washington, the first in that city. Venerable Lucretia Mott was its president; its subject the relative need of Negroes and women for the vote. The convention presented petitions to members of Congress, and as a result woman suffrage was for the first time brought up in the Senate, and a bill for a Sixteenth Amendment to enfranchise women presented to Congress. The absence of Lucy Stone at the meetings was notable, and she was not represented even by a letter of encouragement. A week later Congress passed the Fifteenth Amendment restricted to male suffrage.

On February 4, 1869, *The Revolution* printed an attack on Lucy headed "Stones Holding Their Peace." Its theme was that, while senators and representatives were "laboring earnestly in woman's behalf, Lucy Stone, instead of joining her voice, is even silencing theirs with her cry of the 'Negro's hour.'" A letter from an unnamed congressman bolstered the attack. Next week the paper commented on a letter from a reader protesting that Lucy had recently stated at several conventions "with all her old time enthusiasm, pathos and eloquence, that nothing could be paramount in importance, and nothing should be prior in time to the establishment of woman's right of suffrage." The paper defended its position by replying that "To divide the question now . . . is to deserve defeat, and to invite it."

Meanwhile the woman whom *The Revolution* assailed had, both before and after being shut out of Susan Anthony's personally organized association, been working vigorously for woman suffrage. In April 1868, continuing her conquest of physical and psychological difficulties, she had several times addressed the Massachusetts legislature. The day after a committee hearing she reported to Harry, "I have headache all the time, and did yesterday, though it did not spoil my speech. . . . Several members of the House want to have me repeat my address before the Whole Body next week, if they can arrange it. I was invited to ever so many places, and really might lecture all the time."

A few days later, she wrote in a familiar vein, "God bless you, Harry dear, and give you the large patience you need with me. My blues are gone, I wish they may never return to trouble me or you." And again, "Don't fret about business, we shall do well enough."

In the election of November 1868, after General Grant had beaten out Lucy's friend Salmon P. Chase for the Republican Presidential nomination, the women suffragists of New Jersey decided to go to the polls. When Henry's mother died two years later, her obituary included a moving account of that election day. "Mrs. Blackwell's life fulfilled the most conservative conception of the sphere of woman. . . . As wife and widow, she was the presiding genius of a beautiful home. She reared nine sons and daughters to vigorous and useful maturity. She . . . never wavered in her adherence to the literal verities of the Calvinistic faith. . . . Mrs. Blackwell will long be remembered in New Jersey for her testimony at the polls on the occasion of General Grant's election. In company with her daughter-in-law, Lucy Stone, and leaning upon the arm of her son, the venerable lady, aged 74, walked quietly to the place of voting in Roseville, and offered a straight Republican ticket. The Inspectors of Election received it respectfully, but declined to let it be deposited in the box."

In November, too, Lucy and Henry had gone to Boston, where they had been asked to help form a New England Woman Suffrage Association. The call for this convention had already been sarcastically greeted by Mrs. Stanton because it stated that the society proposed to work "in a wise, systematic and efficient way." Mrs. Stanton and Susan were by now wrapped in a cloak of intransigence from which they snugly attacked with the nasty word "conservative" anyone who disagreed with them. Yet when the convention took place, even *The Revolution* admitted it was a success.

A month after *The Revolution*'s slap at Lucy, their Mr. Train, stumping New England in an effort to defeat the Fifteenth Amendment, a task congenial to his anti-Negro views, reported that Lucy had addressed a meeting of the Rhode Island legislature considering a resolution for woman's suffrage. "L.S. in R.I. is having everything her own way. She speaks to-night at City Hall. Her address to the legislature was well received, and made many converts."

In May 1869 the Equal Rights Association held what turned out to be its last annual meeting. At the meeting *The Revolution* was attacked by no less a man than Stephen S. Foster, who criticized its emphasis on educated suffrage, and objected to the continued participation of a man like Train in the movement. In a characteristic communication printed in *The Revolution*'s first issue of 1869, Train had technically withdrawn from the paper to spare his co-workers criticism. " 'Crucify Him,' " he modestly wrote, "is no new reward of virtue. All great men must expect the malice of little minds." And then more realistically, "When I come back I shall be too busy to devote much time to the Woman Question, but will do all I can." He continued to supply lengthy accounts of his exploits until May 6, when he again announced his resignation, an event the paper lamented editorially.

Foster also revived an attack made by Henry the year before on Susan's slipshod manner of keeping accounts and on her use of funds collected in the name of the Equal Rights Association. Now, in an effort to free the situation of personal antagonisms, Henry himself came to Susan's defense on these issues.

Susan was not having things her own way. She did not like Henry's resolution deploring the omission of women from the Fifteenth Amendment but approving its gains for Negroes. She did not like the fact that Ernestine Rose's resolution to change the name of the organization to the Woman's Suffrage Association was defeated.

Susan and Mrs. Stanton in their *History of Woman Suffrage* give one account of what happened next. "At the close of Anniversary week a meeting was called . . . which resulted in reorganization under the name of 'The National Woman Suffrage Association.'" This seems straightforward enough. What is omitted is that the meeting was a minority gathering, secretly called, and without authority to represent or change the name of any organization, a fact *The Revolution* admitted at the time.

A different account is contained in a statement by Mrs. Hannah M. Tracy Cutler, a member of Lucy's unauthorized debating society at Oberlin, president of the Ohio Woman's Rights Association at its first annual meeting in 1853. In unprinted reminiscences, Mrs. Cutler tells a tale of double-dealing never publicized because Lucy was afraid it would harm the movement. Her scruples have proved costly to her reputation.

According to Mrs. Cutler, during Anniversary Week, Susan, Mrs. Stanton, Lucy and several others "had agreed to correspond with the known suffragists throughout the country, and after this to call a convention and if practicable, to form a society for the advancement of suffrage." On the last day of the convention "Mr. H. B. Blackwell heard that Mrs. Stanton and Susan B. were inviting parties then in the city to come . . . that evening and aid in forming a National Woman Suffrage Society. When he mentioned this to his wife, she assured him there must be some mistake." Unable to convince her, he went himself to Mrs. Stanton, who assured him that "no such thing was intended." The same day Susan told another delegate, Mary A. Livermore, that there was no such plan. Yet that very evening the meeting took place.

At the meeting, Mrs. Cutler says, one of the invited members "asked where Mr. Blackwell and Lucy Stone and Mrs. Livermore were. Mrs. Stanton, with apparent surprise, looked over the audience and said she did not see them; she thought they must have gone out of the City." Henry, in his reminiscences thirty years later, said only that Mrs. Livermore told Lucy and him early on that eventful day that there was to be a meeting; but later announced that because the plan had been abandoned she was going to leave the city; and this she did.

A further view was published a year later, in a letter signed by William Lloyd Garrison, Julia Ward Howe, Henry Blackwell and Mary Livermore. After the adjournment of the Equal Rights Convention, a group of about twenty members from outside New York and forty from the city met and "then and there organized what they called the 'National Woman Suffrage Association.' They were not sent by any state or any society as delegates for any such purpose. No public notice had been given. . . . The control of the Association was vested in an executive committee, resident in New York City. . . . The result was . . . a local society . . . the organ of a few persons. . . .

"The subsequent proceedings . . . were in accordance with its irregular and irresponsible origin. Weekly meetings were held to discuss a variety of questions, often not germane to the question of suffrage—such as the causes of deficiency of offspring; marriage, divorce, the social evil, &c. . . .

"At one of these meetings, a resolution was . . . adopted, repudiating the Fifteenth Amendment; thus committing the movement upon a most important question . . . by the action of a few individuals."

Susan Anthony and Elizabeth Stanton were great and heroic women; they were also self-willed and erratic. Because they refused to accept political defeat, they made an enormous contribution to American life; because they could not accept personal defeat, they often injured the movement to which they gave their lives. They had not hesitated to estrange so valuable a potential ally as Horace Greeley nor to enlist the aid of a convinced Copperhead like George Francis Train. They had declared their newspaper to represent an unheard-of National Party of New America. Now they saw no objection to a national association formed by a small caucus. The many veteran workers who found themselves shut out had an important decision to make. Were they, after years of devoted service, to accept a leadership with whose principles they disagreed, whose tactics made open opposition and democratic vote impossible, or were they to form an organization which would more nearly express their views?

Chapter Twenty

The year 1869, when dissension tore the suffrage movement, saw the first decisive victory of woman suffrage in the United States. At the end of that year the legislature of the territory of Wyoming gave women equal rights with men. Women voted. Women sat on juries. Their first attempts to exercise their rights caused considerable disturbance, but the territory soon accepted women's new status.

For Lucy, too, the movement made great strides in 1869; and her own way of life underwent large changes. Lucy, Henry and Alice vacationed that summer at Coy's Hill and Kennebunkport, Maine, as well as at Martha's Vineyard, where they had gone first toward the end of the war with a party which included Henry's old friend Ainsworth Spofford, whose father was the Congregationalist minister in the island town of Chilmark. They had reached the island by sailboat and, much to little Alice's delight, had stayed as boarders at the Gay Head lighthouse. Later they bought land around a pond near steep sandy dunes which dropped to the blue sea, and there all the Blackwell family summered for many years. Today descendants of Henry's brothers Sam and George still have homes there.

That summer was not an idle one. Since the chief cause for the formation of the minority group, which in effect had destroyed the Equal Rights Association, was its differences with Lucy and Henry, it was impossible to suppose that they could work with it. So the New England Woman Suffrage Association formed a committee, of which Lucy was a member, to confer with suffragists throughout the country for the purpose of creating a new association on a delegate basis. Lucy therefore began an intensive correspondence with other members of the shut-out majority. To a Rhode Island friend she wrote that the new organization hoped "to unite those who can work steadily to one end, who will not injure our claim by opposition to the 15th Amendment, or chase after side issues." These efforts met with immediate success, and a call was issued for a convention to assemble in Cleveland on November 24 and 25 to organize the American Woman Suffrage Association. Its formation, unlike the National's, was announced by widespread notices in the press.

How unaware even intelligent people can be of their own causal connection with events is illustrated by the reaction of Susan Anthony and Elizabeth Stanton, who apparently were honestly wounded and amazed that their old friend Lucy Stone could so hypocritically set about to create a second suffrage association. Did not such an association already exist? Surely, as *The Revolution* maintained after the Cleveland meeting, the only purpose of the new organization must be to count out Mrs. Stanton and Miss Anthony. The paper went further when it disingenuously referred to the "*half score* of getters-up of the Convention," though it had received the call signed by over a hundred distinguished men and women.

In October Lucy wrote to Nette that Higginson had from some "mistaken magnanimity perhaps, told Mrs. Stanton and Susan that he expected to see them at Cleveland." Lucy thought they would not go, but if they should, "it will be so dreadful an incubus to take them up again!" Yet with her usual scrupulousness she had sent Mrs. Stanton a copy of the call, saying, "So far as I have influence this Society shall never be an enemy or antagonist of yours in any way. It will simply fill a field and combine forces which yours does not. . . . Your little girls and mine will reap the easy harvest which it costs so much to sow."

Scrupulously too, Lucy refused to publicize the reasons for the formation of the new association. Again her dedication caused her personal harm, for the uninitiate national press was, not unnaturally, surprised at being confronted by a second suffrage association and startled by the absence of two of the most familiar figures in the movement. History tends to leave its crowns on the heads of those who have placed them there with their own hands. People who wish their point of view presented must leave their own record for future historians to read.

At the Cleveland meeting there were representatives from twenty-one states. Among them were Julia Ward Howe, Antoinette Brown Blackwell, Mary Livermore, Amelia Bloomer, Hannah M. Tracy Cutler, William Lloyd Garrison, Stephen S. Foster, A. Bronson Alcott and T. W. Higginson, a colonel now, since he had commanded a Negro regiment in the Civil War. Susan Anthony was there. Invited to the platform, she asked permission to speak and expressed herself in her usual emotional fashion. "So help me, Heaven," she said, ". . . if you will do this work . . . I will thank God for this Convention as long as I have the breath of life." Of the entire convention, the single audience reaction which found its way into *The Revolution* followed this speech. "Tremendous applause," *The Revolution* announced.

Susan's biographers are as one in their account of her magnanimity, but the paragraph above included words which somewhat reduce its generosity. Susan also said, "Though this Convention, by its action, shall nullify the National Association of which I am a member, and though it shall tread its heel upon THE REVOLUTION, to carry on which I have struggled as never mortal woman or mortal man struggled for any cause which he or she advocated, though you here assembled declare that the one is null and void—a bogus and a sham, and that the other is unworthy of your patronage and should be ground into the dust—still . . . I will thank God for this Convention. . . ."

Returning to New York Susan replied in the same ambiguous vein to those who asked her if they should join the new association. "I cannot advise you one way or another," she wrote, then promptly repeated that the new association had no purpose but to ignore the National Association and *The Revolution,* in spite of the fact that "the old association welcomes to its platform everybody who believes in Equal Rights for women." Yet the "old association" had clearly not welcomed Lucy, Henry and their friends. What of the claim that no difference of principle existed?

The National was ruled by a small group meeting weekly in New York. At its conventions any member paying annual dues of one dollar was entitled to vote. In the American only accredited delegates, whose numbers were based on state populations, could decide on policy. It believed in annual meetings held in different cities. The National was dedicated to a single political end—passage of a national woman suffrage amendment. The American worked for municipal, state and national suffrage, believing that the greater the number of women who had a right to vote on limited issues the more pressure they could exert for national suffrage. The National permitted only women to hold office. The American welcomed the support of sympathetic men. The Cleveland convention elected Henry Ward Beecher president of the association, Lucy Stone chairman of the executive committee.

As time went on, the National, while fighting valiantly for a Sixteenth Amendment, turned its interest to matters other than suffrage. Mrs. Stanton was an advocate of easy divorce, and the association came more and more to concern itself with marriage and divorce. It also continued to ally itself with any group or individual willing to support a woman suffrage amendment.

A revealing sidelight on Susan Athony's attitude is contributed by Antoinette Blackwell in her account of the break. To an objection that the National was in the hands of a few officers under the patronage of a single locality, Susan made the reply always made by those who grow impatient with the slow processes of democracy in a country or an organization. It was the only way to get things done.

For Susan it continued to be the way to get things done. Years later, when the two suffrage associations were again united, Henry and the now grown-up Alice (it was after Lucy's death) were protesting Susan's ruthless method of choosing her own successor when she was about to retire as president of the association. She had set her heart on the election of Carrie Chapman Catt, a younger worker in the movement, so, to get rid of the chief contender, Lillie Devereux Blake, her colleague from the earliest days of the National, Susan illegally disbanded the powerful legislative committee of which Mrs. Blake was chairman.

The formation of the new American Association made an enormous change in Henry and Lucy's lives. As Henry later put it, "Having earned by activities of fifteen years in real estate, book publishing and sugar refining, a moderate pecuniary independence, Mrs. Stone and her husband moved from New Jersey to Boston." For Lucy it was a move of emotional and political importance. It took her back to the surroundings which had always held her heart and the culture which seemed to her the highest the United States had to offer. Politically it brought her and Henry into the center of the most active woman suffrage organization in existence, the New England Association, which only a year before she had helped to launch, and which was already parent to a group of flourishing state societies.

There was another reason for the move. Lucy was about to attain her dream of many years. She was to have a newspaper. It was to be called *The Woman's Journal,* and was financed by a joint stock company with two hundred shares of fifty dollars each. Henry was the largest stockholder. Lucy herself sold the other shares to sympathizers of the movement.

In March 1869 in Chicago, Mary A. Livermore had begun publication of a paper dedicated to woman suffrage and temperance. Now she had agreed to return with her husband and three children to her native Massachusetts, to merge her *Agitator* with the new *Journal,* and to edit the combined paper.

In October Lucy wrote to Nette that they would "set to raise $10,000 to start a paper," and if they did, she would try to work through the paper for the future "and quit this lecturing field nearly altogether. It is not consistent with any proper home life or any proper care of my family. I feel it more and more, and shall certainly not continue this mode of life, tho' it is my natural way. . . . If I were only a ready writer I should be so glad!"

This scheme, never entirely fulfilled, began sadly enough. The first step in creating a closer home life was to break up the one she had. To raise money for the paper and move her household from New Jersey to Massachusetts, Lucy had to be free of family burdens. "You know Alice goes to Newburyport this week. I think it is the best thing for her, but I feel crushed, and torn, and homeless–But I shall make myself very busy–"

Even when, a short while later, Alice moved back, Lucy did not for some time have a home of her own. *The Woman's Journal* began publication on January 8, 1870, on the ground floor of the New England Women's Club building; and for a while the family lived in quarters above the offices. In September 1870 thirteen-year-old Alice wrote to her cousin Kitty Barry, Elizabeth Blackwell's adopted daughter, "We have not very roomy quarters here, one room and a cupboard. I also have the run of the staircases, the office and back office, and two parlors belonging to the club, I believe. Papa and Mama are out or busy a good deal, so I prowl about the house, read newspapers, and scribble."

A few months later they moved into the house which was their home for the rest of Lucy and Henry's lives. It was in Dorchester, a town which had been annexed to Boston only in January 1870. Alice told Kitty it was "five miles from the true Boston, fifteen minutes ride on the steam cars. It has a separate station, and there are no sidewalks." The place as described in the *Journal* years later seems unimaginable in the great city of Boston. "A large, old-fashioned, white house [which] stands on Pope's Hill in Dorchester where it commands a beautiful view of the Neponset River, Dorchester Bay and Boston Harbor with several islands and Boston Lighthouse. There are large grounds full of trees and flowers and grass. There are pine trees, lindens, apple, peach, pear and cherry trees. There are grape vines, currant and blackberry bushes. Morning-glory, honeysuckle, adder lily, rambler rose, moss rose, wild rose . . . violets, lilacs, syringa, hollyhocks, give a beauty that makes one reverent. . . .

"The house has some seventeen rooms. . . . Then there is . . . the little summer-house, a piazza on two sides of the house, the porte cochere, the cupola with the ocean, the Great Blue Hills, Boston and suburbs in panorama. . . . Nearly every room in the house has a fireplace, for they loved cheer and fireside comfort. . . . A large miscellaneous library, many pictures . . . and scores of relics of other generations are here and make the great old house articulate."

Lucy, the farmer's daughter, had a horse, a cow and poultry, and a large vegetable garden; and though they usually had a servant, Lucy dried herbs, preserved fruits and made her own yeast, bread, dried beef and soap. It was truly the home of which she had dreamed, from which she could also carry on the work that had been the focus of her life.

Chapter Twenty-one

The Woman's Journal had an unbroken existence of forty-seven years. Continued by Henry and by Alice far beyond Lucy's lifetime, it was the only long-continued woman's suffrage paper published in the United States. Inez Haynes Irwin, historian of later suffrage years, said in 1934, "It is hard not to become lyrical and rhapsodic when one tries to estimate how much *The Woman's Journal* became to the suffrage cause. It was a burning cloud by day and a tower of flame by night. Just the names of its contributors, unpaid all of them, seem to list the liberal *Who's Who* of the period." The praise is not too high.

It took a while for the new *Journal* to lose a touch of amateurish camaraderie and become the serious, effective paper it remained. Its masthead announced it as "a weekly newspaper, published every Saturday in Boston and Chicago, devoted to the interests of woman, to her educational, industrial, legal and political equality, and especially to her right of suffrage." Mary A. Livermore was its editor; Julia Ward Howe, Lucy Stone, William Lloyd Garrison and Thomas Wentworth Higginson were associate editors; but during the first year Garrison resigned and Henry took his place. In format the paper was eight large pages of five columns. The original price of a year's subscription was $3.00, soon reduced to $2.50, *"invariably in advance."*

"Would the readers of the Woman's Journal like a peep into our office?" the second issue inquired. ". . . Its carpet has a small, neat pattern, of quiet colors. It is the only article we have had to purchase. The substantial and comely black-walnut chairs were the gift of a pleasant young furniture merchant. . . . The sofa, upholstered in green rep

. . . the étagere and the clock are all furnished by one of the earliest friends of the cause. . . . Landseer's companion pieces, 'The Challenge' and 'The Sanctuary' hang one on each side of a fine portrait of Mr. Garrison. . . . A large grate, with an open fire, gives a look of cosy home-likeness to 'our office'." The domestic little article was signed L. S.

This homey tone was part of the paper's early effort to appeal to varied interests. Political articles, news of special concern to women, reports of suffrage activities shared space with stories, poems, correspondence, book reviews, columns of humorous items. "Caution to all ball-goers—never wind up the evening with a reel." There was advice on how summer suits should be washed, recommending tepid water and a pinch of salt to preserve the color. "A little beef's gall will not only set, but heighten, yellow and purple tints, and has a good effect upon green."

Correspondents sent reports from England, Europe and occasionally such remote spots as the Sandwich Islands. Like *The Revolution,* the *Journal* had a regular column, "What Women Are Doing." The first column began with the item: "Rosa Bonheur has made $30,000 by her paintings." "Gossip and Gleanings" was made up of items from other papers. "New Hampshire makes as many bushels of shoe pegs as she raises oats." "Paper was first made of linen rags in 1417."

The first issues contained such items as that there was in Geneva, Switzerland, an International Association of Women whose aim was to point out injustices pertaining to women and to fight for equality with men in every right everywhere. The association desired "to form between the well-intentioned women of all countries and conditions a bond of union and a solidarity of moral interests." The paper carried information about the growing activities of peace societies. It also carried news of the war between France and Prussia, and of the Paris commune.

Toward the end of 1871 there were accounts of the disastrous fire which had destroyed Chicago. In 1872 there were several stories about a Mrs. Leonowens who had recently returned from Siam, where she had gone to teach English to the wives and children of the king. Mrs. Leonowens was lecturing about her experiences, which included a dramatic story of the punishment of a slave girl who had defied the royal command and run away to marry the man she loved.

By 1872 the *Journal* had reached maturity. Mrs. Livermore, now a highly successful lyceum lecturer, resigned as editor, though as corresponding editor she continued her close association with the paper. The *Journal's* original small capital of $10,000 was exhausted, and it struggled to remain solvent by holding bazaars and collecting contributions. It offered premiums for new subscriptions: croquet sets, books, silver-plated tableware. The editors had been taxing themselves two or three hundred dollars a year; yet the paper's economy was so precarious that it could no longer pay contributors. An exception was made for Colonel Higginson, who had an invalid wife and could not afford to work without pay, but was too valuable to lose. Though there was a board of editors, the lion's share of the work was now done by Lucy and Henry. The paper continued to publish short stories, poems and humor, but its columns were fewer. There was still a column "Concerning Women." "By a new law, married women in Pennsylvania may purchase sewing-machines without the consent of their husbands, and the contract will be binding. That is, we suppose, they may purchase the machine if they have sufficient money and security of their own. And truly, this is freedom, this is progress!" On one occasion, in its enthusiasm about new fields for women, this column reported that "A Chinese girl is now undergoing trial in Pekin, charged with being the captain of a piratical craft recently blown up in one of the Chinese rivers." Regular correspondents sent letters from England and throughout the United States. Whatever trace of quaintness or uncertainty had invaded its early pages was gone.

The *Journal* was born in a period of rapid national development. In 1869 the Golden Spike celebration had signalized the completion of the railroad spanning the country from ocean to ocean. It was born at a time too when women's participation in business, professional, artistic and political life was expanding beyond the dreams of those first few valiant fighters. The presence of Julia Ward Howe on the staff of the paper was a tiny testimonial to this fact.

That Mrs. Howe was not only the author of the *Battle Hymn of the Republic* but a philosopher and humanitarian as well must have surprised those who knew her in her early years when, a banker's daughter and cousin of Ward McAllister, who originated the "400" classification of the socially elite, she moved in the best New York society. An attractive girl, small and well-built, dramatic because of her red hair, blue eyes and delicate pale skin, she had intellectual interests even then. Longfellow and Charles Sumner were close friends of her brother; she met Dickens when he came to the United States, and visited the Dickenses in London. Educated by a tutor, she studied exhaustively in every field that caught her interest. At twenty-three she married Samuel Gridley Howe, almost twice her age, a handsome and romantic figure who, Byronlike, had fought for Greek independence. He was, besides, a reformer who had dedicated his life to teaching blind children, and was famous as the teacher of blind and deaf Laura Bridgman, the Helen Keller of her day. Woman's rights was one reform in which Dr. Howe did not believe. A dictatorial husband, he held his wife's money and her life firmly in his hands. Theirs was a stormy marriage. To write, even anonymously, she had to defy him, for he disapproved of literary ladies and believed it her duty to care for him and their large family—she gave birth to six children. Less than a year younger than Lucy, but so much more protected from the erosions of life, she took no part in the suffrage movement until 1868 when, in spite of her husband, she was already famous. She seemed then to try, by her energy, to make up for the lost years.

At her first suffrage meeting she met Lucy, who, Mrs. Howe said, "had long been the object of one of my imaginary dislikes. As I looked into her sweet, womanly face and heard her earnest voice, I felt that the object of my distaste had been a mere phantom, conjured up by silly and senseless misrepresentations. Here stood the true woman, pure, noble, great-hearted, with the light of her good life shining in every feature of her face. . . . When they requested me to speak . . . I could only say, 'I am with you.' "

There were other notable converts to the cause, among them the newspaperwoman Jane Swisshelm who, though an early fighter for woman's rights, had been a harsh critic of Lucy Stone and bloomerism and public agitation for the franchise. In 1871 the *Journal* reported that Mrs. Swisshelm spoke at a suffrage convention, "physically so weak that we scarcely dared trust her to speak at all . . . swaying the large assembly at her will." This conversion apparently failed to endear her to Lucy, because in 1874 she wrote to her friend Margaret Campbell, active agent for the American Woman Suffrage Association, that she was glad Mrs. Campbell had "got the right side of that crooked stick, Mrs. Swisshelm."

Formal education for women was spreading. Swarthmore opened as a coeducational college in 1864; the first student was enrolled at Vassar in 1865; Smith College was chartered in 1871. Early issues of the *Journal* recorded that Michigan State University had "at last" voted to admit women "on precisely the same terms as men"; that John Simmons had left a bequest of $1,100,000 for a girls' college. In 1869 and 1870 one or two women were admitted to the bar, the first women lawyers.

A freer world was also in the making in England, which had moved ahead of the United States in 1869, when women "ratepayers," that is, single women and widows, began to vote in municipal elections. The following year they won the right to serve on the newly constituted school boards. In 1869, too, John Stuart Mill's *On the Subjection of Women,* written earlier, was published and widely circulated on both sides of the Atlantic. A dramatic development in women's political and social influence made its first effective appearance in England when in 1865 a group of fifty leading women inaugurated a discussion group to study such subjects as: should women take part in public affairs? and: what are the limits of parental authority?

Abortive attempts at women's discussion groups had begun in the United States long before. In the early seventeenth century Mrs. Anne Hutchinson had tried to nurture an alliance among women in the Massachusetts colony to discuss "various polemic and political questions." Indignant Puritan Fathers had disbanded the society and banished its subversive leader to Rhode Island, where the indomitable lady promptly organized another discussion group.

Over the years other women had formed local literary societies and discussion centers, but it was not until the spring of 1868, with the almost simultaneous formation of Sorosis and the New England Women's Club that the idea took hold. Sorosis—the word means aggregation—was begun by Mrs. Jane Cunningham Croly, a working journalist whose pseudonym was Jennie June. When in 1868 she was refused a ticket to the New York Press Club banquet for Charles Dickens on his second visit to the United States, she was not unnaturally indignant at the insult to herself and through her to professional women. Mrs. Croly, whose almost childlike prettiness belied her determination, decided that if intelligent women were not to be permitted to associate with men, they ought to join together to overcome their "want of unity and secular organization." With a group of friends she formed an association to enter a "protest against all idle gossip . . . follies and tyrannies of fashion, against all external impositions and disabilities; in short, against each and every thing that opposes the full development and use of the faculties conferred upon us by our Creator." The idea spread. Throughout the nation societies sprang up, many of which took the name Sorosis. In 1868 too, the New

England Women's Club was inaugurated. Among its early active members were Julia Ward Howe, Caroline M. Severance, Mary Livermore, Louisa M. Alcott and Lucy Stone. The activities of these proliferating women's clubs were regularly reported in the new *Journal.*

Closely related to the club movement was another phenomenon, the lecture bureau. Lecturing had for years been a profitable enterprise. Now, when James Redpath, abolitionist and Civil War correspondent, set up a Lyceum Bureau to supply the huge demand for speakers, lecturing entered the field of big business. Fees soared. Visiting lecturers were lionized.

Women were also entering politics on a new level. The October 6, 1870, issue of the *Journal* carried a report of the Woman Suffrage Party of Massachusetts of which Lucy Stone was a moving spirit. The party would not nominate its own ticket, but would question all candidates as to their convictions about woman suffrage, and support those committed to votes for women.

This burgeoning of the suffrage movement was having interesting repercussions among conservative ladies. An antisuffrage movement was developing in Massachusetts among women who, not content with being themselves unable to vote, were determined to keep their sex free of the pollution of politics, "because we shrink from the notoriety of the public eye," as the *Journal* quoted them, "restrained by that modesty which we esteem our chiefest ornament, and which belongs to us as our most precious, inalienable right." In the *Journal* Colonel Higginson suggested that an amusing dilemma confronted these militant antisuffragists, for "to vote No is to vote, just as much as if you vote Aye . . . you are vindicating your freedom of lung, whether you chirrup one way or the other." The next year, Mrs. Almira Phelps, sister of the late Emma Willard and for years head of the Troy Female Seminary, was loudly calling upon former pupils, in the name of the Anti-Suffrage Committee of Washington, D.C., to join a crusade against votes for women. This developing movement had a modest publication, entitled *The True Woman.* According to Colonel Higginson, "The first thing that surprises the reader, on opening the first number of the Anti-Woman-Suffrage paper, is its extreme smallness. Are true women necessarily diminutive? Are conservative journals necessarily so small?"

The Woman's Journal serves as a diary of Lucy's public life. In the first issue she wrote an article on "Laws in Relation to the Property Rights of Married Women in Massachusetts." In the third, she attacked the barbarism which still gave a father entire control of minor children; and throughout the year she continued to write on subjects close to her heart. The news items show the destruction of her plans for a quiet home life. In February she spoke in Vermont and in New Jersey. In March she was in New York for a meeting of the executive committee of the Equal Rights Association.

The committee decided not to call a public meeting that year, since in effect the association had ceased to function, and since so many of its members were part of one or the other of the suffrage associations, both of which were to hold meetings in New York in Anniversary Week. Instead a business meeting was called for that week.

In June Lucy was in Indiana. In the fall, among her many engagements, she addressed conventions in Pennsylvania and Delaware. There was relaxation too. In July the *Journal* announced that, "The address of Henry B. Blackwell and Lucy Stone, for the present, is West Brookfield, Mass." Throughout the summer both continued to contribute to the paper. That summer the *Journal* consolidated with still another paper, *The Woman's Advocate* of Dayton, Ohio.

The October 8 issue reported that "Republicans of Melrose . . . elected Mrs. Mary A. Livermore . . . one of their delegates [to the State Convention]; and instructed them to advocate Woman Suffrage in the Convention. The Republicans of West Brookfield . . . elected Mrs. Stone one of their delegates. In both cases the action of these towns was unanimous. . . . In the Convention . . . the Committee on Credentials reported the number of delegates duly accredited, and added the significant words, 'among this number are two ladies.' The Convention applauded heartily, and unanimously accepted the report." The ladies had come a long way since the day when little Lucy's hand was not counted in the church vote on Deacon Josiah Henshaw's expulsion, and since the later day when Nette was not considered a fit delegate to the World's Temperance Convention. They had not yet come the entire distance. At the State Convention the resolution on woman suffrage was defeated by a vote of 139 to 196, though the following year the Massachusetts Republican platform endorsed votes for women. The next year too the *Journal* noted that Lucy Stone had received a five hundred dollar donation to the suffrage cause from Josiah Henshaw of West Brookfield.

Meanwhile the last act of the split in the old-line suffrage movement was being played. Theodore Tilton, whose friend and mentor Henry Ward Beecher was president of the American Association, had developed aspirations to lead the movement. He therefore appealed to both the National and American Associations to send delegates to a meeting in New York on April 6, 1870. Lucy, Colonel Higginson and George W. Curtis attended unofficially for the American.

Tilton's proposal was for a new society with a constitution patterned exactly on the National's, without the delegate basis fundamental to the American's plan. Lucy and her colleagues refused to merge with any such society, and Tilton declared the Union Suffrage Society formed without them.

In May Lucy and Henry attended the business meeting called by the executive committee of the Equal Rights Association, of which no public notice had been given to the more than three hundred voting members of the association. Arriving at the meeting place, they were surprised to find some twenty persons, among whom were faces never before seen at the association's meetings. When challenged, these newcomers paid the ten cent dues required to become voting members.

Lucy and Henry felt the time was overripe for dissolving an association which had ceased to function. Tilton had other plans. He wished to merge the Equal Rights Association into his new suffrage society and had packed the meeting for this purpose. His tactics were successful. By the vote of everyone except Lucy and Henry, the defunct Equal Rights Association was merged with the Union Suffrage Society. At its May meeting the National Woman Suffrage Association, apparently expecting the American to do the same, voted to merge with the Union Suffrage Society with Tilton as president. He had attained his ambition, though not for long. Shortly afterward the National Woman Suffrage Association resumed its name, and so it remained for the twelve years of its separate existence.

That May Susan Anthony was forced by a huge burden of debt to give up *The Revolution*. She turned it over to wealthy Laura Bullard who, with Tilton's aid, continued to edit it for another year and a half, during which it lost most of its militant suffragist quality. To Susan the loss of the paper was like signing her "own death warrant." For a long time she worked heroically to repay the ten thousand dollar debt she had incurred, and finally, unaided, paid it to the last cent.

The last scene of the tragi-comedy of the break in the suffrage movement was staged at the American's November convention in Cleveland, where the union of the two organizations was again discussed. Again Susan Anthony, the only representative of the rival group, made an impassioned speech. Why would the American Woman Suffrage Association not join with hers? Was it because of Mrs. Stanton's views on marriage and divorce? How could *The Woman's Journal* logically oppose marital freedom, when "Lucy

Stone—at her wedding, refused to submit to the legal form of marriage, which, on her part was only a conditional one, with a solemn protest against the laws bearing upon woman in her social relation of wife"?

Whether or not she intended to suggest that Lucy was not legally married, her audience certainly believed she had done so. Colonel Higginson expressed outrage. "To say of one claiming to be a married woman that she refused to submit to the legal ceremony of marriage is to bring against her the most cruel attack that can be made." I know that Lucy Stone is "thoroughly and legally married . . . I tied the knot myself."

Susan immediately apologized, saying she had not intended to attack Lucy. It would seem extraordinary if she had. She knew that Lucy and Henry, because of the difference in their names, had been publicly accused of being free lovers, and that such scandal must injure the movement.

Yet in factional disputes it is easy to lose sight of the main end. In those reminiscences which Mrs. H. M. Tracy Cutler sent to Lucy, she told an unsavory story of a gathering at the Tilton home that spring of 1870. Neither Susan nor Mrs. Stanton was there. "We were entertained with a boastful account of how they had tricked Lucy Stone by turning over several of the Equal Rights Clubs, with the names of their members to the National, doing it before the Blackwells could reach the meetings where this was done; and all this was represented as a conspiracy between Mrs. Stanton, Susan and [Mr. Tilton] . . . and they laughed over it as the best joke possible."

She closed her long account with a note:

"Dear Lucy, I have written out my recollections to be used as you may see fit. It was this deep treachery that made me fear them from the beginning, and when I asked you why you did not expose them, you said, 'I would not because they are women.' And for this I honored your loyalty, but I have feared it was, after all, misleading."

Her fears were fulfilled. For nearly a hundred years historians and biographers have accepted the version so fully expounded by Mrs. Stanton and Susan Anthony. Lucy's policy of silence left them no alternative.

Chapter Twenty-two

At the end of 1870 the National Woman Suffrage Association became involved with an adventurer far more dramatic and dangerous than the lavender-gloved Mr. Train. On December 21 of that year, Mrs. Victoria Claflin Woodhull was given a hearing before the House Judiciary Committee on a memorial she had presented to Congress on the enfranchisement of women.

The Fourteenth and Fifteenth Amendments stated that "All persons born or naturalized in the United States, and subject to the jurisdiction thereof, are citizens of the United States . . ." and that "The right of the citizens of the United States to vote shall not be denied or abridged by the United States or by any state on account of race, color, or previous condition of servitude." It was Mrs. Woodhull's contention that this gave women all the rights of other citizens, including the right to vote.

Mrs. Woodhull presented her memorial on the same day that the National Association convened in Washington. Susan Anthony, Isabella Beecher Hooker and Paulina Wright Davis attended the Congressional hearing and invited Victoria and her sister Tennessee Claflin to return to their convention, where Victoria would repeat her speech. The woman's movement had up to then snubbed the two notorious sisters. Now Susan and Mrs. Stanton opened their arms to take them in.

Victoria Woodhull was one of the most striking and unsavory characters thrown up by the turmoil of nineteenth-century America, a beautiful adventuress with a sharp intelligence and persuasive tongue, but so uneducated that there is some doubt whether she could read or write. She was born in 1838 into a poverty-stricken family of unsuccessful charlatans. Her younger sister, Tennessee, claiming occult powers, was exploited as a fortuneteller by their father. At fourteen Tennessee was healing and prophesying, and papa was so successfully selling a cure-all called the Elixir of Life, with Tennessee's picture on the label, that the family expanded its healing operations by opening an infirmary for the cure of everything. When one of their patients died of cancer and Tennessee was indicted for manslaughter, the family decamped, abandoning its surviving patients.

Victoria was not with her family then. She had married at sixteen and moved to California; but one day she heard spirit voices calling her home, and unhesitatingly returned to join Tennessee as a traveling clairvoyant, her contact in the other world being no less a person than Demosthenes. She never underestimated herself.

Victoria now divorced her husband and contracted a "marriage" with a swashbuckling adventurer known as Colonel Blood, though the divorced Woodhull continued as part of the ménage, and Colonel Blood had a wife and children somewhere in his background.

The Claflin sisters' rise in the world came about when Tennessee "cured" Cornelius Vanderbilt by magnetism. The tycoon, who had begun life as a Staten Island ferryman, was old now and seriously ill. An ignorant man, who believed diseases were caused and cured by spells, he was easy prey for faith healers, particularly pretty ones, and Tennie Claflin's laying on of hands seemed to have splendid results. In gratitude, spiced perhaps with a dash of blackmail, the great tycoon gave the sisters tips on the stock market. They made a fortune, and inspired by success set up as lady stockbrokers, creating a sensation in Wall Street.

Along the way, Victoria had attached to her train the eccentric philosopher Stephen Pearl Andrews as well as one of the most controversial of the northern Civil War generals, Benjamin F. Butler who as representative from Massachusetts was publicly the author of a favorable minority report on her memorial, and was privately accorded the honor of having written it himself. Guided by Victoria's brains trust of Blood, Andrews and Butler in this world, and Demosthenes in the other, the two sisters commenced publication of *Woodhull and Claflin's Weekly*. Stephen Pearl Andrews, a man of great learning, believed in a new world order and a universal language. In the sisters' magazine, which spread its wings wide over free love, clairvoyance and Marxism (the *Communist Manifesto* appeared for the first time in the United States in the *Weekly*), Victoria signed articles probably written by Andrews, on these and other subjects. In 1870, so firmly pro-woman suffrage was the *Weekly*'s stand that it announced as its candidate for the next President of the United States—Victoria Woodhull.

This was the woman whom Susan and Mrs. Stanton took up not only as a fellow suffrage worker but as a friend. Elizabeth Stanton, at least, was at the time convinced of the curative powers of magnetism and attracted by spiritualism. She was also increasingly concerned with easy divorce as a main objective of the woman's movement. Since censure had dogged every step of her public life she had perhaps lost the ability to discriminate between unthinking prejudice and social responsibility. If any woman was attacked as too free or radical, it was Mrs. Stanton's first, and thoroughly decent, impulse to defend her.

Susan Anthony had said she would align herself with the devil if he would support woman suffrage, and beautiful, unsatanic Victoria Woodhull had done more. By her memorial, she had given the cause a new direction and nationwide publicity. When, at the National's Anniversary Week meeting in 1871, Victoria proclaimed, "We mean treason; we mean secession . . . we will overthrow this bogus Republic and plant a government of righteousness in its stead," Susan and Mrs. Stanton remained unperturbed. The press did not. Conservatives everywhere were delighted to associate the suffrage movement with Victoria's far-flung doctrines and unsavory activities.

Six months later, at the National's Washington convention, Susan was troubled when, from the platform, Victoria nominated herself as the Presidential candidate of a new party. Though Elizabeth Stanton and other leaders were ready to enter a political party with the disreputable Mrs. Woodhull, who had now given new fodder to the press by turning to blackmail and to court battles with her own family, Susan took a firm stand, even defying Mrs. Stanton, in order to dissociate the movement from Victoria Woodhull; but by then it was too late to avoid a shocking scandal.

At the time they became interested in Victoria Woodhull, Susan and Mrs. Stanton were worried about two of their close friends, allies in the suffrage movement. Handsome, blond Theodore Tilton was married to Elizabeth Roberts, a wistful, birdlike creature who, when he met her, was teaching Sunday School in Henry Ward Beecher's church in Brooklyn. The Tiltons shared an almost worshipful attitude toward Beecher, whose flamboyant personality had won him a huge following both in the pulpit and on the lecture platform.

Though in their home life Beecher and his wife were models of puritanical morality, it seems probable that Beecher had a life of his own, for in July 1870, according to Tilton, his wife confessed that sometime earlier their preacher had convinced her that Heaven had ordained she should give herself to him, and that, so instructed, she had become his mistress. Tilton forgave them both, but his agitation became perceptible in a series of articles he wrote for *The Independent* on love, marriage and divorce, in one of which he directly attacked Beecher. "Mr. Beecher's views on the proper punishment of adultery would have great interest just now in their application to the case of a certain clergyman whose name is in all the newspapers . . . [who] has at a most unseemly time of life been detected in improper intimacies with certain ladies of his congregation."

Tilton also confided his woes to his friends, Elizabeth Stanton among them; and Susan witnessed a heated scene between the Tiltons about which she told Mrs. Stanton.

To her new-found friend Victoria Woodhull, Elizabeth Stanton confided the sad story of the Tilton-Beecher entanglement. But Victoria was not the type of woman with whom Mrs. Stanton was used to dealing; and when one of Beecher's sisters attacked her, she retaliated by printing innuendoes about Beecher and his pretty parishioner.

Lurid events followed in rapid succession. Beecher had Tilton removed as editor of *The Independent,* then repented and helped him to the editorship of a new paper, *The Golden Age.* Tilton went to Mrs. Woodhull to plead with her not to expose the affair further. It seems likely that he became her lover—she later said he did, but she said the same of Beecher. Certainly he fell in love with her and wrote her biography from highly imaginative material which she supplied and which the enraptured Tilton believed and published. His public support of her ruined him, while she, preaching free love and enlightened radicalism, became increasingly popular.

When rumors of the sisters' blackmailing activities spread, Victoria, to divert criticism, lashed out. Now she publicly told the story of the Tilton-Beecher affair, then twice published an intimate account in her *Weekly,* because she explained, "I am engaged in officering a social revolution on the marriage question." Henry Ward Beecher denied the affair, making Susan and Mrs. Stanton angry. "What a pity it is," Lucy wrote to a friend, "that Mrs. Stanton should put her nasty foot in the Beecher scandal." Theodore Tilton refused to deny the story, making everyone angry.

Finally the situation assumed such proportions that the church authorities investigated. Elizabeth Tilton now maintained that she had told her husband only that she loved Beecher with a pure love. She left her husband in order to defend Beecher, who rejected her and further ruined Tilton by his attacks. In desperation Tilton sued Beecher for alienation of affection. To the satisfaction of the sensation-loving press, the trial, which began in January 1875, lasted six months, ending in a hung jury. From the day in 1870 when Elizabeth Tilton had allegedly confessed her transgression to the end of the trial was almost exactly five years. Tilton was ruined. Elizabeth Tilton's life was destroyed. Only Beecher, secure in the protection of the church, continued to flourish with such effect that in 1877 the *Journal* announced that he had earned $40,000 on a western lecture tour—a huge sum in those days—and that when he preached in Chicago twenty thousand people were turned away.

For most of this period *The Woman's Journal* remained judicious. Attacked early in 1871 by Mrs. Woodhull's *Weekly* for having too "pure hands" because it suggested that women of damaged character should not be accepted in the suffrage movement, the *Journal* defended itself and the dignity of the movement. At about that time, in personal letters, Lucy expressed the opinion that "the Woodhull and Claflin tribe are a real curse, but they make only a temporary nuisance." And again, "Please say . . . that my one wish in regard to Mrs. Woodhull is that she nor her ideas may be so much as heard of at our meeting."

In the summer of 1874 the *Journal* briefly entered the controversy when Julia Ward Howe wrote a scathing attack on Tilton, later quoted by the church committee who exonerated Beecher. "Wishing to fill the horizon with the blaze of a sudden glory, Mr. Tilton, a man of fair ability, with a gift of rhetoric, and a desultory culture, sought to make himself at any price, the popular deity of the hour." Mrs. Howe described Tilton's arrogant role in the suffrage movement, and his biography of Victoria Woodhull "which would have sunk any man's reputation anywhere for common sense." Then "it occurred to him to invent a disgrace so great that his own would be small in comparison."

In the next issue Lucy herself breathlessly expressed unsullied faith in Elizabeth Tilton's innocence and her husband's guilt. "Smarting under blows which human eyes could see, and bearing others which, though not seen, give the most cruel hurt . . . Elizabeth Tilton said what her tormentors required her to say, against herself, against her pastor, to her apparent certain ruin, just as men in burning buildings, to escape the torturing flames, leap from the top to certain death." In a letter to a friend Lucy asked help for Elizabeth. "She has no money . . . and her heart, aching for her children, may yield again to the power of her old tormentor. . . . She needs *occupation*. . . . Tilton has no legal right to the children, since he disclaims being their father, but I fear he will give her all the trouble he can."

That fall Henry, writing to Lucy about events in Michigan, where woman suffrage and a new constitution were to come before the voters in November, said, "This Beecher-Tilton affair is playing the deuce with [woman suffrage] in Michigan. No chance of success this year I fancy." The involvement of Victoria Woodhull in the suffrage movement was unquestionably damaging. Her candidacy for the Presidency was ridiculous, her advocacy of free love and spiritualism an incubus, and her exposure of the Beecher-Tilton affair a blight, since all three principals had been identified with woman suffrage.

The divergency of tactics in the two associations again reflected a divergence of principle. From the time of Victoria Woodhull's memorial to Congress in 1870, the National had put its main weight behind her interpretation of the Amendments. The American believed that, even if the new interpretation was valid, it was without practical significance. The hope that Congress could be induced to enact legislation which would permit voting under the Amendments was too weak a straw to grasp at.

The American believed in spreading outward from a smaller base, on the principle that every wedge driven into the block of disenfranchisement brought women closer to total citizenship, that on a state and local level the movement could have a greater influence on the nomination and election of politicians favorable to suffrage. Also, because

Presidential electors were chosen on a state level, they hoped, by act of state legislatures, to win the right to vote in Presidential elections.

The change in attitude toward women's demands was everywhere perceptible. Not only were the ranks of sympathizers enormously augmented, but this increase of interest was making itself felt politically. National and state legislatures were bombarded by petitions, and the prosuffrage vote in these bodies, though not yet a majority, showed increasing strength. After each small gain *The Woman's Journal* printed a picture of a dove on an olive branch.

In 1872 Henry went to the National Republican Convention in Philadelphia, which nominated Grant for a second term, to urge them to adopt a woman suffrage resolution. Under prosuffrage pressure, the party adopted a plank: "The Republican party is mindful of its obligations to the loyal women of America, for their noble devotion to the cause of freedom; their admission to wider fields of usefulness is viewed with satisfaction; and the honest demands of any class of citizens for additional rights should be treated with respectful consideration."

Lucy wrote in the *Journal,* "In the whole history of the Woman Suffrage Movement, there has been nothing so touching as the eager grasping at the first recognition we have ever had from any national party that had the power to help. . . .

"Just as drowning men clutch at anything that *seems* to have substance, so have women caught at this; and in spite of long neglect, and repeated rebuffs, they forget it all, in grateful recognition of this first small sign of good-will." Yet this small sign was enough to win Lucy's support. Susan Anthony referred to it as a splinter rather than a plank. Yet, though it cost the party nothing and was not even a promise of future action, the splinter was enough to win Susan's support as well. Then, at their state convention, the Massachusetts Republicans adopted a plank forthrightly endorsing the extension of suffrage "to all American citizens irrespective of sex." Each week the *Journal* headed its editorial page with both planks printed in capital letters.

The words of the National Republican platform, pussyfooting though they were, played an important part in radical women's stand in the Presidential campaign. Decisive too was the fact that the candidate opposing Grant was Horace Greeley. Greeley had been nominated by a split of Liberal Republicans who could not stomach a second administration of Grant's venal henchmen, and his nomination had been endorsed by the Democratic party. Though Greeley was a liberal and a reformer after their own hearts, it was difficult for liberals and reformers who had viewed the Republican party as the banner bearer of emancipation, patriotism and a better world, to place their hopes on the Democratic party with its tradition of proslavery conservatism. It was more difficult still for women suffragists to support Greeley. "We shall not decry Mr. Greeley," Lucy wrote in the *Journal*. "He is a man of great intelligence, great personal excellence, and purity of character. . . . But *because* he hates Woman Suffrage, and as President of the United States would veto a Sixteenth Amendment to the Constitution, every woman suffragist, of whatever party, should withhold his vote from Horace Greeley."

Greeley had said that everyone knew that woman suffrage meant free love, a silly statement by an irritable man. How had this man, so sympathetic to women's rights when the tiny movement was taking its first heroic steps, come to this position? Partly it must have been due to his marriage to a neurotic, domineering woman, who made his life difficult when she was at home, and went away with her two daughters (five of their seven children had died), leaving him for months alone in their large house in Chappaqua, New York. She believed in woman suffrage, and aided by Susan and Mrs. Stanton had contrived to humiliate him at the 1867 convention. It is said that the fiery Greeley always treated his wife with gentleness. He was less forbearing with the woman suffrage movement, and as the years passed his bitterness toward it increased.

Women suffragists therefore were nearly unanimous in their opposition to Greeley, and further solidified in opposition when both the Liberal Republican and the Democratic conventions refused any recognition of women's right to vote. Lucy had advised women to use their influence against any "candidate who is against suffrage for women, no matter how worthy he may be in all other respects," but not therefore to advocate "mean and unprincipled men" whose only virtue was their support of woman suffrage. Yet in the 1872 campaign suffragists found themselves in almost this position.

During that summer Susan and Mrs. Stanton corresponded at length with Lucy and Henry about the possibility of co-operative effort to aid the Republican party. As usual the negotiations ended in renewed suspicion and fear. The year before Lucy had begged a co-worker to discourage Mrs. Livermore from attempting a reconciliation with the National. Tell her that you think it best "not to strike hands with those people at Washington. They were our late enemies; we don't know that they are our friends." In the fall of 1872 Susan, similarly alarmed, wrote to a friend asking her to distribute the letter throughout the organization. Susan had already sent copies to many people because she "wanted one and all to know the spirit of Boston."

"Here is the *finale* of all the *loving, fraternal* letters of *Lucy* and *Harry* to Mrs. Stanton, this summer, *refusal* to be present at this *first Campaign* meeting, tho' append *their price* to do so. I do hope Mrs. S. will not be *so fooled with them again,* but it is no use hoping. She will be. All in the world they want, is just what she has given them, over and over again this summer, an acknowledgment *from her,* that she has been wrong, and they immaculate in their management of affairs."

Susan's annoyance was not surprising. She had had a letter from Henry advising her how to conduct her meeting, lest the women with whom she worked, "a somewhat different class of women from ours," undo the success Henry himself claimed of leading the Republicans toward recognition of women's demands. "Don't let them try to drive, bully, or threaten the party. Women can *persuade* men . . . they cannot scold them into compliance."

The theory that, as citizens, women were entitled to vote caused many throughout the country to attempt to do so. In Rochester Susan and her sisters went to the polls to register. After a considerable argument Susan was able to convince two election inspectors that they should register the sisters. Immediately Susan went to find more women willing to try. The papers picked up the news, and when registration closed about fifty women had registered in Rochester. On election day Susan and a few others succeeded in voting.

Shortly thereafter a criminal charge was brought against Susan for knowingly voting without the legal right to do so. Her case was tried before a judge, described in the *History of Woman Suffrage* as "a small-brained, pale-faced, prim-looking man," who illegally directed the jury to find her guilty. The jury was not even polled. Susan was fined one hundred dollars and costs, which she refused to pay. The inspectors who permitted her to vote were found guilty too. Later President Grant pardoned them all.

The *Journal* freely printed articles and letters about the case, and in her annual report to the American Association Lucy commented, "Thus the Law holds that to be a crime, when done by a woman, which is praiseworthy and right when done by a man"; but the paper did not take the position that Susan had acted with great heroism. The *Journal* and its editors were by then convinced that spectacular action and sensational news were harming rather than aiding their cause. About the trial Susan delivered herself of one of her more immoderate opinions. It was, she wrote in her diary, "the greatest outrage History ever witnessed."

Meanwhile the Presidential election was long past. Grant was in the White House for a second scandal-ridden term. Mrs. Greeley, ailing for years, had died shortly before election day. Greeley, a broken man, died in a sanitarium less than a month after his defeat.

Letters in the *Journal* in April 1873 sharply criticized its support of Grant and pointed out how weak had been the promise of "respectful consideration" made by a party which had thereafter accorded woman suffrage neither respect nor consideration. "Oh," exclaimed one, "there has never, in the history of our government, been such absolute pollution! from the shameless, vulgar head, down to the leanest tributary Post-master. The President's relatives are now all peacefully feeding at the crib again."

Henry justified the *Journal's* position. "Politically we are for Woman Suffrage first, last, and all the time."

Chapter Twenty-three

In that spring of 1873 Lucy and Henry's only daughter was sixteen. What kind of child had her surroundings bred—the home so different from her schoolmates', the parents loving but all too often busy at their chosen work of making a better world? She was a shy, wistful girl who adored her father, that sociable, joking man, miraculously able to talk to anyone, to make friends so easily. In appearance Alice was thin and small-boned, with a tiny, almost peaked face, further diminished by huge blue eyes. It was the face of an intelligent girl, infinitely vulnerable, eager for life, yet afraid to meet the world. Alice suffered from headaches, an ailing stomach and weak eyes.

Family tradition has it that, as a child, Alice Stone Blackwell was far from enthusiastic about women's rights. "Suffrage, suffrage, suffrage. I'm so tired of suffrage," was the way she put it then. Later she dedicated her life to the cause, but when she was little it was her rival, and a successful rival, for her parents' attention.

She was twelve when the family moved from New Jersey to Boston, and she was sent to a school in Newburyport. Lucy, desolate at Alice's absence, wrote frequent, affectionate letters to her "Dear Cub" or "Cubikin." "Here is a kiss for you, and a hug, and a cuddle, and a great deal of love." But letters were necessary only because she had been sent away so that the new suffrage paper could be started. It was not an unfamiliar situation; she had often been left with relatives while her parents went off to lecture or campaign.

Returning home, Alice found a devoted mother, a dedicated housewife, who was concerned with what her daughter wore and ate and did, but who was usually occupied in editing, soliciting funds, and writing for *The Woman's Journal.* Frequently too, both mother and father were away. Lucy's letters were full of such loving details as where to find the blue socks that matched the dress for the party next day; but they were letters from a mother busy and away from home.

For the effects of Lucy's childhood on her development there is only the evidence of her life. For Alice's childhood picture of herself there is her diary, recipient of her fears and hopes. She began it in 1870; significantly enough, on her mother and father's wedding anniversary. The entries for 1872 and 1873, when she was fourteen, fifteen and sixteen, still exist. They begin with an account of the fire which on December 10, 1871, destroyed a large part of the family's new Dorchester home.

According to *The Woman's Journal,* Lucy and Henry were attending a series of conventions when they received a telegram telling them of the fire. Many "cherished keepsakes and family heirlooms" were lost. "It has been a dreary homecoming for them."

The loss was estimated at about ten thousand dollars, much of it covered by insurance. "Papa says his loss by the fire is $3,000," Alice wrote. "Mama thinks it will come to more. Papa's pet plan . . . is to rebuild the house with improvements and alterations and live in it. . . . Mama I think would like best of the various plans that are talked over to sell the place as it is, take lodgings in Boston and there go on editing the Journal."

Papa's plan carried the day, and while the repairs were being made the family moved to a small house where they stayed until June. There Alice began her 1872 diary. Like so many growing girls, she believed that a more romantic name would have changed her fate. ". . . I, Alice, Elsie or Alsette, am living in the small house at the foot of the hill, waiting till our large burnt house is built up. Papa and Mama . . . are generally away all day in Boston . . .

"That is about enough introduction, and if Posterity

wants more, Posterity will have to do without. Not that I mean to have P. read it—at least not miscellaneous P."

She was adolescent, a creature of volatile and violent emotions. Sadie was her schoolgirl love that spring. "I being intoxicated with love and doing all sorts of idiotic things without rhyme or reason, such as tumbling against trees, telegraph poles and fences, and glaring at the sky, which was overclouding blackly from the west." Mary was her enemy. Alice challenged her to a duel, "which challenge she accepted," but when the time arrived, "I waited in state with my weapons around me, but Mary Fifield did not come." A few days later Alice squirted her with water from a syringe at twelve paces, and the mock duel over, the two girls became friends.

There was love and hate for older people too. About a Miss Tucker, living with them in the spring of 1872, she wrote, "I'll beg borrow or steal money enough to pay my passage to England . . . for I won't stay here to be insulted by that conceited old mischief-maker—I won't, that's flat!" There was loyalty to her family and their tradition. A friend said Alice was bad because she sewed on Sunday, to which Alice replied that the friend was bad because she did not believe in woman's rights. " 'Why Alice Blackwell!' cried she, 'do you mean to say you think it's as wicked not to believe in Womens Rights as to sew on Sunday?' I said 'I think it's quite as much of a mistake.' " And a year later, "Papa introduced me to Parker Pillsbury and I spoke to him rather cordially, and found out after to my disgust, that he is a Woodhullite, by both theory and practice; and I wanted to wash my hands."

Whatever the emotion happened to be, there was a great deal of it. One day that spring Lucy surprised her daughter with an issue of *The Woman's Journal* in which a poem of Alice's appeared over the initials A. S. B. "I was prepared for it," Alice admitted, "yet sat down on the floor and shrieked, after my usual style. Mama seems rather disgusted that I am not pleased, and showed signs of turning blue;

and so decided to *be* pleased, and abated my wrath." And after a physical fight with a schoolmate, she commented on her own uncontrollable temper, so like her mother's when Lucy was a girl, "In the end I am afraid I shall murder someone."

Besides her diary, Alice had another confidant, her cousin Kitty, ten years her senior, whom Alice sometimes addressed as "Dear Betrothed." Shortly after the move to Boston, twelve-year-old Alice had written to Kitty, "One of my shoulders is certainly higher than the other, and Mama thinks of asking Aunt Emily's advice about shingling my hair, dressing me as a boy, and send me to military school to straighten me." However seriously Mama entertained this extraordinary idea, it is clear that Alice believed she did, and clear too are the frightening implications of such an idea for a young girl.

In fact, in the autumn of 1873, when Alice was sixteen, her life took a turn which indicates that Lucy's plan may not have been sheer fantasy. Alice entered a boys' school now accepting a few girl students. The *Journal* explained: "The Chauncy Hall School has begun its new term with an increased number of ladies among its students. It is a disgrace to Boston that the public high school for girls does not fit them to enter college. This deficiency Chauncy Hall School supplies." Alice recorded that the first day she was "the only girl in a Latin class of small boys, among whom I towered up like a watermelon among peaches." Next day she added, "I who would as lief have a garter snake near me as a boy am the one girl in classes of from 20 up to the 50's." She continued to be the only girl in her class during her first two years at Chauncy Hall; a second girl joined her in her two final years there. There were other girls in the school though, for the girls "drilled with guns for the first time," with doors closed so that the boys could not see.

She was an excellent student, but a nervous one. At the beginning of 1872 she was first in her class at the Harris Grammar School in Dorchester. In the spring of 1873 she was class valedictorian. Yet, though top of her class from first to last, she suffered doubts throughout. She had taken examinations and had failed history and almost failed geography; but this may not be quite realistic, for later, after receiving 100 in history, 91 in grammar and 90 in arithmetic, she was "very dismal because of my bad examinations."

Her insecurity was everywhere. After a Ladies' Club tea, she wrote, "I having had a splendid time, and decided that if one smiles at people they are very apt to smile back again, and that there may be other poor little cats shying about in strange garrets who relish a friendly look as much as I do."

Like her father in his adolescence, she attributed her moods of despair to religious doubt. "Am feeling unhappy . . . I think—I want—God. Not the 'Spiritual Consciousness' or 'Pervading Power' that one *supposes* about; I want . . . one to *love,* to really believe in and trust to utterly. Mama believes in a Guiding Influence, and gets along somehow; but I shouldn't wonder if her blues came somewhat from the want of—something in that direction. As for Papa . . . I think he supposes that creation is a sort of machine set going once for all. . . . The God I should like to believe in wouldn't squash individuals for the good of the whole if it wasn't for their own good as well. . . . And being a Blackwell, I keep all the worry to myself; there really seems no one to tell—who I could tell."

A few months later she did have a religious talk with Mama. " 'Set spinning and let go' is her theory. I'd rather be blue orthodox and believe in Hell than believe what she does. She'll have a pleasant surprise when she dies."

She went to hear Robert Collyer, Unitarian clergyman and reformer, a friend of her parents. Collyer, born in England, had in his youth been a blacksmith. Now as preacher and lecturer this simple, earnest man with his healthy, beaming face was enormously popular and much loved. Alice had a schoolgirl crush on him, feelings intermingled with the religious experience through which she was passing. At one of his lectures Collyer gave her a fatherly kiss, which left her much flustered. She made an armlet with his initials on it and wore it "for love of him . . . who once and again pulled me out of the slough of despond."

Glimpses of her parents come through. Unlike her mother in her girlhood, Alice read a great deal of fiction. Indeed, in the evenings, while Lucy mended, Henry would read aloud to his little family–*Nicholas Nickleby, The Newcomes* and *Middlemarch,* which in 1872 was appearing for the first time in the United States. On the rare occasions when papa and mama had a disagreement, it was papa who won Alice's allegiance. Yet when Lucy told the story of the slave mother who killed her child, and added that she thought Margaret Garner must be one of the tallest angels in heaven, " 'Mama,' said I, 'I think *you* will be tall in heaven!' And so I do."

There is a record too of her parents' constant comings and goings. "I am to be alone most of the rest of this week. Therefore coming home from school I bought chocolate, with which to comfort myself evenings."

Henry was much involved with an appeal of the Dominicans to have their country annexed by the United States as protection against its neighbor Haiti. In the spring of 1871 he had gone to Santo Domingo with an investigating commission appointed by President Grant. Another member of the commission was Julia Ward Howe's husband, Dr. Samuel Gridley Howe. Both Henry and Dr. Howe had fallen in love with the island. In November Henry had written a long letter to Charles Sumner attempting to convince him that annexation or a protectorate was essential for the island's safety; but Sumner continued to oppose it.

In March 1872 "Papa [again] left for Santo Domingo." He wrote from there to Lucy that the country needed the example of American family life to redeem it from "its present immorality," but whether the trip furthered his plan for "opening up a colonization enterprise from New England" would depend on whether the island was annexed. Dr. Howe's interest in this project had taken him back to the island too, and Mrs. Howe had gone with him. From there she wrote long, fascinated descriptions to the *Journal.* A joint passport issued to her and Henry by the Santo Domingo government shows that she returned to the states with him. Alice reported that Papa brought back "a pineapple, guavas, bananas, and two pods of cocoanut beans."

That November the pre-election rapprochement between the American and National Associations which had so troubled Susan Anthony had an interesting side issue. Mrs. Stanton and her daughter Hattie came to visit. Mrs. Stanton, the pretty young matron of early woman's rights days, was now fifty-seven, and to Alice's eyes "a pleasant, short, excessively fat little old lady with white curls." Except for the white curls, Hattie might quite easily have described fifty-four-year-old Lucy in the same words. Four years later Lucy wrote to her brother, "I am getting fatter all the time, and weigh at least 170 lbs, so that I go puffing, with a red face."

In June of 1873—Alice was to enter Chauncy Hall school that fall—Mama gave her advice about boys. From Alice's account, it seems odd advice to have given so shy and timid a girl. "Mama told me all sorts of queer things about boys—how if you show them any attention they immediately think you want to marry them, and that they would like to marry you. How very inconvenient!" Alice was to have no ultimate concern with such inconvenience. On August 2, 1873, there is an entry in the diary describing "a pleasant shady room such as I am hoping to set up housekeeping in with Kitty when we are two old maids and live together." This plan she carried out.

Part Four

New World for Women

Chapter Twenty-four

The era in which Lucy and Henry's daughter grew to young womanhood and the *Journal* became a solid and continuing publication was very unlike that in which young Lucy struggled alone. Though in the North and Southwest severe Indian outbreaks still occurred, railroads now spanned the country, telegraphic communication covered miles in seconds and in 1878 the first commercial telephone exchange began operation in New Haven. The following year Captain A. B. Tuttle of New York sailed past the northern ice barrier into polar seas.

It was a highly mechanized world of steel and iron, harvesters and flour mills; a society where the demand for women's labor was so great that, by thousands, they had achieved the doubtful freedom of working in sweatshops and factories unlimited hours a day, unlimited days a week. There were many new household aids; the sewing machine alone had liberated the housewife from the burdensome necessity of sewing each stitch of her family's clothing by hand.

European travel was becoming a commonplace. In 1878, with a Paris exposition as special attraction, the *Journal* reported the departures of Mary Livermore and her husband; the Reverend Robert Collyer; Thomas Wentworth Higginson; and Julia Ward Howe with her youngest daughter, Maud. The following year Henry and Alice made the trip which, since his marriage, Henry had hoped to make with Lucy.

Colonel Higginson, writing to the *Journal,* commented that Americans, invading Paris by the thousands, had become a subject of controversy. Were American tourists better mannered than English or worse? The controversy was not permanently settled. Fuel was added by the publication of *Daisy Miller;* and debate raged as to whether Henry James's view of the unconventional behavior of American girls was an accurate one. Americans were becoming self-conscious about themselves and about their relation to a larger sphere.

The end of an old order and the beginning of a new were made dramatically clear in the deaths of the old guard. The list of obituaries in the mid-1870's reads like an honor role of reformers of an earlier day: John Stuart Mill, Charles Sumner, Sarah Grimké, Harriot Hunt, Lydia Mott, Samuel Gridley Howe, Harriet Martineau, Paulina Wright Davis. In 1879 Angelina Grimké Weld died. So did William Lloyd Garrison; and the story of that day when the great abolitionist had so nearly been lynched by an antislavery mob on the streets of Boston was retold as history unknown to men now in their forties.

Lucy and Henry had not entirely bridged the gap. In a period of infinite change they remained the same, maintaining their innocence and singleness of purpose in a sophisticated, complex and often corrupt world. Because the Republican party had been the advocate of freedom, they remained loyal to it through the corruption of the Grant administrations. "It is impossible not to hate the party which, omnipotent in power, has shamelessly and cruelly trampled on . . . the sacred rights of half the people," Lucy said in 1873, after repeated antisuffrage action had proved Republican mouthings of women's rights no more than pre-election bids for the votes of prosuffrage men, ". . . because, as loyal women, it degraded them below the worst rebels . . . with all the legal inequality which grows out of such degradation." Yet after the election of 1876, when the Democrat Samuel J. Tilden received more popular votes than Rutherford B. Hayes, and Hayes became President by Republican manipulation of doubtful electoral votes, Henry entirely approved the maneuver. As young men in Cincinnati he and Hayes had been members of the same literary club. He knew Hayes to be prosuffrage, and though the Republican platform had been weak on suffrage, the Democrats had spurned it altogether. It was not until January 1878 that Henry stated that he, an "original Republican," was repudiating the party whose loss of moral tone was illustrated by its abandonment of impartial suffrage; but even this resolution did not last.

It was a period of awakening social consciousness. *Das Kapital* had appeared in 1867. In the supposedly classless United States, it was an era of great poverty and great fortunes, of robber barons and mass immigration of unskilled workers. Andrew Carnegie had made a fortune before he was thirty. When he turned to producing steel the men at his furnaces worked twelve hours a day seven days a week; their wages were pitiful.

The Woman's Journal lacked social awareness. The panic of 1873, followed by five years of depression, had a strong impact on the paper, which had to struggle to keep alive. Yet the surrounding poverty and unemployment found little space in its pages. Nor did the *Journal* link the fate of women to the growing labor movement. Its concern was that women should be treated as men's equals, with no distinction in wages or legislation. "Equal rights, not special privileges. Justice, not favors." But the *Journal* seemed not to realize, as Susan Anthony did, that a better life for workers might mean a better life for women. Lucy and Henry, so aware of the fate of slaves, were not concerned with the concept of wage slaves.

In 1877, when wage cuts caused a widespread railroad strike with resulting violence, Lucy condemned the "riotous proceedings." With her naive faith in the ballot, she actually suggested that the strikers, being men and enfranchised, should turn to the vote to gain their ends. "This insurrection must be suppressed, if it costs a hundred thousand lives and the destruction of every railroad in the country." Only after law was restored would discussions of the workers' dissatisfaction be in order. So spoke the woman to whom John Brown had been a hero.

Fifteen years later, at the time of the bloody Homestead Steel strike, Lucy was still incredibly naive. "If men are not satisfied either with the hours they work or the price they are paid, is it not better that they should combine their capital, establish business of their own, in a small way at first, if need be . . . than to resort to the wasteful and bloody way of the strike at Homestead . . . ?

"If the wages which have been lost by strikers in the last dozen years could have been saved and combined, there might have been many a thrifty business now, where each workman might be one of the capitalists. . . . It may be urged that a man can save but little from his wages. But many littles combined amount to much."

There is evidence that Lucy and Henry feared that the vast army of ignorant immigrants, bringing with them a reactionary European outlook toward women, would turn back the tide of growing rights. This feeling was part of a general resentment that uneducated naturalized citizens could vote while American-born women could not.

Their identification with the rapidly expanding farmers' organization was far greater than with the budding labor movement. The farmers, who had undergone a machine revolution less advanced than industry's, were inadequately represented in Congress. In the mid-sixties a co-operative association developed which by the depression years had grown powerful. By 1873 the Grange, a semisecret society with a Masonic type of ritual, had a membership of three-quarters of a million. What aroused Lucy and Henry's enthusiasm was that in the Granges women had complete equality with men.

They liked less the fact that southern Granges were for white farmers only, for they never swerved from the radicalism of their youth. And when, in the late seventies, the Chinese question came to the fore, they unequivocally supported the Chinese, attacking a judge who had decided that a Chinese man was not a citizen, indignant at the move in California to oust the "yellow" race. Chinese and women, the *Journal* declared, were now the two disenfranchised classes left in the nation. They were also consistent in their indignation at religious discrimination, never wavering in their basic tenet, the equality of man and of woman.

The woman suffrage movement had reached a plateau. In state referenda and in legislative votes it continued to show gains, though rarely winning a majority. There was every reason to suppose that with continued pressure this growth would steadily increase until it attained the desired end. Lucy's moods varied between hope and gloom as a favorable omen was followed by a defeat. After the Massachusetts House of Representatives turned down a suffrage petition, she commented bitterly that "they spent four times as many minutes in discussing the size of barrels of cranberries and the branding of boxes of fish, as they gave to the demand of Suffrage for women." But again, "The eternal forces, truth and right are on our side, and by their omnipotence, spite of all delay, and of all our mistakes, we shall yet have equal rights for women." In general the spirit of the *Journal* and the American Association was one of judicious optimism.

Throughout the world women were attaining many of the goals Lucy had dreamed of. In the mid-seventies the *Journal* noted two woman's rights papers in Italy, one in Geneva, a new paper in Germany and woman's papers even in Turkey and Roumania, though these two lasted only a brief time. Zurich University opened its doors to women. The University of Copenhagen admitted women, though from Denmark came the complaint that, after graduation, they were not permitted to practice their professions. To a young Peruvian lady asking to study law, the Minister of Justice there replied that Peru placed no restrictions on women. In India a medical school for women was opened, of crucial importance since Indian women and their children died unnecessarily rather than be attended by male physicians. In 1877 the *Journal* said that in Russia in the past few years 430 women had studied medicine. In 1878 it announced that London University, where education "goes far beyond that of any American institution for either sex," had been opened to women. In Austria, Holland and Sweden women with the required property qualifications voted in municipal elections.

In January 1876 Lucy wrote that, since 1870, the laws of almost every state had been radically changed in regard to women, that two-thirds of United States colleges accepted them, that in some churches they now voted with the congregations. That spring, when a bill for municipal suffrage was before the Massachusetts legislature, the Boston papers were in the main favorable or only mildly critical. The *Boston Daily Journal* felt that since this right had been granted to women in several European countries, "it would be singular if the State which is confessedly behind no others in the American Union for intelligence and general developement should not be ready for such a reform." The bill, debated for more than three sessions, lost in the senate by a small vote. In a few states women were already eligible to serve on school boards, though the fight to seat them in Boston was for a time valiantly resisted by the board's male members.

In 1878 New Hampshire became the first New England state to permit women to vote in school elections, and the next year the women of Massachusetts made the first small break in their disenfranchisement by winning the same right. The *Journal* occupied itself with teaching women how to register, how to pay the poll tax—there was much confusion over whether the amount was $1 or $2—or, if they were property owners, how to be sure their property was assessed in time for election. The paper proudly announced that Louisa M. Alcott was the first woman to register in Concord; but after Lucy herself registered, she was notified that her name would be "annulled" unless she signed herself Blackwell, "which," she told Henry, "I shall never do." So, sadly, with two precious principles in conflict, Lucy lost her vote.

Disappointingly too, because of shyness, indifference, the complications of registration and its cost, only a small proportion of eligible women went to the polls. In some places petty officials deliberately tried to keep women from even so limited a vote, and women went as often as six times to be assessed and then, on some technicality, found themselves debarred. One woman declared that public pressure in her town was so great that only she and one other woman dared go to the polls.

In 1880 New York State passed an even more limited school suffrage bill, and Vermont a more liberal one. In 1881 the poll tax for school suffrage was reduced in Massachusetts, and the voting process somewhat simplified. By 1883 the *Journal* announced that women in twelve states now voted in school elections.

On the national scene women now had an established place in public life. In 1879 Congress passed a bill permitting qualified women to practice before the Supreme Court. Mrs. Belva Lockwood, who had long fought for this right, was the first woman admitted to practice. Julia Ward Howe had inaugurated Mother's Day as a yearly peace festival. Women's congresses, peace societies, clubs, were normal in the social scene.

With this changed attitude toward women throughout the civilized world, what happened to delay the attainment of woman suffrage in the United States for forty years? The single most responsible element was probably the linking of woman suffrage with the temperance movement which, having for years jogged ineffectually along, erupted in the Midwest in the middle seventies. "Oh, the agony, the tears, the sleepless nights, the heart-breaking anguish that wives and mothers suffered during those long, bitter years of sorrow and silence, when few seemed to care that the demon had come into their houses and was doing his bloody work," wrote a historian of the temperance crusade. "Suddenly the world was startled by a flash of heavenly light. Hands of faith had touched the hem of power, and a mighty spiritual swirl came down upon the people."

The crusade, though encouraged by the churches, started almost spontaneously. Throughout the Midwest women organized themselves into praying bands which entered saloons when they were permitted to, and, when their way was barred, knelt on the sidewalk outside, to pray and sing hymns. Sometimes bands of women, lifted beyond prayer, entered saloons and smashed whisky barrels with axes. Sometimes even saloon keepers were wafted along by this hysteria. Early in 1874 the *Journal* reported thirty-seven cities and towns freed of liquor traffic; seventeen hundred and sixty-one saloons closed in Ohio, Indiana and Illinois; eight hundred liquor sellers "not only reformed but hopefully converted."

In December the *Journal* announced that delegates from temperance societies had met to form a Woman's National Christian Temperance Union which preferred prayer to politics and direct action to legislation. Yet the *Journal* continued to hail the woman's temperance movement as "a powerful auxiliary to the direct movement for the Enfranchisement of Women."

In the days just after the Civil War many antislavery leaders had been afraid to tie the Negro's fate to the unpopular woman's rights movement, and in the fifties temperance leaders had created a scandal rather than let Antoinette Brown speak at a temperance meeting. Even in 1878 the W.C.T.U. decided not to confound its campaign by the injection of woman suffrage. Yet the suffrage movement had always embraced both reforms. Indeed Susan Anthony and many others had come to the woman's movement by way of temperance. Newspaperwoman Jane Swisshelm and young Mrs. Abigail Scott Duniway, who was editing a woman's paper, *The New Northwest,* in Portland, Oregon, and almost singlehandedly building a suffrage organization there, expressed their fears of linking the suffrage cause with temperance. Mrs. Howe and Colonel Higginson were opposed in principle to prohibition. Higginson, though himself an abstainer, believed that abstinence should not be enforced by law. The other suffrage leaders continued to hail prohibition.

Henry congratulated women for having "left the 'sacred privacy of their homes,' generally with the approval of their husbands." But he pointed out that only by voting could they act effectively to attain prohibition. Hannah M. Tracy Cutler admitted that some manifestations of the crusade were "singular," but believed no one should criticize the effort to rescue men from the "satanic power" of alcohol. In the late seventies Mary A. Livermore, so closely identified with the *Journal* and woman suffrage, became president of the Massachusetts W.C.T.U. In 1880, when asked why suffragists did not join the prohibitionist ranks, a note in the *Journal,* signed *Ed.,* stated inaccurately that "Suffragists are all temperance people, but one great reform is quite as much as one set of people can undertake to carry." Yet they continued to carry the burden by insisting that women, if enfranchised, would inevitably vote for prohibition.

In 1875, after woman suffrage and the new constitution were defeated in the Michigan referendum, Henry had analyzed the defeat astutely enough. Not only had the "Tilton-Woodhull conspiracy culminated in a shameful scandal" at the crucial moment, but the liquor interests had persuaded the German and Irish populations to vote against woman suffrage which, if granted, would swing the state to prohibition. The *Journal* recorded that in Wisconsin, where the liquor interests were defeated, the saloon keepers boarded up their doors and hung up "articles of feminine wearing apparel" and placards reading "TEMPERANCE! PETTICOAT GOVERNMENT! ! ! GONE TO THE BLACK HILLS! ! !"

Why then did the *Journal* not advocate that the suffrage movement dissociate itself from temperance? Partly it was because this would have antagonized many of their supporters. Women flocked far more readily to temperance than to suffrage because, Lucy said, it is so much easier to see a drunkard than a principle. Partly, too, their support sprang from a principled belief in temperance and in the fact that wherever women banded together in militant action a woman's rights movement was bound to grow. But they also underestimated the liquor interests which, now aroused, organized nationwide campaigns to combat woman suffrage. They failed fully to realize that, with so much of the work of public pressure already done, the time had come when they must depend on votes to win their cause, and the votes were in the hands of men, most of whom cared more for their glass of beer than they did for the right of women to full citizenship.

Chapter Twenty-five

The *Journal* was caught up in other crusades which bore the stamp of Lucy's girlhood and Oberlin's moral reform. In 1877 the Reverend S. W. Bush, guest editor of the paper during an absence of Henry's, became alarmed about advertisements of immoral books which were being sent to boys and girls. "Mr. Anthony Comstock," he wrote, "is engaged in a work which deserves the aid of every well wisher of society . . . the suppression of vile literature." He appealed for funds to help in this fine undertaking. In 1879, when Sarah Bernhardt was to appear in the United States, this same gentleman warned American women that Bernhardt, as the unmarried mother of four children, assailed the "sanctity of marriage"; and the *Journal's* editors supported his opinion. Lucy herself wrote to inform Boston University that coeducational Oberlin used expurgated texts of the classics, "as much in the interest of the boys as of the girls. It is a thousand pities that there should be a spot on the soul of either." She suggested that Boston University do the same.

Lucy and Henry worked as vigorously as ever to keep the issue of suffrage before the people. Lucy, a roly-poly lady approaching sixty, dashed from meeting to meeting, addressed legislature after legislature, edited her newspaper and often wrote as many as three articles a week for it. In September 1877—woman suffrage was to be placed before the voters of Colorado in October—Lucy and Henry traveled through that state, speaking in a different town each day, riding in rickety carriages over hazardous mountain roads to reach some small mining town. It was like the days of 1867 in Kansas. The results were much the same too.

Woman suffrage received only about a third of the popular vote.

Though the fresh-faced girl was lost in the matronly woman, Lucy was still an appealing speaker with an entrancing voice. A report of a meeting in Detroit said that she came "into *rapport* with her audience readily, and was the life and magnetism of the platform."

The mid-seventies presented a dramatic setting for protest in the centennials of the Boston Tea Party, Bunker Hill and the Declaration of Independence. "The opportunity cannot come to us again," Lucy said, "to make the contrast so vivid between the men who, a hundred years ago, fought and bled and died to secure the right to govern themselves, and the men who today deny to all women the right to govern themselves, and at the same time praise those old dead heroes."

"If it was tyranny to tax the Colonists a century ago, and deny them representation," she wrote to Mrs. Campbell, "it is tyranny to do the same to women now."

In 1873, when the Boston Tea Party was celebrated in suffrage tea parties throughout New England, Lucy repeated the theme that women, disenfranchised, were classed with "felons, fools, Indians, lunatics, and Jefferson Davis." The anniversary of the colonists' refusal to pay taxes led to dramatic rebellion on the part of a few courageous landowners. Most notable were two old ladies of Glastonbury, Connecticut, Abby and Julia Smith, survivors of a family of five maiden sisters. In their youth they had worked for abolition; Abby had attended an early woman's rights convention; Julia had taught at Emma Willard's Troy Academy. Otherwise they had led unnoteworthy lives on their substantial property for nearly eighty years, until they decided to pit themselves against the tax collector. Then, imbued with the rugged pioneering quality of their ancestors, they continued their fight over years during which town and tax collectors entered into a combination to harass them. Though the law required that movable goods be disposed of first, eleven acres of their best land was sold, without bidding, to a neighbor who for years had been trying to obtain it. And this to satisfy a tax of forty dollars! Their most valuable livestock was driven away and sold. Refused the right to speak in town meeting, they addressed their fellow citizens from a cart in the street. "Did England do anything to our forefathers in the way of taxation without representation so iniquitous as this?" Finally, when a tax was placed on bank deposits, Julia, preferring to spend her money in any way other than taxes, published at her own expense a translation she had made of the Bible.

Perhaps the most astonishing episode in this saga occurred in 1879. The year before, Abby Smith, the more aggressive of the sisters, had died at the age of eighty-one, leaving Julia, aged eighty-six, alone. On her deathbed Abby asked Julia, reluctant to continue the battle without her support, not to give up the fight, and Julia obediently continued her lonely work. In 1879 this amazing lady married Mr. Amos A. Parker, described by the *Hartford Times* as a good-sized, broad-shouldered man in ruddy health. Mr. Parker explained his energy by the fact that he had never used tobacco or liquor and drank neither tea nor coffee. It was Mr. Parker's third marriage. Miss Julia was the only one of the five Smith sisters ever to marry.

Stephen and Abby Kelley Foster had allowed their home to be sold for $100 in taxes. The law gave them two years to redeem it, and when Foster paid $2400 to recover his property he was ridiculed by the press. In reply, he maintained that he had never said he and his wife would not pay taxes if forced to, but that they intended to continue to make the government collect their taxes by legal process. The Worcester officials, he admitted, had been "very courteous and kind," and had "shown none of the contemptible meanness exhibited by those of Glastonbury toward the Smith sisters." Shortly thereafter the Foster house was again sold for taxes, and the entire process commenced once more.

Of the Centennial Celebration of 1776 held in Philadelphia, Lucy wrote in her initial indignation, "I say that women should take no part in it. Let them shut their doors and darken their windows on that day, and let a few of the most matronly women dress themselves in black and stand at the corners of the streets where the largest procession is to pass, bearing banners . . . 'We are governed without our consent; we are taxed without representation.' "

Women had been asked to prepare a pavilion of which they bore the work and expense, but they did not otherwise share in the centennial. When the pavilion opened, Julia Ward Howe found it "very encouraging." Besides the needlework "which might have been anticipated," it included inventions patented by women, some excellent wood carving, exhibits by European women and an art gallery which "showed more effort than achievement."

Lucy had asked for space to exhibit women's tax protests; but, since to most of its descendants any successful revolution is the last, she was told "that anything which savored of 'protest' was not suited to the time and place." The committee finally consented to accept a frame about two feet square; but when the exhibit opened, the "Protests of Women against Taxation without Representation" was hung so high that it could not be read.

On July 3 in Philadelphia the American Association held a meeting to celebrate the New Jersey Constitutional Convention which in 1776 had enfranchised unmarried women and widows in that state. The honors of the centennial, however, went to Susan Anthony. Lucy reported that "Miss Anthony's society held a public meeting" on the Fourth, and read a *Woman's Declaration of Rights* and *Articles of Impeachment against the Government of the United States.* "By some means Miss Anthony and Mrs. Joslyn Gage obtained access to the platform where the great National celebration was being made and presented . . . the above Declaration. . . . So quietly was the whole thing done, that very few even on the platform saw or heard anything. . . .

But the fact received wide and favorable notice by the press."

In these years *The Woman's Journal* continued to wage wars long ago begun. The debate about coeducation went on, though on a far different level. In 1873 "more than seventy American Colleges and Universities [were] now open alike to young men and women." Coeducation was spreading in other countries too. Yet so eminent an educator as Harvard's President Eliot refurbished the old argument that doctors agreed women could not bear the stress of mental labor. The *Journal* was therefore delighted when in 1876 the committee to award Harvard's annual prize for a medical essay—the contestants' names being sealed—declared a woman doctor the winner. The assigned subject, resulting from the current debate on sex in education, had been "Do women require mental and bodily rest during menstruation, and to what extent?" In 1879 Harvard, while refusing a proffered ten thousand dollars rather than admit women to its medical school, opened a department where women would receive equal but separate undergraduate education.

Though the *Journal* believed separate education of the sexes to be wrong, it welcomed the new little colleges of the early seventies, Smith and Wellesley. Secondary education for girls was still so inferior that Smith College had rejected all but eighteen of the hundred applicants for its entering class. Even these eighteen overflowed its small dormitory. Vassar had had to offer preparatory classes because most applicants were unprepared for college studies. In 1878 Elizabeth Stanton's daughter Harriot was graduated from Vassar with high honors. Next year Antoinette Brown Blackwell's daughter Florence was reported making her mark as a successful elocutionist.

Another old battle had been revived. Though men's clothes had through the century become simpler and more comfortable, women's were, if possible, more cumbersome and lavish than in bloomer days. In the early seventies skirts were narrower and dresses very tight, with a bustle or draped skirt trailing on the ground. Charming, romantic, feminine as ever, they made activity a burden and required suffocating corseting which continued to be a menace in an age when tuberculosis was rampant and childbearing still hazardous. Now the New England Women's Club and the *Journal* launched a fresh effort to free women from the bondage of fashion. They had learned much from the humiliations of bloomer days. "Any singular and pronounced style of external dress would inevitably limit us in our good work, and very likely defeat it altogether."

The club had an exhibition of clothes which were simple, graceful and not eccentric. Their most important reform was to take the weight from the waist and hips and place it on the shoulders. Their designer, the club announced, had worn such garments for years without causing excitement, though—since legs must be covered—she could not eliminate some sort of pantalette. However, tucked into boots for street wear, her version hardly looked like pants at all. Controversy raged about a name for a new loose undergarment. Should it be a *chemiloon,* a *shimmerloon,* a *chemelette* or an *underall?*

Amelia Bloomer, still an optimist in dress reform, wrote to Lucy that Mrs. Livermore had recommended a skirt supporter with "straps for the shoulders, and a belt around the waist in which hooks were inserted on which hang the skirts." Mrs. Bloomer would like to know where the garments were manufactured, and become an agent for their sale.

Two new crusades which had been agitating English suffragists engaged the *Journal* in the late seventies and early eighties. One was a campaign for laws, like the bill passed by Parliament in 1879, protecting wives from physical assault by brutal husbands; the other was a battle against laws licensing houses of prostitution. The protection such laws afforded immoral men, while condemning the women who shared their illicit conduct, outraged suffragists. In England Elizabeth Blackwell dedicated years to achieving the repeal of a national "Contagious [Venereal] Diseases Act." In the United States Doctor Emily, aided by the *Journal,* tried to arouse public opinion against the passage of laws "in accord with the European system of regulation."

How to organize political pressure was a chief concern of the Massachusetts Association. Through the seventies their tactics fluctuated. They formed an abortive political party, decided such action was premature, then turned to political clubs in various townships. "Organize! Organize!" the *Journal* urged, to help elect friends of woman suffrage. In November 1873 Lucy and Henry spoke at eleven political conventions throughout the state, enrolling 1087 members. In 1877, against opposition within their own ranks, they organized a party which decided to endorse the prohibitionists, firm supporters of woman suffrage. Next year they again abandoned the idea of a political party. By the early eighties Lucy and Henry had decided that pressure within the major parties was more effective than support of single-issue parties like the prohibitionists, and were once more advocating support of the Republicans. Of the Democrats Henry wrote, "A party which is in fellowship with the bulldozers of the South will be equally in fellowship with the bulldozers of women."

The antisuffragists still insisted that politics would "unsex women," that women, who could not bear arms, should not vote. Some years later the *Journal* outlined their conflicting arguments. Women's votes would undermine the structure of government; their vote would not change anything. Women's voting would cause dissension in the home; they would vote as their husbands and fathers told them to. Women were too emotional for politics; women were too indifferent.

Yet even here were signs of changing times, for when in 1879 Francis Parkman turned from writing history to criticizing current events in an attack on woman suffrage, the *North American Review,* in which his article appeared, asked a group of leading suffragists, including Lucy Stone, to answer him. The controversy ran to fifty pages in that most reputable of magazines; and the *Journal* mentioned that newspapers throughout the nation had denounced Parkman. Replying to another attack, Lucy commented that "ever since Adam found it convenient to lay the blame of a certain transaction, in which he had a large share, upon Eve, there has been a long line of his male descendants, who have followed his example at every possible opportunity."

In 1881 Queen Victoria, at the urging of Sir William Jenner, declined to be Lady Patroness of the International Medical Congress in London unless physicians of her own sex were excluded; but this extraordinary Victorian move was only necessary because the arrangments committee had decided to admit women.

The same year a young Massachusetts Republican, opposed to seating Mrs. Livermore as a delegate to the Republican State Convention, had the misfortune to ask whether, if a "trained monkey" had been sent, it would have been accepted as a delegate. The young man lost the nomination for state senator he was seeking and was dropped from the State Central Committee. His chief supporter in this move to unseat Mrs. Livermore was young Henry Cabot Lodge. That fall Mr. Lodge was defeated for state senator by a progressive young Democrat, the first Democratic senator elected from that district in ten years.

Chapter Twenty-six

Throughout her life Lucy's appearance had amazed strangers who expected to encounter some large and aggressive female. At sixty her appearance deviated more than ever from the popular concept of a strong-minded woman. Composed in manner, round-faced, round-bodied, she was the most motherly-looking of women. Lately she had begun to wear a lace cap on her head and a shawllike lace collar over her simple dark dresses. These she abandoned at places like Martha's Vineyard for a red shawl and a captain's hat.

Mrs. Doris Mayhew, widow of Samuel Blackwell's grandson by adoption, recalls her as "one of the nicest looking ladies of that age there was"; and Mrs. Anna Belden, daughter of George Blackwell, says that "Nobody who saw Aunt Lucy at home in those days could even have imagined her on a lecture platform."

The impression was not deceiving. In those moments when Lucy's commitment was not driving her, she was indeed the most domestic of women. Her letters to Henry were, as always, full of homey details. "The lower lot is plowed, and the peas are up. The milk comes in regularly and you must not forget, in spite of your load of care, that the sky is blue, and the birds sing, and the spring has come, and we have a good daughter and many other things to be thankful for."

Years after Lucy's death, one of her servants remembered her almost with reverence. Her reminiscences of Lucy are a paean of praise to a woman who seemed more a mother than a mistress. "Mrs. Stone wouldn't let me wear corsets. She used to say, 'Mary, you have only one gizzard and you must save that.' " Wages were low, but "she paid the very highest," even while her maid was being trained. She "urged me to go to night school and when I wouldn't she taught me herself. . . . If I was sick she sat up with me herself."

More remarkable is the story of Mrs. Hagar, a poverty-stricken widow who, in the late 1880's, was dying in a home for consumptives near Boston. Fearful for her two adolescent daughters, the unhappy woman told the home's matron that she would die content if she could find a good woman she had worked for when she first came from Germany. It had been in New Jersey, and the woman's name was Lucy Stone.

When Lucy learned of the strange destiny that had followed her over the years, she arranged for one of the girls to be taken in by a woman who brought her up. Henry and Lucy took the other, Beth Hagar, who lived with them as household helper "to take steps" for Lucy. "The little German girl," Henry wrote to Alice in the summer of 1890, "is a very helpful, gentle, bright child, and suits your mother." Lucy and Henry never legally adopted Beth—indeed, none of the Blackwells legally adopted the children they took as their own—but they came to consider her their child; and even Alice, who resented her parents' affection for this interloper, remained her friend after Lucy and Henry died.

By 1890 Lucy was in need of someone to save her steps. Late in the 1870's she had begun to suffer from the rheumatism which plagued her for the rest of her life, and from the constant colds and sore throats which forced her to leave her work, and sometimes her home, for long periods. In the spring of 1880 one of these infections was so severe that from New York, where she had gone to recuperate, she wrote to Alice that she was spitting blood. Not unnaturally, in those days when death from tuberculosis was so common, she believed she was dying. In 1880 Alice was twenty-two, a junior at Boston University, and her parents' confidante on many subjects. "I am not at all afraid for myself," Lucy wrote. "I should like to stay till you are older, and for the need papa has of me, and may be I shall." One of the results of these throat infections was that Lucy's voice, never loud, could no longer be heard in large halls.

In 1881 she confided to her friend Margaret Campbell another symptom of advancing years. "I am not sick. . . . But I have had turns of something. I do not know what. A sense of faintness runs all through me, lasting not more than half a minute, but while it lasts, I feel as though I was dissolving, just as you see milk dropped in water spread all through it. . . . A week ago Thursday it came upon me twice . . . and again on Saturday evening while I sat quietly by the sitting room fire."

In the light of her declining health, the record of Lucy's activities throughout these years is extraordinary. Nor had her psychological problems diminished. "Every meeting she undertakes to get up," Alice told Kitty, "gives her several weeks of anxiety, blues and general distress." But since, without her work for women, survival would be meaningless to Lucy, she continued to travel and speak as best she could.

In fact, in the late seventies and early eighties, her burden increased, because Henry was again engaged in a project for manufacturing beet sugar. How strongly Henry's childhood memory of his father lured him irresistibly to such endeavors, how much it was his reformer's belief, as it had been his father's, that the success of beet sugar would end slavery in countries which raised sugar cane, how large the hope of making a fortune loomed in his plans, Henry himself never seemed to know. Whatever the reasons, he was enthralled by this renewed enterprise, though it took him endlessly from home and caused him untold worry. For a while the ample grounds of the Dorchester house were devoted to growing beets for Henry's experiments, experiments so successful that in 1877 he was granted a patent on the basis of which he proceeded to set up a manufacturing business.

In 1878, as their summer vacation, the Blackwell-Stones took a nine-day boat trip to St. John in New Brunswick. As always they combined pleasure with suffrage, and this time with Henry's sugar business as well. The *Journal* mentioned Henry as a founder of the Maine Beet Sugar Company, and its treasurer. Henry was full of optimism. In October he sent Lucy a telegram from Maine: "Beet sugar manufacture a success slavery in Cuba is doomed." The next June the paper reported the business an unexpected success, and the following winter Henry's company was "working up about 150 tons of beets a day."

Henry was away on May 1, 1879, their twenty-fourth wedding anniversary. "How long a time we have jogged on pulling together!" Lucy wrote. "Well, the last part has been much the best to me. May it grow better and better for both of us till the end!" He was away all that summer. From the earliest days of their marriage he had planned to take Lucy to visit his English homeland. Now, forty-seven years after he came to America, he found an added excuse for the trip because in Germany he could buy machinery for making sugar. So, in the summer of her sophomore year at college, Alice took her mother's place and went with her father to England.

To Lucy, almost singlehandedly editing the *Journal* and keeping the suffrage association alive, Henry wrote that his exploration "into the dead past . . . has given me inexpressible pleasure and pain." He had gone to his old home in Bristol with his sister Anna, whom he had not seen in thirty-seven years, reliving his childhood with the help of her older eyes and her memory of landmarks he had forgotten. To Sam he described Anna as having the "same bright face . . . her hair white but abundant and beautiful, an anxious shade of expression, but graceful and well-dressed as of old."

While her father went to Germany Alice stayed in England with her Aunt Elizabeth. It must have been an exciting adventure for a wide-eyed, intellectual young woman. Her distinguished aunt numbered among her friends Florence Nightingale, Herbert Spencer, George Eliot, Dante Gabriel Rossetti and Barbara Leigh Smith, prime mover of the first Feminist Committee twenty-two years earlier.

Henry's return in the fall of 1879 found him more than ever involved in the beet sugar industry, and the next years were like the early days of their marriage when Henry was, though rebelliously, traveling about on that earlier financial-philanthropic enterprise of opening farmers' libraries. Henry's passionate bitterness at his absences was lacking now. Lucy wrote the same long, affectionate letters to her "dearly beloved" and her "dear little boy." She was as busy as she had ever been, and by 1880 appeared on the masthead as sole editor of the paper, with Colonel Higginson, Mrs. Howe, Mrs. Livermore and Henry as contributing editors. She was less lonesome, though, than in those early days, for Alice was now a companion who already helped with the *Journal* and on her graduation from college in 1881 devoted all her time to the paper.

The world was still not Alice's oyster. She remained a shy girl, easily wounded. The Victorian morality that bound her mother and the *Journal* held her too, and in 1899 she described to Kitty a ballet in *Lucia di Lammermoor* as "utterly uncalled for, having no connection with the plot. . . . I was almost ashamed to look, though I was alone. The first time Mother saw it, she says she put her head down on the seat and wouldn't look."

For Lucy and Henry there were many elements in Henry's financial venture reminiscent of their early days together: the extremes of hope and despair, the ultimate failure. In March 1880 he wrote from Maine, "We cleared last year about $12,000 over and above my salary, including the State Bounty [of $7,000], which shows that the business might be made profitable if we could get an abundance of Beets even at last years prices." But only a day later he admitted that they couldn't get acreage, prices had risen and the business would probably collapse.

Growing sugar beets was difficult, and the Maine farmers who had been induced by free seed and subsidies to try it returned to more familiar crops. A Canadian attempt failed too. By the middle of April the situation was so precarious that Henry had put his real estate in Lucy's name so that it could not be taken for debts if the company failed.

Meanwhile the necessity for making money had grown because of family pressures. Samuel and Antoinette Blackwell had a large family and so little mony that in 1879, with her children growing up, Antoinette reluctantly decided to return to the ministry, even if it meant being separated from Sam for a while. Henry gave Sam an opportunity to sell beets, but he sold almost none. Anna in England was old and needed money too, and because she had dedicated her youthful years to supporting the family after their father died, Henry felt he must help her now. There were problems closer to home. In 1880, just after she became the *Journal*'s sole editor, Lucy's health was so bad that for several months no article of hers appeared. She went to Delaware to recuperate that spring, and wrote to Henry that the countryside along the Brandywine was beautiful with buds and flowers. Alice was with her. "Alice gets frequent communications from the girls at college, and goes on with her lessons with praiseworthy persistency, while her care of me is a miracle of thoughtfulness. She *is* a good child. She enjoys herself, takes a hand at anything that is going, croquet [and other games], and walks off for long walks, but not in the evening." Even when Lucy returned to Boston and her writing, she did not immediately resume her editorial duties.

She kept urging Henry to give up the sugar business, but in the spring of 1881 he had reorganized the company—"I am to have my salary $5000 for 2 years"—and moved operations from Maine to Schenectady, New York. Lucy, at work in Boston, wrote that she hoped at least to spend her vacation with him. He answered, "If God has given me a wife and child who love me so much, I must 'buckle to' and be worthy of them. Whatever may be the issue of this strange half-crazy infatuation which has dragged me away from home and happiness and comfort and peace of mind—it will not be long in coming, and whether the enterprise succeeds or fails it will restore me to you." But the next year the grounds of their house were planted with sorghum, a grain from which he hoped to obtain sugar.

"Ever since supper," Lucy wrote to Alice, "Papa has been at his sugar. He brought out a little hand centrifugal. *He* turned at it, and I turned, and Maggie [the current servant] turned, and now past bed-time, the sugar is separated from the syrup and the triumph is complete. Sorghum *will* make sugar."

That September of 1882 Lucy and Henry again crossed the country to conventions in Wisconsin and Nebraska. Both suffrage associations were holding their conventions in Omaha that year, because a suffrage amendment was to be submitted to Nebraska voters. Lucy and Henry planned to stay for ten days to campaign for the amendment. From their tour of the state Lucy wrote to Alice, "We have good audiences, but in this country the foreign population is nine-tenths of the whole, and there is not a ghost of a chance to carry the Amendment. . . . We would not have staid if we had known how it was." Even so, they extended their trip to more than a month and spoke in twenty-five counties. Mrs. Cutler lectured for a month in Nebraska too, as did Susan Anthony and other members of the National. In these changing times one hundred and twenty-five Nebraska newspapers supported the amendment, yet it was defeated, as Lucy had predicted.

Meanwhile Alice was editing the *Journal.* By now in any case she was signing her initials to the Literary Column and writing weekly articles in her clear, fresh style. Her reply to an attack on independent women might well be taken as a tribute to her mother. "The woman who is described is independent, but has neither tact, common sense, nor consideration for other people's feelings, that, and not her independence is the matter with her. The woman who thinks for herself and follows her own conscience and convictions, provided only she has good judgment, will 'diffuse more happiness about her', and a higher kind of happiness, than the most charming woman in the world who has no independence of character." It was one of her early ventures in the polemical writing characteristic of her, which combined stringent attacks on the enemy with gentleness toward her friends.

When her parents returned Alice continued to share their editorial tasks; and in January 1883 Lucy's, Henry's and Alice's names began to appear on the masthead as joint editors. The following New Year the editors announced that the paper "owes no man anything except good will."

Turning from the school suffrage victory to the battle for municipal suffrage, the Massachusetts suffragists were harassed by increasingly militant remonstrants, the same strange manifestation which appears in Switzerland today, where women assume the political burden of imploring voters not to force them into political activity. In the 1880's the Massachusetts antisuffragists, ably abetted by such men as the young lawyer, Louis D. Brandeis, carried their campaign to a national level. A small number, with disproportionate money and influence, they vulgarly boasted of "wealth and social position." The *Journal* rightly saw the increased resistance as a sign of the growth of prosuffrage feeling, yet the appearance of such impressive objectors at legislative hearings was a deterrent to the passage of suffrage bills.

The *Journal,* continuing to waver in political tactics, in 1882 found itself in an almost untenable position. Victoria Woodhull's mentor, General Butler, was running for governor of Massachusetts, and he and his party both declared themselves in favor of woman suffrage. Lucy, Henry and Alice, though maintaining that they would not back a prosuffrage candidate who had no other virtues, enthusiastically endorsed Butler. Colonel Higginson, writing his thoughtful lead articles with clocklike regularity week after week, was shocked at their support of an irresponsible demagogue, and after Butler's election wrote a violent attack on the new governor, condemning his inaugural speech as misinformed on every subject and ridiculous on woman suffrage. For some time there had been minor disagreements between Higginson and Henry or Lucy. Now, below Higginson's article, appeared a biting reply signed Eds. W. J. It emphasized the policy which Henry and Lucy had now adopted, of supporting men of either major party who were in favor of votes for women. The vehemence of the attack was too much for Higginson. Next week the paper announced that his commitments had forced him to stop writing for a while; and it was two months before his weekly article reappeared.

After the defeat in Nebraska Henry had reached another important political conclusion. Though legislative votes on woman suffrage were increasingly favorable, and laws improving woman's status constantly passed, no popular referendum had yet been successful. Apparently legislatures were more progressive than their constituents, and suffragists should concentrate on them, redoubling their efforts to win the vote in municipal and Presidential elections, rights in the power of legislatures to confer. This faith was strengthened when in November 1883 the legislature of Washington Territory passed a bill striking the word male from the voting laws. This, the first major victory in years, was short-lived. The courts declared the law unconstitutional. It was repassed in strengthened form, again declared unconstitutional, and in 1888 popular vote abolished woman suffrage in Washington when it was about to become a state. This was a second reversal of the few suffrage gains. In 1870 the Territory of Utah had given its women the vote. In 1887 the National Congress, in a battle against Mormon influence, withdrew the vote from Mormon and gentile women alike.

Henry had less clearly formulated his views on another problem. When friends of suffrage, among them Charles Robinson of Kansas, again warned that linking the woman movement to prohibition had defeated the amendment in Nebraska, Henry agreed. But he continued to urge prohibitionists to work for woman suffrage as the surest road to temperance.

On labor Lucy continued as reactionary as ever. In 1882 she and Antoinette argued at a meeting that workers should be educated so that they might be freed from "the dominations of unions, which claim the same wages for each man, so that he who can shovel five loads of dirt can only have the pay of the man who can shovel one load."

Yet a year later a strike of telegraph workers was so differently greeted by Henry that the difference can be explained only by the fact that women's rights were involved. Henry hailed the strike as hastening the "development of the organization of labor for the great impending battle of the people against the monopolies. This battle will be one of the hardest ever fought, but its results will be beneficent." Later Lucy wrote that the strike had failed and that, though many men had been re-employed, no striking women had been taken back. The *Journal* was attempting to help them find employment.

In July 1883 Lucy, Henry and Nette were in the Midwest on a mission which must have delighted the two women. They were to be speakers at the Oberlin jubilee. Henry submitted a minority report to Alice. "It is my impression (entre nous) that I shall be the worst bored man at Oberlin who ever visited it at a Commencement–One day I could stand; yea two;–but a whole week of contact with people who believe in hell and also mention the devil will, I fear, be too much of these good things for a person of impaired spiritual digestion like myself."

The occasion belonged to Lucy and Nette. Lucy found hardly a trace of the old poverty-stricken Oberlin. The college square was filled with buildings now and shaded by trees. The greater change was that Lucy, refused permission to read her essay at graduation, was now an invited speaker at the great Fourth of July celebration. She spoke in praise of Oberlin old and new, catalogued women's gains in the fifty years of the school's existence and begged Oberlin to support woman suffrage as it had woman's education.

There was triumph for Nette too, when the alumni enrolled her and one of her classmates as graduates of the theological school, though they had still not received the degrees for which they had qualified so long ago.

After her parents' return Alice went for her usual summer visit to Aunt Emily at Martha's Vineyard. A letter from her father to "Dear Alicekins" renews a picture of Lucy still burdened by a sense of inadequacy, still perhaps uncertain whether she met the standards of the cultivated family into which she had married twenty-eight years before. "Will there be a week when there will be any spare room where your Mother might be made comfortable . . . ? I rather think it would be well for such an invitation to be sent to her as she may otherwise feel that she *has not been invited*. For myself, I wish most heartily that she could be removed from the cares of housekeeping and paper pottering—for a week—by an absence somewhere. She will never take any holiday here." And this appeal came just after a doctor friend had prescribed the dry climate of New Mexico for Lucy's troublesome throat, not damp, foggy island air.

By this time Lucy understood the meaning of those symptoms she had described to Margaret Campbell two years earlier. "I have a heart trouble," she told her now. "When I lie on my right side, I feel such a weight hang in the left side. . . . Dr. Emily says . . . there is a weakness in the muscles that should send the blood onward. . . . I have too a trouble with my kidneys."

Lucy was growing old. Most of her old reformist friends were gone, and in 1884 two more were lost. Wendell Phillips died; Alice said it was the only time she ever heard her mother sob aloud, like a little girl. The other loss, not caused by death, was in its way sadder. Thomas Wentworth Higginson, who almost thirty years before had performed Lucy and Henry's unique marriage ceremony, resigned from the American Association and *The Woman's Journal.* Lucy's statement that he had resigned without explanation was disingenuous indeed. No one who followed the *Journal* could have doubted that his resignation was the result of a bitter political disagreement.

When, in the Presidential contest of 1884, the Democrats had nominated Grover Cleveland and the Republicans James G. Blaine, many Republicans, unable to stomach Blaine's unsavory political reputation, supported Cleveland. Higginson was among them. It was a scandal-ridden campaign. Very early it was disclosed that Cleveland had an illegitimate teen-aged son, and this charge of immorality was blown up into claims of perpetual debauchery and drunkenness. The level of political thought was exemplified by torchlight processions which chanted, "Ma, ma, where's my pa? Gone to the White House, ha, ha, ha."

Into this morass of charges Lucy fearlessly stepped. If Cleveland was a despoiler of women, he must be dropped as a candidate; if the charges were false, their authors must be sued for libel. When Cleveland refused to enter into the controversy, the *Journal* morally kept the immoral debate alive, Lucy writing article after article based on the unspoken premise that all women were pure unless defiled by impure men. Higginson, horrified to find mudslinging in the chaste pages of the *Journal,* indicated that Cleveland's record of public service was admirable while Blaine's was not, and that in a President political virtue was the more important. He even hinted that in a sexual lapse a man and woman might be equally responsible.

The lady suffragists disagreed. "We must regard the effort

to place him at the head of the government," wrote a leader of the American, "as an indignity offered to the women of this nation which ought not soon to be forgotten." And Lucy said, "Women must be opposed, at all other cost, to that which is the destruction of the home. They know with an unerring instinct that the purity and safety of the home means purity and safety to the State and Nation."

The disagreement between T. W. H. and L. S. grew sharper, until, the election over, Higginson resigned from the paper he had served so conscientiously for fifteen years; and Lucy expressed annoyance that Higginson had regularly been paid six hundred dollars a year by a paper "so poor that HBB and I gave all our time for nine years without compensation." The *Journal* announced that Colonel Higginson would write a column for *Harper's*. It republished long excerpts from these columns, and Higginson did appear from time to time at suffrage meetings, but the close bond was broken. Throughout the controversy Henry had remained silent, but just before election day he reaffirmed his allegiance to the Republicans and warned defectors that Cleveland could be elected only by suppression of freedmen's votes in the South.

Now Lucy's contributions to the *Journal,* though still many and vigorous, were fewer and shorter than formerly. Her health grew steadily worse. In December 1885—she and Henry had just returned from a lecture tour in Indiana, Minnesota and Michigan—she was crippled with rheumatism, and a month later could not attend a local convention because of a severe cold. This seesaw of activity and illness expressed a courage no less striking than that of her early life, for she must have known that there was less hope of conquering the enemies of old age and illness than there had been fifty years before of changing an intransigent social system.

In the summer of 1886 there was a reunion at the Dorchester house which made the passage of time very clear to

Lucy. A tiny group of surviving antislavery fighters came together. There was Samuel May, Mr. and Mrs. Samuel Sewall, Elizabeth Buffum Chace, leader now of the Rhode Island suffragists, Miss Southwick and Abby Kelley Foster. Representing their dead father were the four Garrison sons. Six months later Abby Foster was dead, and Lucy was commenting sadly that "the group of last summer will never meet again."

"I long," she told Margaret Campbell that fall, "for younger hands and for personal release from the work. I suffer with rheumatism and I am near 70 years old, and that is time to rest." The younger hands were reaching out to help, not only her own daughter, but such newcomers as the Reverend Anna H. Shaw, an indefatigable speaker, and Garrison's son and namesake, a dedicated worker for woman suffrage. In January 1887 Alice inaugurated a new and successful service which sent suffrage news items free to newspapers throughout the country. In February she announced the response to her *Woman's Column* to be "almost alarmingly large," as several hundred papers had already agreed to publish weekly suffrage columns.

Two months after her discouraged letter to Mrs. Campbell, Lucy was again in the West, and wrote to Alice that in Iowa in cold November she and Henry had reached a town at 5:00 A.M., rested and gone to a scheduled meeting; but in the spring of 1887 she was so ill that she had to go for several months to Thomasville, Georgia, where George Blackwell and his family spent the winter. George's wife Emma was Lucy's own niece, daughter of her sister Sarah.

Lucy was so sick when she arrived that the sense of death overtook her again, and from "a thousand miles away" she wrote to Harry, "For the abundant and unselfish work you have done for women, Harry dear, you know how thoroughly I appreciate it and how grateful I am for it. Few men would have done it, leaving business, friends, pleasure for it! . . . I wish I could have made it more agreable [sic], or less hard, but it could not be easy because it was all up-stream against wind and tide."

A few weeks later she wrote to Alice, "My pain from rheumatism is nothing compared to what it was at home"; and this respite had already led her to activity. Invited to speak on woman's rights, she had suited her "speech to beginners and the locality," with such success that a month later she contemplated organizing a small suffrage center.

She visited a Negro school taught by two Yankee women, "excellent women, but so unfit for the place!" " 'Do you believe in Gawd?' " she quoted them. " 'If you do not believe in Gawd you will go to h-e-l-l.' " Though the lesson was geography, the women made no attempt to teach anything. Yet when Lucy herself told the pupils about Yellowstone Park, "The whole school lighted up with interest, eager and all alive, showing how far removed they were from the dull stupid set they appeared to be before the ghastly solemn face of their two pious teachers." She went to the Negro church too. "The pastor, a tall yellow man, hopped about a great deal trying to keep his congregation still. 'Now if you must cough, cough now all you want to and then stop,' said he. Whereupon a volume of coughs swelled up till he said 'There, there, that is enough. . . . Recollect what I told you before about manners. . . . We have done better since emancipation than any other race ever did—so mind your manners.' . . . Every person there seemed respectable. . . . But they are utterly poor. And the whites here do not want them to learn from books. They like to have them inferior. . . . As long as the blacks are content to be inferior there is no trouble."

Lucy's letters included detailed instructions about scrubbing window screens, cleaning the cedar closet, and washing shelves. She worried too about Alice and Henry carrying the burden she herself had placed upon them, the burden they were to carry throughout their lives. Hearing that Henry had traveled to a school suffrage meeting, she wrote to Alice, "Papa's letter telling me of his hurried trip to N.J. . . . show[s] me that in spite of my years, and my rheumatics, and my adipose, I may be left a widow to mourn a man who was hurried to death." And again, "It is a great immortal work, and well worth weariness and fatigue. Nevertheless I do not want the sole daughter of my heart to be drawn to death in it, nor the man whose name I do not take harried to death by it–"

Henry had other concerns as well. The year before, he had advertised for sale three modern houses each with bathroom, stationary tubs and range. He was still attempting to manufacture sugar; and that summer, when Alice was traveling with Aunt Emily in Europe, Lucy told her, apparently without impatience or skepticism, about a scheme "to get sugar out of molasses at an infinitesmal cost that they are now trying for."

Lucy was again hard at work editing the *Journal* and journeying about New England to speak at suffrage meetings, though illness had prevented her, for the first time in eighteen years, from attending the annual convention of the New England Suffrage Association. Yet, encouraged because that year Kansas had become the first state to grant women municipal suffrage and New Jersey the fourteenth to give them school suffrage, she wrote, "It matters little now. The workers in the cause are a host."

To these workers Lucy Stone had become a tradition. After a visit to Oberlin she wrote to Alice, "Old and young women have kissed and thanked me and some brought their children, telling them to remember they had shaken hands with me–all was for love of our cause which they knew I had served."

Chapter Twenty-seven

"My dear child," Lucy wrote, "To-morrow is to be my seventieth birthday. . . . I trust my Mother sees and knows how glad I am to have been born, and at a time when there was so much that needed help, at which I could 'lend a hand.' Dear old Mother! She had a hard life, and was sorry she had another girl to share and bear the hard life of a woman. But I am wholly glad that I came, and she is too, if she sees. . . .

"It seems all a wonder, and not possible that I am really three score and ten! It seems a little while ago that I skipped with the lamb and ran down hill, bounding like a cork, my flesh so light that I scarcely knew I had it. Now, at a slower pace, I still go on with downright good-will to help on as long as I may." No public celebration of her birthday had been arranged, yet, to her surprise, testimonials came from far and wide.

Because of Lucy's declining health, a notice in the *Journal* early in 1888 had requested that letters be addressed to her at Dorchester. She would be at *The Woman's Journal* office on Mondays from eleven to three "to meet any persons who may desire to see her." Yet the following fall and winter she traveled to Iowa, to Illinois, to Rhode Island and to Maine, where she and Henry were caught in a heavy snow-storm.

That summer and fall of 1889 Henry, in an extended tour, had attempted to persuade the four territories, Montana, Washington and the Dakotas, about to become states, to include woman suffrage in their constitutions. He had no sooner returned from this dedicated journey than Alice wrote to Kitty that Papa had been buying land in Dorchester on which he intended to build houses for sale, and that Mamma was disgusted with his renewed commercial endeavors. But, said Alice, "Papa takes a lively interest in . . . anything by which there is a hope of making money. This new tract of land will furnish him with an occupation much more congenial to him than editing a reform paper, for he does not naturally take to reform. Now Mamma and I do. I like to work on the W. J.—can't think of any line of work open to me that I should like so well." So simply did his daughter perceive in her father's nature a trait with which neither he nor her mother had ever come to terms, a trait for which Henry blamed himself throughout his married life and suffered anguish of spirit at Lucy's death.

Part of the work Alice so much enjoyed was her offering of suffrage news, *The Woman's Column,* now advanced from a broadside to a small newspaper. It was sent free to newspaper and magazine editors; individuals could subscribe for twenty-five cents a year. After dropping those editors who had not been using the material, six hundred and four free copies were still distributed weekly, and the service was now to be extended to libraries.

Alice was also an official of the W.C.T.U. franchise department, of which Anna Howard Shaw was head. Frances Willard had been converted by Lucy, and now the Temperance Union was working to enfranchise women, thereby making an ever stronger link in the public mind between the two reforms.

From the West that summer Henry had written, "Miss Willard and her third party associates are the most dangerous enemies of our cause, because just so far as they educate the women, they array them *against the men* as a means of *coercing* the habits of the other sex. . . . I never before realized the necessity of respecting personal *liberty,* even when that liberty takes injurious forms." And, "They have incurred the active ill will of the politicians of *both* parties and have compelled a choice between them and the saloons – The men are overwhelmingly for the saloons." Yet on his return Henry was active in a group of antisaloon Republicans he had helped to organize.

In Massachusetts, school suffrage for women had taken a strange turn. In 1885, fearful that women voters, predominantly Protestant, would exert religious influence in the school system, the Catholic Church began putting pressure on Catholic women to vote. This was reported in the press, and the non-Catholics in turn became alarmed at this effort of the Catholic Church to extend its influence. An enormous increase in women registrants was the result.

In 1888 a new storm broke out when a high school history text was dropped because its account of the Reformation was said by the Catholics to exhibit a Protestant bias. In the resulting furor, which thrived on the prejudices of both sides, more than twenty-five thousand women registered, twenty thousand of them in Boston. It was an unfortunate reason for women, formerly uninterested in school elections, to flock to the polls. The *Journal* and the suffragists tried to keep clear of the religious issue, only rejoicing that for whatever reason women had been roused from political apathy.

The most important event of these years was the attempt to reunite the two suffrage associations. The movement's pioneers were growing old, and to the generation coming of age, the conflicts which twenty years before had created the split were the unreal history of a dead era. Surveying the pitifully insufficient funds and workers marshaled for so huge a battle they demanded a reunited movement. Alice played a leading role in the effort toward reunion, and its success was later credited largely to her.

In the years since the split there had been inevitable contacts between the two factions of the old guard. They found themselves at competing conventions in the same city, agitating concurrently for the passage of legislation in some state or territory, sometimes even speaking from the same platform.

In 1882 Francis Jackson's daughter, Eliza Eddy, died, leaving the residue of her estate, close to sixty thousand dollars, to Susan Anthony and Lucy Stone. Mrs. Eddy had every reason to believe in greater rights for women; years before, her husband had carried their daughter off to England without Mrs. Eddy's consent. The will was contested by a son-in-law; but the litigation, which lasted more than three years and used up ten thousand dollars of the legacy, was settled when Mrs. Eddy's daughters announced that whatever the result, they intended to fulfill their mother's wishes.

When the dispute was concluded in 1885 Lucy and Susan met intimately for the first time in years. Lucy found Susan "just as egotistical" as ever. "When Susan came here to get her share of the Eddy fund, I invited her to come and spend the day with us. . . . Instead, she sent a hateful note that made me feel the last plank between us had broken. I am too busy with the work that remains to take time to mend broken cisterns." After the money was divided, Susan left Boston at once, carrying her share of the large inheritance on her person to Rochester.

Whether they met or not, there was a recurrent note of ill will on both sides. "I have received an astonishing letter from Mrs. Stanton," Lucy told Higginson in 1873, "begging me to lay aside my 'personal feud with Susan.' She asks me to 'give up my petty revenge' &c. All this because the Journal does not publish in extenso the 'Call' for their National Convention in Washington. Think of that from *her* to *me*."

In 1876, when Elizabeth Stanton, Susan Anthony and Matilda Joslyn Gage were collecting material for the *History of Woman Suffrage,* Lucy wrote to Elizabeth Stanton that no such history could be written "by any one who is alive to-day. Your 'wing' surely are not competent to write the history of 'our wing', nor should we be of yours, even if we thought best to take the time while the war goes on; rations, recruits and all are to get as we go." When she was asked for biographical material, she responded formally, "Mrs. Stanton. Madam . . . I have never kept a diary or any record of my work, and so am unable to furnish you the required dates. . . .

"I commenced my regular public work for anti slavery and woman's rights in 1848. I have continued it to the best of my ability ever since, except when the care of my child, and the war prevented."

On the other side she wrote, "In your postal card you say, 'I' must be referred to in the history you are writing.

"If you will publish the letter which is on the opposite page, it will be a sufficient reference.

"I cannot furnish a biographical sketch, and trust you will not try to make one.

"Yours with ceaseless regret that any 'wing' of suffragists should attempt to write the history of the other."

Nor did Lucy cease to regret it. Several years later she stated that she was "more than content to be left entirely out of any history those ladies may publish of the suffrage work." The first volume of the *History* appeared in 1881, the second, containing a short account of the American, taken from printed reports of its meetings, in 1882. When the third volume was published, Lucy wrote to Margaret Campbell that a suffrage friend had told her that Susan and Mrs. Stanton's speeches had been corrected for the book, but that newspaper scraps had been used for the rest. "It is a shame to publish such a one sided history—But the good work exists all the same and will just as truly have done its part in this great movement."

In the summer of 1880 Lucy had told Margaret Campbell that a big campaign had developed to get the two societies together, and that Susan and Mrs. Stanton were visiting various leaders with this in mind. Lucy declared herself opposed to union with those who "advocate buying and selling votes, and going for any party that will go for them. It is a great deal better to be separate."

In 1882, without public announcement, the National Association unexpectedly set up a Massachusetts society, though the work for suffrage had been diligently pursued in Massachusetts by the American for more than a decade, and had achieved school suffrage. The National gave as its reason that the American's Massachusetts society was not dealing with national issues. Henry replied that this was untrue. The Massachusetts society, with the American, customarily petitioned Congress for a Sixteenth Amendment, though it believed this effort less important and less likely to succeed than work on a local and state level.

That year, when the suffrage amendment was before the voters of Nebraska, there was a conflict of dates in the annual meetings of the two associations, both to take place in Omaha. Lucy told Margaret Campbell that although the American's meeting had been arranged first, they would have to change the date; but a few days later she wrote that though their meeting was now rearranged, she had such a "dread lest there should even *seem* to be a disagreement among suffragists themselves and hence our good cause be hindered of success that I half regret the last arrangement. . . . I think we must not admit even in our thoughts that 'they meant to be hateful' . . . and we will if needful hold meetings with them." After the conventions Lucy said that the National's speeches had been good, and had received more publicity than the American's. "They know better than we do how to make a noise." Yet neither association made enough noise to pass the amendment.

When Lucy did not vote in the Massachusetts school elections, Susan Anthony openly attacked her, though she must have known it was because Lucy would not use Henry's name even to vote. It was true that a few women like Abby Kelley Foster had refused to vote under the "shameful conditions" of the limited suffrage law, but Lucy, who had fought for its passage, could hardly have been among them.

In 1883 Lucy expressed dismay because Susan and Mrs. Stanton were spreading rumors that she was making difficulty in the movement. In 1884 the two leaders of the National again tried to reach the delegates to the American's annual convention and to urge union upon them. That year a small but real advance in unity was made when a New York report began to appear regularly in the *Journal.* At first it was signed L. D. B., but later the author used her full name; Lillie Devereux Blake was one of the leaders of the National Association.

There were other signs that the two organizations were drawing closer, though mutual distrust continued unabated. In the summer of 1886, only six months after Lucy had been told that Elizabeth Stanton had called her "the biggest liar and hypocrite she had ever seen," Mrs. Stanton wrote to Alice that her daughter Harriot was attending the Concord School of Philosophy and would like to visit the Stone-Blackwell family. Lucy wrote to Alice, who was on vacation, that Hattie had come to the office and everyone had fallen in love with her.

When, in the spring of 1887, while Lucy was in Georgia, she and Alice corresponded about the possibility of union, it was Lucy who soothed Alice's fears. Rachel Foster, a rich and gifted young woman, one of Susan's aides, who had been writing for the *Journal,* had acted in a fashion Alice considered treacherous. Though Lucy suggested that this was characteristic of the other group, she went on to say, "You need have no fear of our being 'gobbled' up. We can at any time make a statement of the facts which divided us . . . and it would be proof of the need of the separation that was made in 1869." Lucy felt that the fortieth anniversary of the movement would be a proper time for reunion, "with an American Branch and a National Branch . . . each . . . responsible for the management of its [own] work, but all *meeting* upon occasion, and working together as friendly societies, and in this way escaping . . . responsibility for their false moves or for their indiscreet ones. . . .

"But this is the cause not of one woman but of all women—and of the whole race—It[s] success and prosperity have always been more to me than any personal feeling—and any damage to *it* far more than any personal ill will to, or misunderstanding of myself."

In moments of despair Lucy had always overestimated the National and depreciated the American. In 1878, discouraged by lack of funds, she had written to a co-worker, "Now after ten years of better doing by the other society, the old alert sense which rose up so vigorously to form this society seems to have gone to sleep. I know it would wake up actively again if there were danger." And in 1881, "I do not think the American Society *can* continue. It is too much for Harry and me to lift it bodily as we have to. But this is not to be said." Perhaps such thoughts influenced her now, in 1887, when she was older and sicker. In any case, that November the American passed a resolution that Lucy should confer with Susan Anthony about reunion, and that if they agreed, committees should be appointed by the two organizations to decide on the terms.

The suggested conference took place in the office of *The Woman's Journal* on December 21. Susan Anthony brought young Rachel Foster with her, and Alice was with Lucy. The two younger women recorded the conference. At this first meeting the name National-American Woman Suffrage Association was agreed on. It was agreed too that the new association should be organized like the American on a delegate basis, and that the new union should fight for a Sixteenth Amendment and for municipal and Presidential suffrage as well.

Lucy maintained that old wounds could more quickly be healed if she and Susan and Elizabeth Stanton refused to accept the presidency of the new society. Miss Anthony, according to the *Journal,* "expressed strong repugnance to this proposal." Miss Foster thought that a triple presidency of the three ladies might be acceptable. Instead, Lucy urged Mrs. Howe or Mrs. Livermore as president. They were rejected. Miss Foster suggested that all matters should be decided by votes of members of the two associations in convention. Miss Blackwell pointed out that, since in the National every auxiliary member voted, while in the American only authorized delegates had a vote, the National would inevitably swamp the American.

It was Susan who brought up the subject of a newspaper. In 1883 Clara Colby of Nebraska had launched a monthly newspaper, *The Woman's Tribune,* which had recently become a weekly. Now Susan said that since Mrs. Colby had struggled on with her paper for four years, they could hardly ask her to give it up. Neither, Alice answered, could her family be supposed to give up the *Journal* which had been solvent and continuous for almost twenty years. She suggested that both papers continue on an equal basis. To this Susan blandly replied that if both papers were offered, subscriptions would not be gotten for either. Apparently Mrs. Colby's four years of struggle counted for more than Lucy's twenty years of success.

Susan's allegiance to the *Tribune* was not unnatural, for it offered undeviating devotion to her and her views. In 1890 it went so far as to suggest that her seventieth birthday "should be celebrated as a *holy day* by every suffrage society in the land," and a month later referred to Mrs. Stanton as "our reverend mother."

After the exploratory meeting between Lucy and Susan there were various delays. The National renewed its effort to gain control by insisting that details be decided at a joint convention, and for some months it seemed as though the whole scheme might fall through. In March 1888 Lucy confided to Margaret Campbell, "Now about a union with Susan as president. I do not think I *can* accept that. To do so would be to justify her, to say we had no cause for separation . . . and *historically* it would put our side at great disadvantage." At the moment Mrs. Colby seemed unable to sustain *The Woman's Tribune,* and, according to Lucy, the National was preparing to accept the *Journal* so that Mrs. Colby could retire gracefully and they would appear to have acted magnanimously. "I wish we had never offered to unite. The difference is in the character. It is like trying to make republicans and democrats work together."

At the end of March a favorite project of Susan's came to fruition when an International Council of Women met in Washington to celebrate the fortieth anniversary of the Seneca Falls Convention. Organizations from many European countries were represented as well as United States societies, such as the Woman's Christian Temperance Union and the Peace Union. The leaders of the American had been invited and had accepted. At a formal reception on the first evening, Julia Ward Howe, Mary Livermore, Antoinette Blackwell, Anna Howard Shaw and Lucy Stone were among the distinguished guests who stood with Susan Anthony and Elizabeth Stanton on the receiving line.

In their speeches at the opening sessions, Susan Anthony, Frances Willard and Julia Howe testified that they had been converted to woman suffrage by Lucy Stone. Mrs. Howe recalled her early aversion to suffrage and suffragists. "I remember very vividly the woman suffrage meeting held in Boston, and to which I went with a very rebellious heart. I came out very meek, indeed, and have so continued ever since." But later Elizabeth Stanton, outlining the history of woman's rights, failed to mention Lucy's name: "After Miss Anthony and Lucretia Mott made their advent, other women woke up and began to speak." Surely a curious perversion of a chronology she must well have remembered.

Before the meeting Lucy had written to Nette, "I think we ought to puncture the bubble that the Seneca Falls meeting was the first public demand for suffrage. *You* can do that. Alice dreads these people even more than I do, but wants to have union to take the burden of work of the American from me, and to save it from coming on her when I drop out." At the conference and outside it there was much that revived her distrust. That summer she explained her feelings to Frances Willard. "I cannot forget that at

Washington, without having the delegates consulted, the whole Council had the shame of having *asked* such a male prostitute as Grover Cleveland if he would receive them. . . . I also remember that the Mormon women and not the Gentile from Utah had a hearing . . . and that the same Mormon woman's name stands second on the committee for the Council . . . while the Mormon hierarchy is in direct opposition to the U.S. government . . . sewing [sic] . . . the evil seeds that disrupt the home and degrade women. . . .

"Until the Washington meeting I never had a doubt that the coming of women everywhere would tend to make cleaner, purer and better. Now I see that under the same temptation they do just as men do. . . . I shall not say any of this to the public, but you can see why I am not eager to join the Council."

A newspaper reported Elizabeth Stanton as saying, "The time is not far distant when . . . women will strike hands with labor, with Socialists, with Anarchists, and you will have the scenes of the revolution of France acted over again in this Republic."

"Mrs. Stanton did use the words quoted . . ." Lucy wrote to a friend. "I do not suppose there is another suffragist anywhere who ever thought of such a thing. Mrs. Stanton said . . . she spoke it 'playfully', but it was most unwise and unfortunate." Yet in the spring of 1888, in spite of doubts, the appearance of friendliness between the societies continued. Susan and Mrs. Stanton were invited to the annual meeting of the New England Association, at which Lucy presided; and Susan came.

That summer Alice, concerned about attempts by the National to capture the American's organizations, begged her parents to try to stop them; but in late fall Lucy said that Susan was still visiting American affiliates in the Mid-west to tell "her grievances, make friends, create a split and get our auxiliaries." To Margaret Campbell she admitted that union would have to be considered at the American's annual meeting in November. "Alice thinks that all or nearly all the younger workers will be glad to unite, and that the old ones who remember the causes of division will soon be gone. . . . But all the time I feel that the two societies are different in essence."

That autumn Susan further endeared herself to the editors of *The Woman's Journal* by stating that what the movement "needs most of all is a great newspaper." Apparently, however, the pressures within the National for union were also powerful, and their annual meeting in January 1889 voted by a large majority for a union based on recommendations made by committees of both associations. There was now nothing to interfere with union, which would formally take place in February 1890, at the first annual meeting of the National-American Woman Suffrage Association in Washington, D.C. There was nothing either to change the emotions of the old guard. Not long before the joint meeting, Mrs. Stanton, referring to the original division, spoke of the American as "the party that seceded," and Henry found it necessary to retell the old story of the break.

A month before the National-American Convention Lucy was still disheartened at the prospect. "I dread . . . to try to work with these women. The old spirit is in them." This time "the old spirit" had manifested itself when Susan asked all delegates to send their credentials to her in advance. But of course, Lucy said, the credentials must be presented to "a committee elected *at the* meeting"; Susan was merely trying to take credit for organizing the union.

When it came time for the meeting, Lucy was ill again with a "hard" cough. She was grieving too, for her beloved brother Bowman had died less than two weeks before. Henry and Alice went to the convention, and up to the last moment Lucy hoped to join them, but it was impossible. To Henry she wrote, "I have great sympathy with and for you in the humiliation which will be poured upon our side—only for the cause, we would not bear it." And a few days later, "I fear you may have had a tough time with the enemy"; for, in spite of Lucy's protests, Elizabeth Stanton was to be president of the new organization, Susan Anthony vice-president and Lucy herself chairman of the executive committee. Susan's unremitting energy had captured the top spots for her friend and for herself. In politics, then as now, ruthless determination was the unexpendable ingredient.

The legal document of incorporation was dated April 14, 1890. The old antagonisms were not curable by majority vote or legal papers or the passage of time. From England, where she went immediately after the first session of the convention, Mrs. Stanton wrote to Clara Colby, "I am afraid we made a mistake when we took them in as even partners." And Susan told a friend, "I have not heard from Boston, save through the W. J., which reports HBB as saying the *union* could *now* be perfected because the *Nationals* had *adopted* all of the American methods, etc. . . . But never mind, let him say it, nobody but himself will be able to discover the *going* over of the National to anything but their own plans and ways of the past twenty years. It is too amusing!"

It did not end there. It did not end with Lucy's death. In 1894 Susan Anthony wrote to Clara Colby, "HBB has all he can do to hold himself from openly scorning us!!—he does it gingerly—but don't let him know that I see it—or notice it—" And five years later, "Let the Blackwell[s] talk to the few who pay them more for a special suffrage paper." In 1898, when Ida Husted Harper's biography of Susan Anthony gave an account of the split which made the formation of the American seem, as Henry put it, "a causeless division, prompted chiefly by personal motives," Henry printed again his version of the disagreement; but it was too late. History had been captured by the other side. Reunion had been effected and it continued; but until the old guard died the differences, the mistrust, the anger survived.

Chapter Twenty-eight

In 1888 Alice spent her vacation camping on the shore of Lake Memphremagog in the Province of Quebec. It was an isolated spot, wild and beautiful. The little group of campers, headed by Mrs. Isabel Barrows, whose husband edited *The Christian Register,* lived in primitive tents with a single log cabin where they spent their communal indoor hours. Alice loved the life, so different from any she had known, and returned there summer after summer.

In her everyday world Alice was an editor, pungent and forceful, whose articles, like her mother's, were in demand in these increasingly enlightened days in nonsuffrage papers like the *Boston Transcript* and *The Christian Union.* She had overcome her painful shyness sufficiently to speak regularly at suffrage meetings, sometimes taking her mother's place now that increasing illness made Lucy's appearances less dependable. In the shade of her mother's reputation, poor Alice always believed her own speeches uninspired and uninspiring.

Still the most repressed and moral of women, Alice attacked Edward Fitzgerald for translating into English "a melancholy and unwholesome Oriental poem, which he would have done better to leave locked up in a foreign tongue." She joined her father in praising Lady Burton who, after her husband's death, burned the immoral *Scented Garden* which Sir Richard Burton had spent years translating, and which he had specifically asked her to publish. That Lady Burton had showed fidelity to her principles there can be no doubt, since she had been offered more than thirty thousand dollars for the book. Alice went so far as to hint that it might have been better if Lady Burton had managed to suppress her husband's translation of the *Arabian Nights* as well.

But in the Canadian woods Alice was able to throw off some of the restraints that bound her. There she found a release and gaiety which her dedicated home, in spite of her father's wit and liveliness, had never provided. A few years before, Alice, praising her mother, had written to Kitty, "It would be a shame of me ever to do anything very bad after she has had the training of me. It is like growing up under the shadow of Bunker Hill." Now, out of the shadow, Alice revealed beneath her stiff, woman's manner an unfulfilled little girl. She was in her thirties, yet letters she wrote home often sound like the effusions of an adolescent. The girls threw sand into the boys' tents, put cedar branches and burrs in their freshly made beds, ran from their revenge and wrestled with them. Once Alice so far lost sight of her adult role as to tussle playfully with Mrs. Barrows, to that lady's indignation and Alice's subsequent humiliation.

In the summer of 1890 Anna Howard Shaw and Susan Anthony's niece Lucy joined Alice in camp for a while, and when they left she reported that she was lonesome without her "chums." Two weeks later she was called home by the news that her mother was sick, only to find on her arrival that her chums had given so unglamorous a picture of life in the woods that her parents had feared for her safety. However she was able to persuade them to let her return the next year.

That her parents had divergent hopes for her future is clear from Alice's camp letters. In 1892—she was almost thirty-five then—she wrote to her father, "You will be glad to hear that there is a *young man* here, who wants to talk about suffrage!" And the next year she told her parents, "Papa will be pleased to know that there are four unmarried gentlemen in camp, all of them nice; and that one of them has the seat next me at table, and we do lots of talking together."

To her mother her tone was different. In the summer of

1893 there was an attractive Armenian "theologue," Johannes Chatschumian, at camp. Alice and he became friends, and together translated Armenian poetry into English. "Speaking of the Armenian, Mamma dear, you need not be uneasy about him; I am never alone with him. . . . Besides, Mrs. Barrows says he is a saint, and has told us confidentially various incidents illustrating the purity of his morals."

Alice's father, brother of five unmarried sisters, husband of a woman who had married late and much against her will, longed for a full life for his daughter. Her mother desired for Alice only a life of dedication. It was, significantly, after her mother's death that Alice found herself in love with her young Armenian; but in 1896, on his way to France to study at the Sorbonne, he fell sick on board ship. As soon as they heard the news Alice and "Aunt" Isabel Barrows went to nurse him; but before their boat landed he had died. It was Alice's only romance. Otherwise her long life was dedicated, as her mother desired, to the cause of women.

Until the summer of 1893, in spite of persistent illness, Lucy continued to write for the *Journal.* That spring, with energy unabated, she wrote an editorial, later famous in suffrage annals. "The trout has had his innings in the Massachusetts Legislature. . . . Should the tame trout be eaten at the same time of the year with the wild trout, or might he be cooked earlier? This was the grave question that consumed much time . . .

"But when the question was whether half the people of the State . . . should have even so much as municipal suffrage, the House of Representatives gave a part of one session to its discussion, and then voted it down."

She continued to lecture whenever possible; and in May she and Alice went to speak at the Chicago World's Fair. It was an event she had long anticipated, for in 1891, while lecturing in the Midwest, Lucy and Henry had been invited by the exposition heads to discuss possible suffrage representation at the Fair.

At the Columbian Exposition, unlike the Philadelphia Centennial of 1876, the women's department was active and respected; and the many congresses included women equally with men. There was, indeed, a special congress on woman suffrage. "I think, with never-ending gratitude," Lucy said at the Exposition, "that the young women of today do not and can never know at what price their right to free speech and to speak at all in public has been earned."

The old guard were well aware of the changes the years had made. After a reception at which she had been nearly mobbed by eager admirers, Susan Anthony was asked if it did not tire her to shake so many hands. "Yes, it does tire me," she said, "but not half so much as it did thirty years ago to stand alone with no hands to shake at all."

On exhibition at the Fair was a marble bust of Lucy by the sculptor Anne Whitney. Lucy was, as always, impatient of personal tributes. "Perhaps you know that a marble bust of me has been made," she wrote to Francis, her only remaining brother. "It was not my wish. I would much rather have had the money go to help the cause of Woman. But a committee raised the money, engaged the artist, and then came to me." She did not add that they had warned her that in no event would the funds go to the suffrage cause. The sculpture was later placed in the main reading room of the Boston Public Library.

On May 1, 1893, her last wedding anniversary, Lucy and Henry, as so often before, were separated. This year, perhaps impelled by some awareness of approaching death to settle her affairs, she wrote him what must surely be one of the most extraordinary letters in the annals of matrimony. "This is our 38th wedding day. After this *always,* I shall like to have my rents, interest, etc., put in my bank. It is the *right* way. I shall be just as willing as heretofore to help you out upon occasion. But all my property will be simpler in the final settlement if it appears according to the facts.

"I have never liked the having it put in your bank but

as I have said, you did so much for women that I had allowed it. But now we will let it go into my bank."

It might have been her father speaking. The years of trust, Henry's sacrifices, his profitable handling of her affairs, fell away, leaving the pathology of her childhood and her mistrust of the male's power and superiority. The same emotion had manifested itself less dramatically in 1884 when Lucy had made a new will leaving the bulk of her considerable property to Alice. In that will she left their Dorchester home and two thousand dollars in stocks to Henry; a bequest to be valid only after he returned to the estate six thousand dollars worth of stocks and bonds he was holding.

Two weeks after their wedding anniversary Henry returned from a Republican convention in Kentucky to find that his wife and daughter had left for Chicago. He had thought that they planned to go later. From Chicago Lucy wrote of her constant activity. She had spoken at the congresses and, when they were over, lectured at the Fair grounds and other places. She had also conferred with the vigorous young leader, Carrie Lane Chapman, whom Lucy described as a refined, educated, noble woman, about the coming suffrage referendum in Colorado, in which Lucy was passionately interested, though she believed it hopeless.

By August, when Henry went to Chicago for the woman suffrage programs, Lucy was too ill to go with him. A new and mysterious stomach ailment made it almost impossible for her to eat and caused her to vomit much of what she did swallow. She wrote to Alice at camp that Dr. Emily had prescribed iron pills, but "I am still limp and without appetite." And two days later, "I took medicine yesterday which has had a good effect, and I believe that now I am really beginning to get over the trouble."

With her family away, she decided to go to her sister Sarah's in Gardner to recuperate. From there she wrote hopefully to Henry, "Already I eat more." The relief was temporary. By August 15 the symptoms had returned in force, and Emily was sending prescriptions and advice to "go on with the dandelion and pepsin" and to try quinine capsules which "increase the appetite and act as a tonic." If she could not eat, she was to "make it up with milk." Nothing helped. Nothing could help. Lucy had cancer; and at that time, only two years before the discovery of the X ray, there was no way to diagnose, no possibility of operating or arresting the disease.

Yet she continued to write short editorials for the *Journal.* Her article on the World Fair's congress on religion appeared on September 16, 1893, and expressed her pleasure in the fact that Buddhists, Jews, Confucians and Christians of every sect sat side by side on the platform. "Each day women will have part in the exercises. Behold the change in public sentiment!" It was her last editorial.

By now it was apparent that she was wasting away. On September 20 she sent a long, solicitous letter to brother Francis, advising him on financial affairs. "As I have written you before," she said, "I am very unwell. Growing weak and wasting away because my stomach has so given out that it cannot digest. So very likely this may be the last letter you will get from me. . . . I have no fear or dread of the life beyond, and sometime somewhere I hope to meet you there."

Henry's grief spilled over in a letter to Julia Ward Howe. "Your friend Lucy Stone is very ill, the doctors giving us little hope of her recovery . . .

"Alice has dropped everything, and has devoted herself to her mother. . . . I think Lucy would be glad to hear from you, for you have been to her more than a sister for over 20 years, and she relied on you in her work as on hardly any other. . . .

"Dear Mrs. Howe, what shall I do without her?"

Next day Alice recorded, "Mamma finds herself growing weaker day by day. . . . She is quietly making all her preparations to go. The decline in strength has been rapid. First she sat all day in her chair on the piazza; then she lay part of the day on the lounge in the parlor and only got out on the piazza for a few hours; then she did not leave the parlor; and now she keeps her room and most of the day keeps her bed. Sometimes she is so weak she cannot talk or be talked to. Then she rallies, and is bright and looks like herself, and gives minute directions . . . looking out for Papa's comfort and mine after she shall be gone."

On September 30 *The Woman's Journal,* "in answer to many inquiries," reported that Mrs. Stone is "much reduced in flesh and in strength, but suffers no pain, and generally passes comfortable nights." On October 7 "a council of doctors" had finally "pronounced the trouble to be a tumor affecting the stomach." On October 14 "she is able to speak only a few words at a time; but her mind is clear.

"A flash of joy passed over her face when we told her that the Democratic State Convention in New York had adopted a woman suffrage plank; and she said: 'That ought to make the Massachusetts Republicans ashamed.'" She was suffering now, but "entirely fearless." "I look forward," she said, "to the other side as the brighter side, and I expect still to be busy for good things."

On her deathbed Lucy recalled that youthful time when, vote after vote, the minister in the West Brookfield church had refused to notice her upstretched hand. Raising "that one uncounted hand," she spoke of the victories women had won since that far-off day, though the franchise, to her the greatest victory, was not to come for many more years.

Chapter Twenty-nine

"Died at her home on Pope's Hill, Dorchester, on Wednesday, [October 18] at 10:45 P.M., Mrs. Lucy Stone, aged 75 years, 2 months and 5 days."

The *Journal* of October 21 carried a short tribute by her husband, *She Leads Us Still.* A long article, *A Beautiful Death,* by her daughter, told of Lucy Stone's last days. "On the last afternoon . . . she looked at me and seemed to want to say something. I put my ear to her lips. She said distinctly, 'Make the world better.' They were almost the last articulate words she uttered. Whether they were a simple exhortation, or part of a sentence the rest of which was inaudible, there was no means of knowing."

With the next, a memorial issue, there appeared on the editorial page beneath the title *The Woman's Journal* the words, Founded by Lucy Stone.

A few days after Lucy died her sister-in-law Emily wrote to her sister Elizabeth in England, "I saw in our paper at breakfast the news of Lucy's death. It was characteristic of Harry and Alice—newspaper people—that fifteen minutes after her death Harry sent the notice of it to the Associated Press, and it was in the papers all over the country next morning, and within 24 hours Alice had sent obituary notices with sketches of Lucy's life to several papers. And yet they were almost broken down by it. But it was second nature to think of how it might be noticed by the press. . . .

"No one could have met death with more calm and cheerful serenity, with more undoubting faith. . . . And no one could have been more absolutely patient and uncomplaining, more appreciative of service, more desirous to spare and save those about her. . . . Her mind was absolutely bright, active and unclouded to the last, until she sank into a state of unconsciousness some two or three hours before the end."

During her last illness Lucy had given her family detailed instructions about her funeral, suggesting that a few friends gather in the Dorchester house. When Henry and Alice told her that many would be disappointed if the services were closed to them, Lucy was amazed. There would surely not be enough people to fill a church, she said, but they might do as they chose.

Services were held at 2:00 P.M. on October 21 at the Church of the Disciples. "It would have been a complete surprise to her gentle spirit," one of the *Journal*'s associate editors wrote, "to see hundreds of people standing silent in the street waiting for the doors to be opened." More than eleven hundred people crowded the church, and many had to stand.

Lucy had asked that there be "nothing lugubrious" about the arrangements. She lay in her coffin, Dr. Emily said, "dressed as in life, in a soft black silk with lace at her throat and wrists." She wore a gold pin and her best cap, "just as she would have dressed for a reception." In her hands Alice had placed lilies-of-the-valley, Lucy's favorite flower, "very scarce and costly at this season," which had been brought by the man from whom Lucy and Henry had bought the Dorchester house more than twenty years before.

The year before, Lucy had written to Alice about an account sent to the *Journal* of the intellectual achievements of Englishwomen, "I felt my heart in my throat for gladness at the great changes that have come to women. The contrast between the time when I was young and eager for opportunities, and there were none to this day when so much is gained, and I was glad I had lived to help. I used often to think that we girls (in my time) were like the cows we saw which were in barren pastures, but which could look over where grass and waving, growing grain grew beyond their reach, and now the bars are down and open. Thank God!"

Perhaps nowhere were the signs of change more clear than in the tributes paid to Lucy Stone by the press. The young woman who forty years before had been reviled for daring to speak in public, for wearing bloomer costume, for suggesting so ridiculous an idea as that women should be considered adults before the law, was now universally acclaimed for the heroism of those very deeds. *The Christian Register* found that her "very name fits itself to music, as the life which this pleasant name recalls was full of harmony." To the *New York Sun* the "unreasonable and tumultuous opposition at a period so recent seems inconceivable. . . . Lucy Stone's name must be enrolled on the list of illustrious Americans." "It will take generations of coming women," the *Boston Globe* said, "to realize the boon bestowed by such a life." And the *Cleveland Leader,* "When Lucy Stone died there passed from earth one of the noblest women of the century." The *Kansas City Star* remembered how "one of the kindest, best-mannered and sweetest-voiced of women was met with all sorts of ridicule. . . . Now all she did is considered right for women. . . . Lucy Stone will be widely honored and lamented." The list of tributes would cover pages.

In private Susan Anthony entered in her diary what might be considered a minority report. "Lucy Stone died this eve'g at her home—Dorchester, Mass. aged 75—I can but wonder if the Spirit now sees things as it did 25 years ago!!"

In the Dorchester home, Henry and Alice were desolate. Henry suffered not only from bereavement, but from the now magnified sense of inexplicable guilt which had dogged him throughout his marriage. In 1878 he had written to his wife, "I know I have tried you in a thousand ways—but, most of all, by not being able to show you the sincere good will I have had—If it had been necessary I would have *died* for you at any time, but it is far harder to live so as not to wound and grieve the heart that loves one."

Now, fifteen years later, having given over his life to the cause for which his wife had lived, he felt no different. His sister Emily tried to reassure him. "As we came home [from the funeral] Sam said, 'Well, there is one thing, Harry can think of his 40 years of married life without any shade of self reproach, for certainly he has been a most exceptionally good husband.' And that was surely the case. Few men would have modified their whole life to suit their wife's needs and wishes as you did. If there were imperfections on your side, there were also on the other—no one is perfect, and in any close association there must be forbearance, and the acceptance of imperfection on both sides. I sincerely hope the morbidly painful feeling you were suffering from has yielded to a different view of the matter and a truer one." But reason could not reassure a man who must have known that by any external standard he had devoted his life to his marriage.

Less than a month after Lucy's death, in the Colorado referendum, woman suffrage was carried by a substantial majority, the first time in the United States that women were accorded equal suffrage by an all-male electorate.

Even at that late date the last obsequies for Lucy had not been concluded. She had been insistent that her body be cremated, but so unusual was cremation in those days that the nearest crematory was in New York State, and it was thought better to wait until the one being built in Forest Hills Cemetery in the Boston area was completed. Her body, which had been embalmed, was not cremated until December 30, more than two months after her death.

The next day Henry wrote to his three sisters in England, describing the event with gruesome accuracy, apparently to reassure them as to the propriety of this unusual method of burial. The letter described every detail of the trip he and Alice, accompanied by William Lloyd Garrison's youngest son, made by carriage and on foot across the icy countryside. It described the heating of the furnace, the moving of the coffin toward the oven. "I saw for the last time the dear form and face lying in the same peaceful attitude as when the coffin lid was closed in the church 2½ months before. The hands were folded upon the breast, the lace around her throat was undisturbed, the face was discolored but its features were not greatly changed. It was only a momentary view, but one I shall ever remember." There is nothing to indicate that the memory would be a disturbing one. The body was placed in the furnace at 2:00 P.M. The incineration was not completed until three hours later. Then Alice and Henry went home.

Next day they drove back in their sleigh through a snowstorm so wild that they lost their way. The doors of the furnace had just been unlocked. "A few white bones partly retained their shape and partly already crumbled into white dust—in all about two quarts were all that remained." Rather than have the bones further crushed, Henry decided to have the remains temporarily placed in two urns. These were sealed with adhesive tape, and "on the place where the ends of the cloth lapped," Henry himself wrote the words, "Lucy Stone, Dec. 31, 1893," in such a way that "the strips could not be removed without the fact appearing."

In his account Henry was, perhaps, in some strange fashion reassuring himself as well as his sisters, for he admitted to "a profound reluctance to have Lucy's body thus disposed of," and explained that only the glimpse of the body which indicated that the "process of decay had already begun" had reconciled him to cremation. Lucy, he added, was in death as in life, a pioneer—the first person in Massachusetts to be cremated.

He was not, however, reconciled to his loss. Two years later Emily wrote to Elizabeth that Harry "absorbs himself in work because he says he broods as soon as he is not driven. . . . [I]t is sad that he is so absolutely without faith or spiritual life. . . . To him Lucy is simply annihilated, and he sees the same fate staring him in the face. How could he have any happiness with such a blank wall around him?"

With Lucy's only child it was otherwise. "Alice is wonderfully developing her individuality in her independent position. She will always be good and conscientious, but she shows a sort of self-will, and positive determination in everyday life which is quite new, and shows what an unconscious subordination her mother's strong will impressed upon her."

Both Henry and Alice had long lives yet to live, lives passed always to some extent under Lucy's domination. Henry survived his wife by sixteen years, during which he continued to serve in suffrage organizations and as editor of the *Journal*. He was eighty-four when he died in September 1909. The "only man of distinguished talents," the *National Cyclopaedia of American Biography* says of him, "who really devoted himself" to the cause of women. At his death Alice became editor-in-chief of the *Journal*. She died, an almost blind old woman of ninety-two, in March 1950. She alone lived to see the triumph of suffrage. *The Woman's Journal,* Lucy's other survivor, continued until 1917 when, on the eve of suffrage victory, it was consolidated with two other suffrage papers, the *Woman Voter* and the *Headquarters News Letter,* to become *The Woman Citizen*.

Lucy Stone was widely mourned and long remembered. Year after year meetings were held in her honor. In 1903, when her birthday was nationally observed by suffrage organizations, a special memorial service was held at her old home on Coy's Hill; and nearly four hundred people found their way to that isolated spot in the lovely Massachusetts hills, where neighbors mingled with illustrious friends to do her honor. In 1913 a conference of the Council of Women Voters in Washington, D.C., voted her "patron saint" of the council. In 1915 there was again a suffrage pilgrimage to her birthplace. A public school built in Dorchester in 1923 bears her name, as does a chapel at the cemetery where she was cremated. Even today women who keep their maiden names after marriage are often known as Lucy Stoners. The battle for equal suffrage for which Lucy Stone fought so long and so well was not won until 1920, twenty-seven years after her death, when the Nineteenth Amendment to the Constitution was ratified. "The right of citizens of the United States to vote," it declared at long last, "shall not be denied or abridged by the United States or by any State on account of sex." None of the pioneers lived to see their work accomplished, or to see the effects of that accomplishment.

With what high hopes those early fighters faced a future enlightened by a female electorate! Lucy's contribution to a symposium "Is The World Growing Better?" was probably her last published statement. "I believe the world grows better, because I believe that in the eternal order there is always a movement, swift or slow, toward what is right and true—a tendency toward higher things, stronger than the impulses of evil."

The hope for a world made better by the high influence of liberated women was as old as the woman's rights movement. In 1870 the first annual meeting of the American Woman Suffrage Association passed a resolution "That the ballot for woman means stability in the marriage relation, stability for the home, stability for our republican form of government." Two years later the *Journal* predicted that when women entered public affairs, "all the corrupt combinations of politicians will be swept away, and a better state of affairs will prevail."

Women, said the leader of the Rhode Island suffragists, have "a responsibility to help to lift our legislation into the region of morality and justice and humanity, such as the times demand, and such as we believe can never be attained, until women are admitted to participation in the ruling of the State." And a New England minister expressed his faith, "Woman suffrage is that ineffable change, that divine transformation. Of all that Jesus came to do, so far as changes in human society are concerned, to establish his kingdom on the earth, Woman Suffrage is the change which lies right at the core of the whole transformation, and is the central shrine of the sacred life, through the unfolding of which, under the laws of human nature, he would effect all that he came to do."

Henry, in 1875, had said, "Women are foremost in advocating all good causes, peace, temperance, economy, education, all moral reforms. Is it not fair to suppose that they will purify politics and make our country the model republic of the world?"

The clearest total expression of this common faith came from Mary A. Livermore. "With her enfranchisement there will come a nobler era. Then, with interests that are identical, with a humanity common to both, the masculine head married to the feminine heart, wisdom supplemented with love, man and woman shall together work out the great problems of life, and a nobler and better civilization shall come to the waiting future."

Those most dedicated to the future are not always the best prophets.

Bibliography and Index

Bibliography

Manuscript Collections

Boston Public Library

Henry E. Huntington Library, San Marino, California

Library of Congress

Massachusetts Historical Society, Boston, Massachusetts

Mount Holyoke College, South Hadley, Massachusetts

New-York Historical Society

New York Public Library

Radcliffe Women's Archives, Cambridge, Massachusetts

Sophia Smith Library, Smith College, Northampton, Massachusetts

Alice Stone Blackwell Archives (documented by Edna L. Stantial for presentation to the Library of Congress)

Books

Abbot, Willis J., *Notable Women In History.* Philadelphia, The John C. Winston Company, 1913.

The American Railway. (A compilation.) New York, Charles Scribner's Sons, 1892.

Anthony, Katharine, *Susan B. Anthony.* New York, Doubleday & Company, Inc., 1954.

Anthony, Susan B., and Harper, Ida Husted, *The History of Woman Suffrage,* Volume IV. Rochester, N. Y., Susan B. Anthony, 1902.

Austin, George L., *Life and Times of Wendell Phillips.* Boston, B. B. Russell, 1884.

Ballantine, W. G. (Editor), *The Oberlin Jubilee.* Oberlin, E. J. Goodrich, 1883.

Beard, Mary R., *Woman as Force in History.* New York, The Macmillan Company, 1946.

Benton, Josiah H., Jr., *What Women Did for the War, and What the War Did for Women.* Boston, 1894.

Bestor, Arthur Eugene, Jr., *Backwoods Utopias.* Philadelphia, University of Pennsylvania Press, 1950.

Blackwell, Alice Stone, *Lucy Stone, Pioneer of Woman's Rights.* Boston, Little, Brown and Company, 1930.

Blackwell, Elizabeth, *Pioneer Work in Opening the Medical Profession to Women.* New York, Longmans, Green and Company, 1895.

Blackwell, Sarah Ellen, *A Military Genius: Life of Anna Ella Carroll.* Washington, Judd and Detweiler, 1891.

Blake, Katherine Devereux, and Wallace, Margaret Louise, *Champion of Women: The Life of Lillie Devereux Blake.* Westwood, N. J., Fleming H. Revell Company, 1943.

Blanc, Madame, *The Condition of Woman in the United States.* Boston, Roberts Brothers, 1895.

Blatch, Harriot Stanton, and Lutz, Alma, *Challenging Years.* New York, G. P. Putnam's Sons, 1940.

Bode, Carl, *The American Lyceum.* New York, Oxford University Press, 1956.

Bolton, Sarah Knowles, *Famous Leaders Among Women.* New York, Thomas Y. Crowell and Company, 1895.

Bradley, Carolyn G., *Western World Costume, An Outline History.* New York, Appleton-Century-Crofts, Inc., 1954.

Briggs, Charles F., and Maverick, Augustus, *The Story of the Telegraph.* New York, Rudd and Carlton, 1858.

Brittain, Vera, *Lady Into Woman.* New York, The Macmillan Company, 1953.

Brooks, Van Wyck, *The Flowering of New England.* New York, E. P. Dutton and Company, 1936.

Bruce, H. Addington, *Woman In The Making of America.* Boston, Little, Brown and Company, 1913.

Burnett, Constance Buel, *Five For Freedom.* New York, Abelard Press, 1953.

Calhoun, Arthur W., *A Social History of the American Family from Colonial Times to the Present,* 3 volumes. New York, Barnes and Noble, 1945.

Carman, Harry J., and Syrett, Harold C., *A History of the American People,* 2 volumes. New York, Alfred A. Knopf, 1955.

Catt, Carrie Chapman, *Then and Now.* (Speech.) New York, 1939.

Cecil, David, *Melbourne.* Indianapolis, The Bobbs-Merrill Company, Inc., 1954.

Chadwick, John White (Editor), *A Life for Liberty—Anti-Slavery and Other Letters of Sallie Holley.* New York, G. P. Putnam's Sons, 1899.

Chester, Giraud, *Embattled Maiden: The Life of Anna Dickinson.* New York, G. P. Putnam's Sons, 1951.

Child, Mrs. D. L., *The History of the Condition of Women,* 2 volumes. Boston, John Allen and Company, 1835.

Christie, Jane Johnstone, *The Advance of Woman.* Philadelphia, J. B. Lippincott Company, 1912.

Circular of the Medical Institution of Geneva College. Rochester, N. Y., Jerome and Brother, 1849.

Commons, John R., and others, *History of Labour in the United States,* 4 volumes. New York, The Macmillan Company, 1946.

A Compendium of the Ninth Census (June 1, 1870). Washington, Government Printing Office, 1872.

Coutant, C. G., *The History of Wyoming.* Laramie, Wyo., Chaplin, Spafford and Mathison, Printers, 1899.

Crawford, Samuel J., *Kansas in the Sixties.* Chicago, A. C. McClurg & Company, 1911.

Croly, Mrs. J. C., *The History of the Woman's Club Movement in America.* New York, Henry G. Allen and Company, 1898.

Cromwell, Otelia, *Lucretia Mott.* Cambridge, Harvard University Press, 1958.

Daggett, Windsor, *A Down-East Yankee from the District of Maine.* Portland, Maine, A. J. Huston, 1920.

Dall, Caroline H., *The College, the Market and the Court.* Concord, N. H., The Rutherford Press, 1914.

———*Woman's Rights Under the Law.* Boston, Walker, Wise, and Company, 1861.

Dannett, Sylvia G. L. (Editor), *Noble Women of the North.* New York, Thomas Yoseloff, 1959.

Davis, Paulina W., *A History of the National Woman's Rights Movement for Twenty Years.* New York, Journeymen Printers Co-operative Association, 1871.

Dickens, Charles, *American Notes.* London, Chapman and Hall, Ltd., 1900.

Dickinson, Anna E., *A Paying Investment.* Boston, James R. Osgood and Company, 1876.

———*A Ragged Register.* New York, Harper and Brothers, 1879.

Dictionary of American Biography.

Dictionary of National Biography.

Ditzion, Sidney, *Marriage, Morals and Sex in America.* New York, Bookman Associates, 1953.

Dunbar, Janet, *The Early Victorian Woman.* London, George G. Harrap, 1953.

Dunham, Samuel, *An Historical Discourse delivered at West Brookfield, Mass. on the One Hundred and Fiftieth Anniversary of the First Church in Brookfield.* Springfield, Mass., Bowles & Company, 1867.

Early History of Old Brookfield, Mass. An address by the Reverend L. T. Chamberlain. New York, 1895.

Earnest, Ernest, *Academic Procession.* Indianapolis, The Bobbs-Merrill Company, Inc., 1953.

Encyclopedia Americana.

Encyclopaedia Britannica.

Farmer, Lydia Hoyt (Editor), *What America Owes to Women.* Chicago, Charles Wells Moulton, 1893.

Fishman, Nathaniel, *Married Woman's Bill of Rights.* New York, Liveright Publishing Corporation, 1943.

Fletcher, Robert Samuel, *A History of Oberlin College,* 2 volumes. Oberlin, Oberlin College, 1943.

———and Wilkins, Ernest H., *Bulletin of Oberlin College,* New Series 343. Oberlin, Oberlin College, 1937.

Flexner, Eleanor, *Century of Struggle.* Cambridge, Harvard University Press, 1959.

Flick, Alexander C. (Editor), *History of the State of New York,* 10 volumes. New York, Columbia University Press, 1937.

Franklin, Margaret Ladd, *The Case for Woman Suffrage, A Bibliography.* National College Equal Suffrage League, 1913.

Furnas, J. C., *The Road to Harpers Ferry.* New York, William Sloane Associates, 1959.

Furness, Clifton Joseph (Editor), *The Genteel Female—An Anthology*. New York, Alfred A. Knopf, 1931.

Goebel, Julius, Jr., *Cases and Materials on the Development of Legal Institutions*. Vermont Publishing Company, 1946.

Goodsell, Willystine, *A History of Marriage and the Family*. New York, The Macmillan Company, 1939.

Graham, Abbie, *Ladies in Revolt*. New York, The Womans Press, 1934.

Graham, Shirley, *There Was Once A Slave, The Heroic Story of Frederick Douglass*. New York, Julian Messner, Inc., 1947.

Greenbie, Marjorie Barstow, *Lincoln's Daughters of Mercy*. New York, G. P. Putnam's Sons, 1944.

Groves, Ernest R., *The American Woman*. New York, Greenberg, 1937.

Hamilton, Gail (Mary Abigail Dodge), *Woman's Wrongs*. Boston, Ticknor and Fields, 1868.

Hanaford, Phebe A., *Daughters of America*. True and Company, 1882.

Harper, Ida Husted, *The Life and Work of Susan B. Anthony*. Volumes 1–2, Indianapolis, The Bowen-Merrill Company, 1898; Volume 3, The Hollenbeck Press, 1908.

Hayes, Carlton J. H., *A Political and Social History of Modern Europe*, 2 volumes. New York, The Macmillan Company, 1922.

Hecker, Eugene A., *A Short History of Women's Rights*. New York, G. P. Putnam's Sons, 1910.

Higginson, Thomas Wentworth (Editor), *The Woman's Rights Almanac for 1858*. Worcester, Mass., Baker and Company, 1858.

History of the New England Woman's Press Association, 1885–1931. The Graphic Press, 1932.

History of the State of Kansas. Chicago, A. T. Andreas, 1883.

Hitchcock, Edward, and others, *The Life and Labors of Mary Lyon*. American Tract Society, 1911.

Holmes, Oliver Wendell, *Currents and Counter-Currents in Medical Science*. Boston, Ticknor and Fields, 1861.

Holtby, Winifred, *Women and a Changing Civilisation*. New York, Longmans, Green and Company, 1935.

Howe, Julia Ward, *Reminiscences 1819–1899*. Boston, Houghton Mifflin Company, 1900.

Howe, M. A. de Wolfe, *Classic Shades*. Boston, Little, Brown and Company, 1928.

Irwin, Inez Haynes, *Angels and Amazons*. New York, Doubleday, Doran and Company, 1934.

———*The Story of the Woman's Party*. New York, Harcourt, Brace and Company, 1921.

Jacobs, Albert C., and Goebel, Julius, Jr., *Cases and Other Materials on Domestic Relations*. New York, Foundation Press, 1952.

James, Henry, *Daisy Miller, An International Episode*. New York, Harper and Brothers, 1920.

Jensen, Oliver, *The Revolt of American Women*. New York, Harcourt, Brace and Company, 1952.

Keller, Allan, *Thunder at Harpers Ferry*. New York, Prentice-Hall, 1958.

Korngold, Ralph, *Two Friends of Man—William Lloyd Garrison and Wendell Phillips*. Boston, Little, Brown and Company, 1950.

The Life, Trial and Execution of Capt. John Brown (Compiled from Official and Authentic Sources). Robert M. DeWitt, 1859.

Livermore, Mary A., *My Story of the War*. Hartford, A. D. Worthington and Company, 1890.

Lowell Offering: A Repository of Original Articles Written exclusively by Females Actively Employed in the Mills. Lowell, Powers and Bagley.

Lutz, Alma, *Created Equal—A Biography of Elizabeth Cady Stanton*. New York, The John Day Company, 1940.

———*Susan B. Anthony*. Boston, Beacon Press, 1959.

Macy, Jesse, *The Anti-Slavery Crusade*. New Haven, Yale University Press, 1920.

Marx, Karl, and Engels, Frederick, *Manifesto of the Communist Party*. (Preface by Engels.) Chicago, Charles H. Kerr and Company.

Maxwell, William Quentin, *Lincoln's Fifth Wheel, The Political History of the United States Sanitary Commission*. New York, Longmans, Green and Company, 1956.

May, Samuel J., *The Rights and Condition of Women*. (Speech 1846.) Syracuse, Stoddard and Babcock, 1846.

Mansfield, Edward D., *The Legal Rights, Liabilities and Duties of Women*. John P. Jewett and Company, 1845.

Mathews, Mitford M. (Editor), *Dictionary of Americanisms*. Chicago, University of Chicago Press, 1956.

Merk, Lois Bannister, "Boston's Historic Public School Crisis." *New England Quarterly*, June 1958.

Mill, John Stuart, *On the Subjection of Women*. London, Longmans, Green and Company, 1869.

Modern Women and What Is Said of Them. (Reprint of a series of articles in the London *Saturday Review*.) New York, J. S. Redfield, 1868.

Monroe, Paul, *Founding of the American Public School System*. Ann Arbor, University Microfilms, 1940.

Montagu, Ashley, *The Natural Superiority of Women*. New York, The Macmillan Company, 1953.

Morris, Richard B., *Studies in the History of American Law*. New York, Columbia University Press, 1930.

Morse, John Torrey, Jr., *Life and Letters of Oliver Wendell Holmes*. Boston, Houghton, Mifflin Company, 1896.

Mott, Frank Luther, *A History of American Magazines*, Volume III, 1865–1885. Cambridge, Harvard University Press, 1957.

Mott, Lucretia, *Discourse on Woman*. W. P. Kildare, 1869.

Mount Holyoke College–General Catalogue of Officers and Students, 1837–1911.

Muzzey, David Saville, *The United States of America*, 2 volumes. Boston, Ginn and Company, 1933.

Myers, William Starr (Editor), *The Story of New Jersey*, 3 volumes. New York, Lewis Historical Publishing Company, Inc., 1945.

National Cyclopaedia of American Biography.

Nevins, Allan, *Grover Cleveland, A Study in Courage*. New York, Dodd, Mead and Company, 1941.

———*The Emergence of Lincoln*, 2 volumes. New York, Charles Scribner's Sons, 1950.

———and Commager, Henry Steele, *A Short History of the United States*. New York, Random House, 1945.

Nye, Russell B., *William Lloyd Garrison and the Humanitarian Reformers*. Boston, Little, Brown and Company, 1955.

Oberholtzer, Ellis Paxson, *A History of the United States Since the Civil War*, 5 volumes. New York, The Macmillan Company, 1917.

Oberlin 1833–1923. (Pamphlet.)

O'Connor, Lillian, *Pioneer Women Orators.* New York, Columbia University Press, 1954.

Orcutt, William Dana, *Good Old Dorchester.* Cambridge, England, Cambridge University Press, 1908.

Parrington, Vernon Louis, *Main Currents in American Thought.* New York, Harcourt, Brace and Company, 1930.

Parton, James, Greeley, Horace, and others, *Eminent Women of the Age.* S. M. Betts and Company, 1869.

Paxson, Frederic L., *The New Nation.* Boston, Houghton, Mifflin Company, 1927.

Peck, Chauncey E., *The History of Wilbraham, Massachusetts.* n.p., 1914.

Penny, Miss Virginia, *How Women Can Make Money.* John E. Potter and Company, circa 1862.

Previté-Orton, C. W., *The Shorter Cambridge Medieval History,* 2 volumes. Cambridge, England, Cambridge University Press, 1952.

Putnam, Emily James, *The Lady.* New York, G. P. Putnam's Sons, 1921.

Quinquennial Catalogue of Officers and Students of Mount Holyoke College, 1837–1895.

Richards, Laura E., and Elliott, Maud Howe, *Julia Ward Howe,* Boston, Houghton, Mifflin Company, 1916.

Robinson, Harriet J. H., *Massachusetts in the Woman Suffrage Movement.* Boston, Roberts Brothers, 1883.

Ross, Ishbel, *Child of Destiny, The Life Story of the First Woman Doctor.* New York, Harper and Brothers, 1949.

Roosevelt, Eleanor, and Hickok, Lorena A., *Ladies of Courage.* New York, G. P. Putnam's Sons, 1954.

Rourke, Constance Mayfield, *Trumpets of Jubilee.* New York, Harcourt, Brace and Company, 1927.

Rowson, Susanna Haswell, *Charlotte Temple.* New York, Funk and Wagnalls Company, 1905 ed.

Sachs, Emanie, *The Terrible Siren—Victoria Woodhull.* New York, Harper and Brothers, 1928.

Schlesinger, Arthur Meier, *The American as Reformer.* Cambridge, Harvard University Press, 1950.

———*New Viewpoints in American History.* New York, The Macmillan Company, 1922.

Seldes, Gilbert, *The Stammering Century.* New York, The John Day Company, 1928.

Sprague, Julia A. (Editor), *History of the New England Women's Club*. Boston, Lee & Shepard, 1894.

Stanton, Elizabeth Cady, *Eighty Years and More*. London, T. Fisher Unwin, 1898.

———Anthony, Susan B., and Gage, Matilda Joslyn, *History of Woman Suffrage*, 3 volumes. Rochester, N.Y., Susan B. Anthony, 1889 ed.

———and others, *The Woman's Bible*. European Publishing Company, 1895.

Stoddard, Henry Luther, *Horace Greeley*. New York, G. P. Putnam's Sons, 1946.

Stowe, Harriet Beecher, Cooke, Rose Terry, and others, *Our Famous Women*. A. D. Worthington & Company, 1885.

Strachey, Ray, *"The Cause": A Short History of the Women's Movement in Great Britain*. London, G. Bell and Sons, Ltd., 1928.

Squire, Belle, *The Woman Movement in America*. Chicago, A. C. McClurg and Company, 1911.

Suhl, Yuri, *Ernestine L. Rose and the Battle for Human Rights*. New York, Reynal and Company, 1959.

Tharp, Louise Hall, *Three Saints and a Sinner: Julia Ward Howe, Louisa, Annie, and Sam Ward*. Boston, Little, Brown and Company, 1956.

Thorp, Margaret F., *Female Persuasion: Six Strong-Minded Women*. New Haven, Yale University Press, 1949.

Tocqueville, Alexis de, *Democracy in America*, 2 volumes. New York, Alfred A. Knopf, 1945.

Train, George Francis, *Great Epigram Campaign of Kansas*. Kansas, Prescott and Hume, 1867.

Trollope, Mrs. Frances, *Domestic Manners of the Americans*. New York, Alfred A. Knopf, 1949.

Tyler, Alice Felt, *Freedom's Ferment*. Minneapolis, University of Minnesota Press, 1944.

Underwood, Sara A., *Heroines of Freethought*. New York, Charles P. Somerby, 1876.

Victory—How Women Won It: A Centennial Symposium. New York, The H. W. Wilson Company, 1940.

Vital Records of Brookfield, Mass., to the end of the year 1849. Worcester, Mass., Franklin P. Rice, 1909.

Webb, R. K., *Harriet Martineau: A Radical Victorian*. New York, Columbia University Press, 1960.

Webber, Everett, *Escape to Utopia.* New York, Hastings House, 1959.

Whitton, Mary Ormsbee, *These Were the Women.* New York, Hastings House, 1954.

Willard, Frances E., and Livermore, Mary A. (Editors), *American Women—Fifteen Hundred Biographies.* New York, Mast, Crowell and Kirkpatrick, 1897.

Williamson, Francis P., *Beecher and His Accusers.* Philadelphia, Flint and Company, 1874.

Winslow, Helen M., "Story of Woman's Club Movement." New England Magazine, July 1908.

Winsor, Justin (Editor), *The Memorial History of Boston,* 4 volumes. Boston, James R. Osgood and Company, 1881.

Wittenmyer, Mrs. Annie, *History of the Woman's Temperance Crusade.* Philadelphia, James H. Earle, 1882.

Wollstonecraft, Mary, *Vindication of the Rights of Woman.* Boston, Thomas and Andrews, 1792.

Woodham-Smith, Cecil, *Florence Nightingale.* New York, Grosset and Dunlap, 1951.

Woods, Lucy R., *A History of the Girls' High School of Boston.* Boston, Riverside Press, 1904.

Woodward, Helen Beal, *The Bold Women.* New York, Farrar, Straus and Young, 1953.

Wyman, Lillie Buffum Chace, and Wyman, Arthur Crawford, *Elizabeth Buffum Chace,* 2 volumes. Boston, W. B. Clarke Company, 1914.

Newspapers and Magazines

Columbian Centinel

Godey's Lady's Book and Magazine

The Independent

The Liberator

The Lily

New York Daily Tribune

New York Evening Post

New York Herald

New York Weekly Tribune

Punch

The Revolution

Thomas's Massachusetts Spy or Worcester Gazette

Una

The Woman's Advocate

The Woman's Column

The Woman's Journal

The Woman's Tribune

Woodhull and Claflin's Weekly

Index